The Nature of Alexander

MARY RENAULT

The Nature of
Alexander

Pantheon Books
New York

Library of Congress Cataloging in Publication Data
Renault, Mary, pseud.
The Nature of Alexander
1. Alexander the Great, 356–323 BC   I. Title.
DF234.R46 1975   938′.07′0924[B]   74–15152
ISBN 394–73825–X

2468C97531

The publishers are indebted to the following for permission to quote from their publications: Mrs. George Bambridge and Eyre Methuen, and Doubleday & Co., Inc. (Rudyard Kipling, "The Young British Soldier," from *Barrack-Room Ballads*); Liverpool University Press (E. W. Marsden, *The Campaign of Gaugamela*); University of Chicago Press (Richmond Lattimore, tr., *The Iliad of Homer*).

(frontispiece) Reconstruction of Alexander's funeral car by Edward Mortelmans

CONTENTS

IMAGES 3

MACEDON 19

TROY 69

PERSIA 125

INDIA 189

THE MARCH TO BABYLON 203

POSTSCRIPT 267

ANCIENT SOURCES 269

INDEX 271

THE
MACEDONIAN SUCCESSION

from *c.* 450 BC to *c.* 310 BC

ALEXANDER I	died *c.* 450
PERDICCAS II	*c.* 450–414; died
(PERDICCAS	son of above, believed murdered at age seven by Archelaus)
ARCHELAUS I	414–399; murdered by his favourite, Craterus
CRATERUS	king for four days; executed
ORESTES	son of Archelaus I, 399–396; murdered by his guardian, Aeropus II
AEROPUS II	descent uncertain, 396–392; fate unknown ⎫
AMYNTAS II	descent uncertain, 392–390; fate unknown ⎬ Civil wars in progress
PAUSANIAS	son of Aeropus II, 390–389; fate unknown ⎭
AMYNTAS III	descent uncertain, 389–369; died

ALEXANDER II	eldest son of Amyntas III, 369–368; murdered by his mother's lover, Ptolemy
PTOLEMY	368–367; killed by Perdiccas III
PERDICCAS III	second son of Amyntas III, 367–359; killed in battle, or by his mother
PHILIP II	third son of Amyntas III, 359–336; assassinated
ALEXANDER III	the Great, son of Philip II, 336–323; died
ALEXANDER IV	son of above, 323–c. 310; murdered by Cassander
PHILIP ARRIDAEUS	son of Philip II, 323–317; murdered by Olympias

Joint kings

It is a lovely thing to live with courage,
and die leaving an everlasting fame.

ALEXANDER

You know that the more magnificent the prospect,
the lesser the certainty, and also the greater the passion.

SIGMUND FREUD

The carriage . . . appeared more magnificent when seen than when described. Because of its wide fame it drew together many spectators; for from every city it came to, the people came out to meet it, and followed beside it when it went away, never wearied of their pleasure in the sight.

Diodorus, Book XVII, 28

The Nature of Alexander

IMAGES

On a hot June day in Babylon, in 323 BC, Alexander died. Wailing spread through the city; his body-squires wandered about in tears; the Persians shaved their heads in mourning; the temples quenched their fires. His generals plunged into a dazed and chaotic power struggle. In one of its episodes they fought about his bier, where he may have been still alive in a terminal coma, for the freshness and lifelike colour of his corpse, left some time untended, were much wondered at. At length the embalmers came, approaching him with awe; and "after praying that it might be right and lawful for mortals to handle the body of a god" began their work.

Roxane's child was still unborn. If he named his successor on his deathbed, no one admitted to having heard. There was no established heir whose own prestige would be invested in the splendour of his obsequies; for decades, Greece and Asia would be riddled with intrigue and shaken with the tramp of armies, as his generals tore off their portions of his empire. Yet steadily for two years, as war elephants moved ponderously in the train of war leaders changing sides, gold and gems by the talents' worth poured into the workshop where Greek master craftsmen were perfecting a funeral car worthy of its burden. It was accepted like a law of nature that the catafalque must be unsurpassed in memory, history or legend.

The coffin was of beaten gold, the body within it em-
bedded in precious spices. Over it was spread a pall of
gold-embroidered purple, on which was displayed Alexander's panoply of arms. Upon all this was erected a
golden temple. Gold Ionic columns, twined with acanthus,
supported a vaulted roof of gold scales set with jewels,
topped with a scintillating gold olive wreath which flashed
in the sun like lightning. At each of its corners stood a
golden Victory holding out a trophy. The gold cornice
below it was embossed with ibex heads from which hung
gold rings supporting a bright, multi-coloured garland.
Its ends were tasselled, and from the tassels hung large
bells with clear and carrying voices.

Under the cornice hung a painted frieze. Its front
panel showed Alexander in a state chariot, "a very
splendid sceptre in his hands," attended by Macedonian
and Persian bodyguards. Another had a procession of
Indian war elephants; a third, cavalry in battle order; the
last a fleet of ships. The open spaces between the columns
were filled in with golden net, screening the draped
sarcophagus from sun and rain, but not from the viewers'
eyes. It had an entrance, guarded by golden lions.

The axles of the gilded wheels ended in lion heads
whose teeth held spears. Something had been devised to
protect their burden from shock. The edifice was drawn
by sixty-four mules, pulling on four yoke poles in teams
of four; each mule had a gilded crown, a gold bell hanging at either cheek, and a collar set with gems.

Diodorus, who apparently took this description from
an eyewitness's, says it was more magnificent when seen
than when described. Alexander himself had always buried
his dead with splendour. Funerals in his day were more
gifts of honour than displays of mourning.

"Because of its wide fame it drew together many
spectators; for from every city it came to, the people

came out to meet it, and followed beside it when it went away, never wearied of their pleasure in the sight." Week after week, month after month, at the pace of its labouring mules, preceded by roadmakers and pausing while they smoothed its passage, fifteen, ten, five miles a day; stopping at towns where sacrifices were offered and *epitaphions* sung, the huge gold shrine, ringing and glittering, trundled across a thousand miles of Asia; the shock absorbers, whose construction has defeated scholars, protecting in death the body so careless of itself in life. North along the Euphrates, east to the Tigris; stopping at Opis, that crucial station on the Royal Road to the west; northward to skirt the Arabian Desert. "Ptolemy, moreover, doing homage to Alexander, went to meet it with an army as far as Syria."

Ptolemy's homage was a reverent hijack. Kings of Macedon had been buried by ancient custom at Aegae, its ancient hill-fort capital; there was a prophecy that when this failed the royal line would end. Ptolemy, a kinsman of the house, must have known it well. But he had shrewdly chosen his share of the fissured empire: Egypt, where the Macedonian conquest had been hailed as a liberation; where Alexander had honoured the shrines profaned by a Persian king, and received divinity; where Ptolemy himself had got rid of a bad governor and was very popular. To Egypt, he declared, Alexander had wished to return; where else but to his father Ammon?

Ptolemy was probably right. Since he crossed the Hellespont eastward at twenty-two, Alexander had shown no disposition to go home. He had planned to centre his empire on Babylon; he had turned himself from a young Macedonian conqueror into an impressive Persian Great King; he was *déraciné*, and so without exception were the ambitious young officers who had followed him. Ptolemy's loyalty had been proved in early years when, materially, he had had more to lose than gain by it. If now the prestige of entombing his friend was immense for Egypt, if it enabled Ptolemy to found a dynasty, he had fair cause to think that Alexander would be grateful. Had his body reached Macedon, sooner or later it would have been destroyed by the implacable Cassander. In Alexandria it would have centuries of veneration.

Southward from Syria, therefore, went the awe-inspiring cortège, augmented now by a satrap of Egypt and his army; past the patched-up walls of Tyre, on through Judaea. At city after city the mingled host of the escort, Macedonian, Persian, Egyptian, set up its tents about the tabernacle of the dead god, from whose divinity Ptolemy, Saviour-Pharaoh to be, would later derive his own. He would take care it was well displayed and its advent heralded. One cannot suppose that Alexander would have wished it otherwise. He had loved his fame. Like Achilles, he had traded length of days for it. He had trusted in the gods to keep their bargain; and, like Achilles, not in vain.

Children who had been unborn or in arms when he rode that way alive gaped at a sight they would still be talking of in sixty years. Pointing to the pictures on the painted frieze, they asked the story, and believed whatever they were told. In that progress must have begun a thousand years of legends.

In Egypt the sarcophagus, still in its famous car, rested some years in Memphis, a magnet for sightseers, while in Alexandria they built The Tomb. (When the mausoleums of the whole Ptolemaic dynasty had been assembled round it, The Tomb it always remained.)

Perdiccas, Alexander's deputy when he died, was extremely angry with Ptolemy, and made war on him in due course. But Alexander's proverbial fortune, which caused people to wear his image cut in rings, passed like a grateful bequest to his boyhood friend. Of all the great generals who contended for his empire after his death, Ptolemy alone died peacefully in bed. He was eighty-four; had kept his people's regard, completed his respected History, and established in his lifetime the succession of his favourite son.

For nearly three centuries, while Macedon became a Roman province, the Ptolemys ruled in Egypt, and the priests of the deified Alexander served his shrine. At last in 89 BC, when the line had grown degenerate, the effete and bloated Ptolemy IX, rejected by his army and needing pay for mercenaries, took the gold sarcophagus and melted it down for coin. All Alexandria was outraged; to no one's surprise, he was killed within the year.

The embalmers had been master craftsmen; Alexander's three-hundred-year-old face had set into distinguished beauty. The Alexandrians piously rehoused him in a sarcophagus adorned with coloured glass. Fifty years later, the house of Ptolemy was extinguished by Cleopatra's asp.

The Tomb remained. Caesar visited it; no doubt Mark Antony too with envy; Augustus left an imperial standard as tribute. The legends gathered.

In his lifetime they had begun, springing up in his wake from the Hellespont to the Himalayas. Through his torn empire and far beyond its fringes they grew like tropical jungle, throwing up exotic flowers of fantasy. Myth says that the robber Sciron, whom Theseus threw off the Isthmian cliff, was rejected by earth and sea, which tossed him back and forth. To possess Alexander, there was an inter-continental tug of war.

Egypt quickly annexed him. He had been thirteen years old when the last native Pharaoh, Nectanebo, fled into exile at the Persian conquest; but now it was told that he had been an adept in magic who, instructed by his art, had voyaged to Macedon, there to beget an avenger of his people's wrong. Olympias, hearing of his fame,

summoned him to cast her horoscope. He foretold her a
hero son from the seed of Zeus-Ammon; his harbinger
would be a monstrous serpent. It appeared, startling the
court. Next night, Nectanebo put on the ram-horned mask
of Ammon and fulfilled his own prediction. The stars
were about to sign a portentous birth; when Olympias was
in labour, he made her hold back till they were in the
right conjunction.

Alexander had spent a few months of his life in Egypt.
In Persia, his adopted kingdom, his memory was fresh
and green. Careless of chronology, legend fathered him on
Darius II, who had received a daughter of Philip of
Macedon after a (wholly fictitious) victory over that
king. In spite of her beauty, Darius only kept her for a
night because she had bad breath; so Alexander was born
in Macedon. Later on she improved her breath by chew-
ing *skandix* (chervil) after which she called her son
Sikandar. Since *skandix* is Greek, not Persian, the story
shows that his work on the fusion of culture had not gone
for nothing.

Persia spent upward of a millennium embroidering the
story of Sikandar Dhulkarnein, the Two-Horned, the
World-Seeker. In the pleasure houses, the bazaars, the
inns, the harems, centuries before it got into written form,
it collected fabulous exploits from eras before his birth,
Märchen with which he himself may have been beguiled
by his Persian favourite. Of no one else did they now
appear so credible.

Assimilated at last to Islam, the romance spread out
to enormous length, every rift loaded with ore, till it could
take eighty-five stanzas to describe two opposing armies
before the battle began. He was credited with deeds he
would have disclaimed indignantly, the tendency being to
equip him with whatever qualities seemed admirable to
the poet, including religious intolerance. He is found

galloping about destroying heathen temples and scattering Zoroaster's sacred fires—he, the most cheerfully syncretist of religious men—in the name of Allah. When he gets to Egypt, it is to rescue the country from the black and hideous invading Zangs, drinkers of blood and eaters of brains. To put them in dread he has a Zang head cooked, and after a deft exchange of dishes affects to eat with relish. Victorious, he leaves the grateful Egyptians (there are still small outcrops of history) and defeats King Dara of Persia, who dies in his arms bequeathing him, in return for avenging his murder, the hand of his daughter Roshanak, who stirs his heart to "tumult like a Russian camel bell's." Dispatching Poros of India singlehanded he takes the surrender of the King of China, who bestows on him the Auspicious Horseman, a gallant warrior later revealed as a lady of dazzling beauty, with whom he spends an elaborately decorated night of love. (So long remembered was his wish to meet an Amazon.) Victorious over monsters and Russian savages, he marches up into the Arctic night, seeking the spring of eternal life, the immemorial quest of Sumerian Gilgamesh. (Probably no part of the legend would have surprised him more than this.)

One thing is constant; in the terms of each epoch, Sikandar is the supreme hero. "To iron men he is iron, but gold towards the golden." When the Dauphin sent Henry V a bat and ball in scorn of his youth, he must have chosen his ill-judged gift with some vague recollection of Dara's challenge to Sikandar. He founds Sikandria, "a city like the joyous spring." He is full of cunning devices, not all of which he would have approved. He invents the mirror—for strategic reasons, but not without some unmeant psychological truth. He venerates the tomb of Cyrus the Great; this was never forgotten in Persia. His tactics are likened to skilful chess, his troop dispositions to enamelled miniatures. Indeed the miniaturists never tired of depicting him, elaborately Persianized with chain mail, pointed helm and scimitar; using a horseman's bow, or catching a giant with an expert lasso; wearing the regal moustache and beard obligatory where a smooth face marked the eunuch; lamented at his death by the sages Aristo and Aflatun (Aristotle and Plato); the Happy World-Possessor, whose cavalcade is like a rose garden. No victor in world history has left an image comparable with this in the land he conquered. Coeur-de-Lion, it may be remembered, survived in Arab memory as a bogyman with whom mothers threatened bad children.

Meantime, while Persian folk memory and fable were putting down the earliest pieces of this extraordinary mosaic, a quite different process, sophisticated and purposeful, was going on to the westward. In Macedon the formidable Antipater, Regent in turn for Philip, Alexander, and the shadowy boy Alexander IV, died like some great rock releasing landslides. His son Cassander, Alexander's bitterest enemy, future murderer of his mother, widow and son, settled down to the serious work of murdering his reputation.

A willing tool was the educational establishment of Athens, bitter at the collapse of the city-states from within, which had left them open to Macedon; blaming on Alexander his Regent's stern hegemony which he had been trying to loosen when he died; smarting at the death of Demosthenes whom he had spared all his life in spite of much provocation, and of the dubious Callisthenes, whose provocation had been too much. They had expelled Aristotle for his links with Macedon. Cassander made it clear, to the lesser men left as opinion formers, that enemies of Alexander were friends of his; and he was a powerful friend. With his encouragement—probably fed by him with misinformation they believed, for he had visited the court at Babylon—they set to work on their own Alexander legend; no organic growth like the Romances, but efficient hatchet work, producing vicious caricatures of an Orientalized, lecherous despot, incongruously active among excesses which might have exhausted Sardanapalus. His failure to beget by this mode of life a horde of bastards was put down to alcoholism; drink made his semen watery, pronounced Theophrastus, Professor of Science at the Lyceum—who, in common with the rest of Athens, had not set eyes on him since he was eighteen.

All this time the involved Wars of the Successors were going on; his former generals were further polluting history by issuing bogus last testaments of his to support their claims. He was a favourite set subject, too, for the schools of rhetoric, which industriously wrote letters for him, describing the marvels of India, lecturing Aristotle, or telling his mother how he was getting on. Modern scholarship has had to labour at extracting these burrs from the cloth of history, in which some of the most striking had become firmly wound.

Romance, however, still kept pace with propaganda. Judaea in the harsh grip of Antiochus thought nostalgically of the Beast with Two Horns who had harmlessly passed that way, and soon pictured him on his knees before the Torah, honouring the One God. The Ethiopians, original models perhaps for the fearful Zangs, evolved their own Alexander story in which, besides conversing with an angel who supports the world, he kills an enormous dragon by getting it to swallow a kind of bomb, and blowing it up. "How is the great Alexander?" the two-tailed mermaid would demand of Aegean sailors, who must hasten to answer "He lives and reigns" if they wanted to save their ship.

In Rome Caesar was struck down in the Forum, to save

the Republic, which promptly died of it. Under Divine Augustus, no one had a motive for praising Alexander. Caesarians cared to eulogize no rivals. Greeks, in Roman prejudice, were lightweights, Greeklings, slick Levantines; panders, procurers and profiteers. To the learned world, on the other hand, Athens was the university where they sent their sons to pick up the intellectual polish of the conquered; and there the dead hand of the Lyceum still wrote on.

But among the republicans, in their bitter underground, interest in Alexander was keen and active. Had he not lived, it would have been necessary to invent him. His was an imperial effigy which could be safely burned.

To this time belongs Trogus, the inaccurate and hostile Justin's now vanished source; and Diodorus. The date most favoured for Curtius is just after the dreadful Caligula, one of whose little conceits was dressing as Alexander. A deified Macedonian, three centuries safely dead, was a propagandist's gift for a tyrannic proto-Caesar. Such monsters did men become who presumed to claim divine honours from their fellow citizens—present company of course excepted.

Here and there the stream of calumny met intractable rocks of fact, too firmly fixed to be washed away. Working this awkward material in, the republican moralists said he had started well, but all power corrupts, and none so absolutely as power over servile, cringing barbarians. The adoption of their effeminate clothes and customs spoke for itself.

There remained the discrepancy of his face. All this while, his statues were being busily reproduced by Roman copyists, the demand being far greater than looted originals could supply. Even the originals had not all been done from life. Yet even with the least talented, something about the eyes shows who is meant.

Perhaps the face, perhaps Greek patriotism, worked upon the young Plutarch long before he embarked on the *Parallel Lives*. Two of his earliest works were essays on the Fortune or Virtue of Alexander, upholding the second above the first—the hostile writers had given Fortune most of the credit. Much later this warm-hearted, charming and long-lived man put Alexander into the *Lives* alongside Julius Caesar. He was, unfortunately, a ragbag of a biographer, scarcely ever discarding a good story, seldom distinguishing primary from secondary sources, deeply concerned to edify. But "books have their destinies," and his account of Alexander's youth and childhood is the only one we have; his sources for it have disappeared.

Some time towards the end of Plutarch's life span, in the second century AD, Alexander was rescued for history by a fellow soldier. He was Flavius Arrianus, a Romanized Bithynian Greek. Hadrian made him governor of Cappadocia, an honour seldom granted to his race; he was a brave and able general who fought off a dangerous barbarian invasion. Epictetus, whose pupil he had been, had taught him:

> Don't you know that all human ills and meanspiritedness and cowardice arise not from death but from fear of death? Against this therefore fortify yourself. Direct all your discourses, readings, exercises thereto. And then you will find that by this alone are men made free.

Perhaps it was Alexander's freedom which attracted Arrian. But the clutter of hindsighted romance and committed lying annoyed the honest general. Happily, he was in time to find the primary sources still intact in unburned libraries. He assessed their value, a chance we no longer have, and settled for Ptolemy, Aristobulus the architect-engineer, and Nearchus, Alexander's admiral and boyhood friend.

> This İ claim; and never mind who I am; never mind my name although it is not unknown among men; never mind my country, or my family, or any rank I have held among compatriots. I would rather say: for me, this book of mine is country, kindred and career, and it has been so since my boyhood.

He did not, in his lifetime, enjoy any conspicuous fame, and it is sad that he cannot know how much we owe him.

Some time about AD 300, on the fertile shore of Alexandria, crossroads of trade and of traditions, all the flotsam of romance, folk tale, rumour, agitprop, and moralistic fantasy, combined with some tattered shreds of history, was gathered by some untalented but limitlessly credulous author, and cast on the waters of time. Implausibly attributed to Callisthenes, who died four years before Alexander, it became the first work of fiction to achieve bestsellerdom in translation throughout the known civilized world. Far beyond its circle of hearers and readers at first hand, illiterates without number heard it retailed at second, third, fourth, or hundredth remove, by bazaar storytellers, itinerant entertainers, people beguiling a journey, pedagogues, court poets, jongleurs and priests. It spread first among the peoples he had known and conquered, then on and on among those he had never seen and only known from rumour, till it reached the Far East which, having been taught that the land mass ended with India, he had not believed to exist.

Greek variants proliferated; versions appeared in Armenian, Bulgarian, Hebrew, Ethiopic and Syriac, the last being done into Arabic. Most significantly, soon after its appearance, one Julius Valerius did it into Latin, the universal language of the literate Western world Greek in the Dark Ages, and well beyond them, was rarer in the West than gold. Latin was everywhere. From Valerius' *Callisthenes,* along with the Roman sources, and from them alone, the image of Alexander came down to the Middle Ages. The Middle Ages split his image in two.

To the Church he was a gift, as he had been to the republicans. Here was Virtue corrupted by Fortune; the lust of the flesh and the lust of the eyes and the pride of life, riding fast to dust and judgment. In an age when Crusaders were proud to approach the Holy Sepulchre up to their horses' fetlocks in Jewish blood; when heretics were burned alive; when holiness was seen in a hair shirt crawling with lice of ten years' breeding; when excommunicate kings, to escape damnation, had to bare their backs to the scourge or kneel in ashes, there were stern useful morals to be drawn from King Alisaunder.

But an age of oppressive orthodoxy, whether under priest or commissar, breeds rebels. "To hell will I go!" cries young Aucassin, defying Nicolete's censorious guardian.

> For to hell go the fair clerks, and the fair knights fallen in tourneys or in grand wars, the good sergeants-at-arms and the men of honour. With those will I go. And there go the fair courteous ladies, who have two friends or three besides their lords. There go the gold and the silver, the vair and ermine; there go harpers and jongleurs and the kings of the earth. With them will I go, so I have Nicolete, my most sweet friend, with me.

There, too, they would go with Alexander. His medieval romances are a vast ramifying theme. Their fascination is that, though their authors had access only to the most hostile sources, their residual relics of fact were enough to seize imagination and cast a spell. Incident might be wildly remote from history, yet the chivalrous knight saluted a kindred soul. In the *Alexandreis* and the *Roman d'Alexandre,* he is the pattern of valour and courtesy, glorious in arms, protective to ladies, fair and generous to enemies, liberal to vassals. God, not Fortune, directs his destiny; envious treachery, not Nemesis, contrives his death.

They had not seen his likeness; though he would have conformed well with their standards of beauty, he is given a conventional face in a conventional helmet, distinguished only by the elegance of his armour. He adventures to Darius' camp, disguised as his own herald, wins Roxane's heart, and escapes across a frozen river, later avenging his foully murdered foe. He flies in a chariot drawn by eagles, and views the monsters of the deep in a glass bell. Seeking the Water of Life once more through forests perilous, he consults the prophetic trees of the Sun and Moon, and with calm courage hears them foretell his end. Warned by an oracle that a close friend will kill him, and urged to purge those nearest him, he protests that he will die by the single traitor rather than wrong the innocent. (Cassander would have learned with some astonishment that he was a dear and trusted comrade.) He is poisoned, and the Seven Sages moralize over his grave.

Constantinople was sacked, its refugee scholars brought westward their salvaged books; the learned world of Italy rediscovered Greek literature and history. It was in the fifteenth century that the scholar Vasco of Lucena, writing to the Emperor Sigismund, told him that Arrian was more to be trusted than the Latin writers upon Alexander

With the Renaissance, therefore, the Romances were consigned to children and the ignorant; the historical Alexander reappeared. But his image was still conditioned by the legends, and by an age without archaeology which, busily excavating all over Italy Roman copies of such Greek originals as had appealed to Romans, admired like

them the soft, late style for its virtuosity, preferring the
sentimental contortions of the Laocoön to the most ma-
jestic classical Apollo. In this spirit, for a century or two
Alexander supplied the painters with subjects for great
setpieces, defeating Darius, protecting the royal ladies,
marrying Roxane. His eager profile is trimmed down to
insipid perfection; his correctly rounded elbow sketches
a stock art-school gesture; a resplendent waxwork in an
impracticable helmet cascading ostrich plumes, he is the
apotheosis of a tinsel-armoured male soprano in Baroque
opera, the vacuous imperial puppet of Dryden's *Alexander's Feast*.

Serious scholars, of course, were meantime reading
the sources and critical appraisal had begun, when in the
mid-nineteenth century the most formidable of them,
George Grote, amid many valuable services to history, disastrously revived the Ideological Alexander. Grote never
set foot in Greece, then without tourist accommodation
and much beset with bandits; a dedicated radical, he had
the fatal commitment which vitiates conscientious fact with
anachronistic morality. His whole capital of belief being
invested in the Athenian democracy, he was resolute in
attributing its fall to external villainy rather than internal
collapse. Demosthenes could do no wrong, Philip and
Alexander no right. For all practical purposes, Grote's
Alexander is back with the Lyceum; a natural tyrant,
forsaking the wholesome Greek virtues at the first taste
of Oriental sycophancy and despotic power.

Commitment breeds counter-commitment; the defence
was pushed too far. Sir William Tarn, active till this mid-
century, was more learned than Grote, and larger minded
But in his sympathy with Alexander, he too applied,
though favourably, his own moral code, often defending
him where he can scarcely have thought his actions needed
extenuation, and when they would certainly have shocked

none of his followers; while his unprejudiced regard for quality in friends or enemies is expanded into an idealistic faith in the unity of all mankind.

Recent scholarship is now restoring a balance; but these discussions, held in circles where it is agreed to respect the evidence, have filtered down as a turbid seepage to levels where only confirmation of the entrenched dogma is sought. An intractable resistance to levelling down has made Alexander the archdemon of egalitarians; while pacifists, well meaning but ill read, have projected on him their horror of modern atrocities (perpetrated after two millennia of Christianity) which this fourth-century pagan would scarcely have credited to savages.

Filtered and refracted by these layers of fable, history, tradition and emotion—a thing inseparable from him alive and dead—the image of Alexander has come down to us.

MACEDON

Alexander's existence was determined in 358 BC, at a celebration of the Mysteries on Samothrace, where his parents met.

Philip II of Macedon, then about twenty-four, was a legitimate but not quite hereditary king. His elder brother, Perdiccas III, had been killed while his son was still an infant. The Assembly of fighting Macedonians had the traditional right to choose in such circumstances a king from the members of the royal house; a fact of primary importance to the country's history. It was a time of civil feud and foreign invasion. A fighting regent was essential, and Philip was proven in the field. Not long after, the situation growing still more perilous, he was asked to assume the throne.

His surviving portrait shows a square powerful face, intelligent, ruthless, possibly brutal, but without the viciousness that chills in some of the Caesars. It has humour; looks capable of charm, and of the amatory success for which he was notorious.

A crucial event of his career had happened when he was sixteen. In the complex wars of the royal succession, Perdiccas, making a treaty with Thebes, had had to supply a royal hostage as security. Childless as yet, he had perforce sent his younger brother. Thebes had been then in its full brief blaze of glory after the overthrow of the

Spartan tyranny. Intellectually provincial, in military lustre it was unmatched in Greece. Lately its cult of heroic homosexual love had reached its apogee with Pelopidas' foundation of its *corps d'élite,* the Sacred Band, made up from pairs of friends who had already taken a traditional vow to stand or fall together. Philip, treated on parole more as guest than prisoner, learned the skills of soldiering from the finest masters. Here too he may have added to his lifelong love of women the taste for young men which was to cause his death.

It is tempting to wonder whether some friendly contrivance of his hosts could have got him, incognito, across the border to Athens. He was a young nonentity and it would have been easy. He was not likely in his days of power to admit having sneaked in under such humiliating conditions; but all his life he showed a deep regard for Athens' history and culture, however great his contempt for her current leaders. Reared himself in a fifth-century palace at Pella, built by Athenian architects and decorated by her painters of the finest period, he could appreciate her material splendours, still in uncorrupted perfection.

His own inheritance was a highland kingdom of great scenic beauty and tall warlike men, where his capital, Pella, was an island of classicism in an archaic society. At his accession (as Alexander later reminded his men) all that the people owned were the sheep whose skins they wore for want of cloth, and even those were hard to keep, border raids from neighbours being constant. As in Homer's day, the lords would follow the king to war— unless just then supporting some rival claimant—bringing each his meinie of tough undisciplined followers armed with what came to hand. The loose law of succession had ensured a series of civil wars and a long record of murders. Perdiccas had got his throne by killing a lover of his

mother's who had usurped it; she was rumoured to have
procured the deaths both of her husband and her son.
From him Philip inherited five rival pretenders to the
throne, some in a state of active hostilities; and two
foreign invasions. No account of Alexander's life can be
understood without remembering the record of his forebears which he must have picked up from his earliest
years.

Philip killed at once the most dangerous of the claim-
ants, who was his half-brother. The others, with restraint
by family standards, he expelled or undermined. His
hands thus free, he set about defending his frontiers. At
some time during these early campaigns, he sailed to
Samothrace.

The Mysteries retain much mystery despite the archaeologists, and it is not clear what benefit he hoped for.
Their chief known gift was protection from shipwreck,
one of the few perils he seldom met. Their "Great Gods"
were pre-Hellenic deities, whose offerings were cast into
a deep cleft, and who were somehow associated with
dwarfs, perhaps by folk memory of an extinct race. The
island is steep and sheer, the sanctuary near the shore;
the rites, which involved corybantic dancing and much
noise, were performed at night.

Legend was bound to make Philip fall in love with
Olympias during the actual celebration; but it may be
true. Such things excited her and must have made her
striking looks dramatic. The visit would keep the initiates
a day or two on the island, giving him a chance to see
her by daylight, find out who she was, and most likely
meet her. Fatefully, she was a girl who could only be had
by marriage.

She was the orphaned daughter of a former King of
Epirus, the region of modern Albania. It was more primi-

tive than Macedon and the hegemony of the kings was
even less secure; but it had important possibilities, and
Philip, if he had hesitated, did so no longer.

No portrait of Olympias has survived which is not
stylized to nullity. Her looks may be suggested by her
son's, which did not come from Philip. Most north Greeks
were fair, red-haired or auburn. Otherwise, our one visual
glimpse of her dates from just before her death, when she
was about sixty. It consists in the single fact that two
hundred of Cassander's soldiers, who had agreed to kill
her and broken into her house to do it, looked at her face
to face and went away.

Her family claimed descent from Achilles. His son
Neoptolemus had fathered their royal line upon Andromache, Hector's widow, his prize from the sack of Troy.
Unaware how momentous this lineage would be for
history, Philip married the princess, and, leaving her
pregnant, returned to his necessary wars.

The prophetic dreams of Philip and Olympias belong
properly to the area of legend. He dreamed he was sealing
her womb with the image of a lion; she, that kindled by a
thunderbolt a fire spread from her body to the earth's
ends, and was suddenly quenched in darkness. Alexander
was in fact born under the sign of Leo, in August 356.

Philip, on campaign in Thrace, got the news along with
two other messages. His general, Parmenion, had soundly
defeated the Illyrians in the west; and his racehorse had
won at the Olympic Games. The right of Olympic entry
was a prized inheritance of the kings of Macedon. The
Games were only open to Greeks; and Macedonians were
not recognized in the south as the offshoots of the original
stock which in fact they were. They were regarded as semi-
barbarous (the actual term "barbarian" was reserved for
Persians) and the royal house had just scraped in on the

strength of a remote Argive ancestry. For Philip, to whom acceptance in the Greek world was a lifelong dream, this news may have been the most welcome item of the three

It was inevitable that Alexander's childhood would later be described as precocious and brilliant; he was certainly not a late developer. Plutarch mentions, without quoting it, a long list of the teachers whom Philip imported for him. More to the purpose is what he learned from his parents.

By the time he was in his teens, they were not merely estranged but open enemies. Their one other child, a daughter called Cleopatra, was born not long after him; thereafter it can be assumed that sexual intercourse ceased. Whether Olympias had ever returned Philip's feeling cannot, of course, be known; like all women of her time she had been "given in marriage." Her pride ensured that if his infidelities did not torment her with jealousy they would be taken as deadly insults. It seems evident that the violent fracture of their relations must have happened in Alexander's early childhood, the time when it would give the deepest pain and leave the deepest impression. It is the age at which the child, given ordinary kindness, will identify with the mother. For Alexander, his father's constant absences on campaign, combined with his mother's possessive love, made this a certainty.

She was a woman of great ability and intelligence, whose judgment was wholly swayed by her emotions; a visionary and an orgiast, though improbably in any sexual sense; she had the pride which does not stoop to common adulteries. The Dionysiac frenzy was for many women a kind of releasing drug trip, though only wine was used, the rest being auto-suggestion and mass emotion. Olympias brought to it a powerful imagination. To the anger and disgust of Philip with his Hellenic aspirations, she kept about her the tame snakes of the primitive Thracian cult. She may have had self-induced hallucinations. Alexander was probably still quite young when first she gave him to understand that Philip was not his father.

Daily life in those days, even for the great, had little privacy. That, in spite of the accusations she invited, no man was ever named as her lover, is significant. Hating her husband, she wished wholly to possess her son. Later events show that whatever mystery he believed to surround his birth, it was supernatural.

It cannot have been long, in a free-spoken society, before he learned what the alternative was; while to be Philip's son may have seemed to him even worse. What hidden agonies he endured remained his secret; suppressed, perhaps, even out of his memory. That he did not emerge a psychopath like Nero is one of history's miracles.

In calm interludes of this life he was taught, like all high-born children, his ancestry. It went back on both sides to Zeus; on his mother's, there was the heroic strain of Achilles, but also the royal blood of Troy. He was brought up to honour both sides in that great war; to treat neither with contempt or hate. Whatever harm Olympias did him, for this at least the world was to be her debtor.

As heir of Macedon, he was reared from his cradle in unquestioning acceptance of having been born to the sword, as a farmhand's son to the plough. Neither to Philip nor Olympias would any other future have been thinkable. It remained only to excel.

Philip had now won the struggle for mere national survival. He began to secure his frontiers by attack. The turning point had been his capture, from the loosely knit tribes of west Thrace, of Mount Pangaeus, with its rich veins of gold and silver. It freed him from dependence on tribal levies. Henceforth he could pay full-time soldiers, and turn them into professionals.

It was a military revolution. The labour of Helot serfs had given Sparta a citizen force in permanent training; but the Spartan mind was inflexible, and the dinosaur was at the point of death. Regular mercenaries existed in plenty: they might be exiles from other cities in the endless oscillations from democracy to oligarchy and back, when each change of government was accompanied by a vigorous settling of old scores; or younger sons whose portion only ran to a suit of armour; or criminals on the run. They would enlist with a mercenary general in good standing (this was important) and follow him where he was hired. But no Greek city-state would pay taxes for a standing army, which was distrusted, too, as a tool of potential coups. Philip now needed little of this casual labour; he could add to regular discipline the force of native loyalties and racial pride. As a matter of course, lords still officered their own tribesmen; it would take the full force of Alexander's personality to bring in promotion on merit. But Philip was now permanent commander-in-chief; and he forged a formidable weapon.

Its solid centre was the infantry phalanx, a deep column (phalanx means finger) armed with the giant spear of his devising, the famous sarissa. Of graded length, those of the fourth-rank line being at least 15 feet long, these pikes enabled four ranks at once to take the enemy at spearpoint, making them virtually immune from all but missile weapons. This was the holding force. The striking hammers were the flanking cavalry wings. Alexander was to be the virtuoso of this instrument; but Philip was its creator.

He had light-armed skirmishers, archers and slingers; Dionysius of Syracuse had made innovations in siegecraft which were not lost on him. His generalship was equalled by his political acumen, which enabled him to intervene in neighbouring wars at the request of one or other party (the ancient tragedy of divided Greece) to his own profit. His influence in Thessaly, his steady extension across Thrace towards the vital corn route of the Hellespont, were already alarming Athens.

One can only speculate what would have been the effect on Alexander if Olympias had died in childbirth; if he had kept her genes but escaped her influence. Such a father and son might have added affection to mutual pride. As it was, this towering figure was the enemy and oppressor; the gross lecher from whose loins some god—pray heaven—had saved him from being begotten; above all the rival, at all costs to be surpassed. All Alexander's story testifies to the effect on natural genius of the deep insecurity felt in these tormenting early years. Compensation for it inspired his greatest achievements; when it took him unawares, it betrayed him into his greatest sins.

That he kept his sanity he must have owed to his capacity for friendship, a solace he turned to while very young. Psychologically his face must have been his fortune; to this attractive boy people were drawn without the pretences of flattery, and his true child's instincts felt it. He grew up with a religious faith in friendship, making it a cult, publicly staking his life on it. The real loves of his life were friendships, including his sexual loves. Though he had the classic family pattern for homosexuality, it was probably the mere availability of men rather than women for friendship which directed his emotional life. To be loved for himself, as he certainly often was, ministered to his constant need for reassurance, and he returned affection so warmly that it seldom let him down. When it did, it shook him to his roots. He had committed too much, and could not forgive.

When he was seven, the recognized end of childhood, his father found him a tutor. He was a certain Leonidas, Olympias' uncle; Philip the diplomat thus avoiding palace brawls. Both parents, it seems, agreed on the way in which the boy should be fitted for his destiny. As a man, he gave his own account of it.

> Ada, whom he honoured with the title of Mother and made Queen of Caria . . . in the kindness of her heart used to send him daily many dishes and sweets, and finally offered him pastrycooks and chefs of noted skill. He said he did not need them; better cooks had been given him by Leonidas his tutor—a night march to make him want his breakfast, and a small breakfast to make him want his supper. "And," he said, "the man himself used to come and look through my bedding-boxes and clothes-chests, to see my mother did not hide any luxuries or extras there."

Spare diet, thin clothing, and the hard exercise his age and nature (as well as the need to keep warm) dictated may have been the chief causes of Alexander's failure to reach the average height of the Macedonians, whatever that was; the great sarissa being a regular weapon suggests that it was impressive. Had he been a really little man, we should read of his being identified by it at a distance instead of by the other means always mentioned, his armour, actions and so on; and the Athenian propagandists could never have let it alone; but that his height was undistinguished, and probably less than his father's, in a society which set great value on stature, must have been bad enough. When later he learned medicine and physiology he may have connected cause and effect. He showed no love for Leonidas after he left his charge, and the only gift he sent him back from Asia was ironical: a sack of incense. As a boy he was offering incense at a shrine, giving extravagantly as he would always do, when Leonidas had told him sharply to be sparing of precious things till he was master of the lands they grew in. He did not take Leonidas along.

He did take, and once risked his life for, an unimportant court hanger-on called Lysimachus, who styled himself his pedagogue. This was of course a joke, for it was servant's work; but Lysimachus did take on the humble duties of the man-nanny from whom no teaching was required. Alexander's gratitude for a personal devotion was always lifelong; but what he got besides is beyond computation, for good or ill. Lysimachus used to amuse the child by calling himself Phoenix, the pedagogue of Achilles. Alexander played his part in the game for life. To the end of his days he kept the *Iliad* under his pillow, along with the dagger for self-defence which was the commonplace bedroom furniture of a Macedonian king.

It seems an odd attraction in a man whose own impulses were to prove more generous. Achilles was merciless to the conquered; asserted the captor's right over royal women; desecrated the body of a noble enemy; sulked in his tent while his friends were falling in battle, a thing rather than which Alexander would have died. But it must be remembered that Achilles was an ancestor, about whom he may have heard many tales not in Homer, embroidering on them in fantasy; the Duke of Wellington in the Brontë children's romances was not the Duke of history, and Alexander's Achilles may not have been ours. His interest in Amazons suggests, for instance, that he knew the Epic Cycle story about the romantic duel between the hero and Penthesilea; and the whole Cycle has now been lost. He knew at any rate what Homer says: that Achilles' mother was a goddess; that he was despoiled and slighted by a king, whom he got the better of;

that he had a comrade whom he loved as his own life; and that he was angry

Plutarch says that from childhood Alexander had a longing to excel, and *philotimia,* the love of honour. Despite his childhood traumas, we hear nothing about fits of rage. Had his love of winning made him an unpleasant loser, he would not have been supported in disgrace and exile by his boyhood friends. Yet the enormous anger of Achilles must have touched some chord in him.

In the year of Philip's accession, a reign had closed in Persia too. The long-lived, weak Artaxerxes II was succeeded by Artaxerxes Ochus his son. A strong but savage ruler, he began at once to reduce too-powerful satraps and to ban their private armies. Rebellion failed; two fugitives were sheltered by Philip and were at his court some years, one of them the important and aristocratic Artabazus, of whom much more will be heard. He was one of those astonishing old men who seem to survive today only in the Russian Caucasus. Already elderly when he rebelled, and getting old when pardoned and recalled, he was to survive, a vigorous nonagenarian, to campaign successively under Darius and Alexander, whose eager welcome when they met again many years later points to warm childhood memories. He had thus known Persians as long as he could remember, not as propaganda monsters but observable humans and friends; with the boys of Artabazus' large family he must often have played. Though Macedonian was a broad Doric patois, the court spoke Greek, as did many travelled or well-bred Persians; so there is likelihood in Plutarch's well-known story that when Persian envoys arrived bringing the exiles' recall, and Philip happened to be absent, little Alexander took it on himself to welcome them.

He won them over by his cheerful friendliness, and by asking questions which were not childish nor trifling, but about the length of the roads, and what the journey was like inland; about the King himself, how he behaved in battle, and about the Persian prowess and strength.

His father had turned Pella into a military base and his palace into a staff headquarters; the child had probably run about among soldiers since he was on his feet. The sublime confidence with which he took command of them in his mid-teens suggests he had long known them with the privileged intimacy of a regimental pet.

It would be as a family guest that he first met a youth who, being eleven years his elder, would have seemed a man to him: his future historian, Ptolemy. He was a kinsman on his mother's side, either in a regular way or, as tradition has it, by a liaison with the adolescent Philip before he left for Thebes, in which case the boys were half-brothers. Later generations of Ptolemys did not disclaim the bar sinister. Born as he was at Pella, Ptolemy I must have known Alexander throughout his life span.

Arrian's History starts at his accession, probably because Ptolemy's did, which is a pity, for his knowledge of earlier years would have been invaluable. Ptolemy is of course his own chief authority for himself, but is respected by ancient authors. He edited out his rivals' exploits—a perennial liability in retired generals' memoirs—and made the most of his own, but was honoured for not inventing any; and he wrote towards the end of a long life, when the tumult and the shouting had largely died, the captains and the kings departed. Arrian recommends him on the grounds that not only did he campaign with Alexander, "but, as he was a king himself, falsehood would have been more shameful to him than to anyone else."

Modern sniggers at Arrian's childish snobbery, evoked
by these sensible words, are themselves curiously naïve.
He is not of course attributing to kings a superior sense
of honour, but stating the obvious fact that they are
vulnerable to public disgrace. Ptolemy was more than a
decade older than Alexander, who in turn had had in
his army, towards the end of his life, many men at least
ten years his junior. In a city like Alexandria, the recitals
of the History—the method of publication in the ancient
world—would have attracted plenty of alert veterans still
in middle life, living on their memories. The founder
of a dynasty cannot afford the ridicule of such an audience.

By then, Alexander had been out of the reach of flattery
for a good twenty years; yet detractors, irked by the fact
that the sources most "favourable" are men who knew
him in life, have sought in Ptolemy for ulterior motive,
apparently oblivious of the fact that their case is based
upon the opposite of what it sets out to prove. Ptolemy's
interest is alleged to lie in creating propaganda for his
own dynasty. But he wrote for a living audience, before
posterity. Why, in the first place, drag all the way to
Egypt the body of a corrupt tyrant about whom thousands of influential people would know the truth? Why not
fill the History with stories to his discredit in which
Ptolemy shone by contrast? Yet anti-Alexandrists have
always assumed that he favours Alexander to bask in his
reflected glory; which is certainly having it both ways.

One need not of course discount the latter motive; it
would be human enough. But Ptolemy's loyalty predates
all possible self-interest and indeed once cost him dear.
Later, though never promoted to the eminence of Craterus
or Hephaestion, this capable and, as it was to prove, very
ambitious soldier remained unswervingly true. Is it too
much to suppose that something in Alexander inspired

these feelings and caused them to outlast his life, and that Ptolemy wrote among men who shared them? He wanted to remember the best, they wanted to hear it. It is after all the simplest explanation.

In 348, when Alexander was eight, Philip captured the Greek-colonized Thracian city of Olynthus, an ally of Athens, after an eventful siege. It had harboured his surviving half-brothers; in open revolt; so he killed them both. "Such tragedies," remarks Grote with irrefutable truth, "were not infrequent in the Macedonian royal family."

The chief reason was the polygamy of the kings. With luck, the Queen Consort's eldest son might hope to inherit; but Macedonian rulers would combine business with pleasure. going through forms of marriage with the daughters of powerful noblemen or new allies to secure the valuable obligations of kinship. All the sons of these alliances were, and had been for generations, potential usurpers. Some had changed the succession. Philip dealt with the problem in the traditional manner. It did not warn him to avoid the cause.

Being both highly sexed and an expert diplomat, he made full use of his royal prerogative; it was a proverb that he had a new wife with every war. In all he had at least a half dozen of these minor wives, several of whom bore children, one being a boy. All sources agree on Olympias' bitter resentment. Whether she felt the jealousy of a woman, the affront of a queen, or both, she watched like a nursing tigress for any threat to her son. The bastard boy, Arridaeus, was mentally retarded; and though it seems unlikely that she brought this about with drugs, people thought her capable of it, as in fact she was. There is no uncertainty about the mark she made upon Alexander.

As a boy, he played and sang to the lyre; for this we

have first-hand evidence from one who heard him. As a man, he was a constant and generous patron of musicians, but we never read of his playing or singing a note. An anecdote of Aelian's gives the reason. He had a rather high-toned voice, later to be much imitated, like all his other mannerisms; and Greeks preferred a sweet singing tone to a deep one. But one day his father heard him, and told him he should be ashamed to sing so well. Since someone recorded it, there was an audience. The slur of effeminacy must have been intended, and was certainly so received. It was probably not the only time his parents took out on him their hatred of one another.

The natural watershed between his boyhood and adolescence is the famous episode of his taming Bucephalas. It is a well-worn tale: the fiery charger offered at a high price to Philip, refusing to be mounted, and turned down as useless; the boy insisting that a great horse was being wasted; the father's challenging him to do better than his elders; their bet on it, the horse to be bought for him if he could manage it, and if not, paid for by him; its instant trust when it felt his hands. But the popular notion is still of high-spirited youngsters meeting; the more interesting truth is that Bucephalas was twelve years old.

The horse must therefore have been trained, and no doubt for war. What this entailed in ancient Greece is vividly described in Xenophon's treatise On Horsemanship. Neither saddle nor stirrups were yet known; the rider sat bareback or on a cloth. Thus the spear could not be used for an impact charge as in medieval war, but only for thrusting (Alexander himself favoured the sabre). Even so, the horseman needed a well-disciplined mount if he was to stay on; apart from knee grip, control was by the bit alone, and surviving examples are often horrible. Besides steadiness in battle, the high-class charger was expected to caracole on parade; and here Xenophon, who was fond of horses, has some revealing "don'ts." "Some teach the curvetting action either by striking the horse with a rod under the hocks, or by having someone run alongside with a stick and hit him on the quarters." He also deprecates simultaneously dragging up the head, spurring and whipping. It seems possible that someone, trying by such means to prepare this brave and spirited animal for a royal buyer, had got more than he bargained for. Arrian says that it never let anyone but Alexander mount it as long as it lived; for him, adds Curtius, it would lower its body to help him on.

No other incident of Alexander's life is related by Plutarch in so much detail; it reads like total recall. Perhaps on nights when the world conqueror, sitting late over the wine, fell "into a kind of soldierly boasting," this was a favourite tale which some memoirist got to know by heart. Its interest, however, is historical as well as human. At the battle of Gaugamela, Alexander, then twenty-five, was nursing his twenty-four-year-old charger, which was famous enough for this to be recorded. The years of its prime were those of his youthful wars before his accession; its exploits, and his, must already have been celebrated.

Philip, buying him the horse as agreed, showed great pride in his son's achievement. Unluckily for their improved relations, at about the same time the King involved himself in the most unpleasant of the scandals his way of life invited. From Diodorus' account of it, it seems that his homosexual love life had retained the pattern of Thebes only in that his favourites were socially presentable; he lacked the constancy of the Sacred Band. A certain Pausanias had been discarded for a new fancy; furiously resentful, at some drinking party he called his young rival a paid whore. Had he been right it would have altered history. He was wrong. With fierce Macedonian pride, the youth threw away his life to reject the insult. In the next Illyrian border war, having left a message to explain his action, he ran ahead of the King to certain death among the enemy.

A noble called Attalus, a friend of Philip, perhaps the dead man's kinsman or tribal chief, devised a black farce by way of retribution. He got Pausanias dead drunk at his house, threw him out in the stable yard and invited the slaves to rape him.

Unable to kill Attalus in the midst of his retainers, Pausanias went to the King demanding vengeance. Since Attalus could not legally be executed without a public trial even had Philip wished it, he naturally refused; but, Pausanias being an Orestid of almost royal family, offered him some kind of compensation in land or rank. He accepted it and the affair seemed closed. It is unlikely that Alexander, by now twelve or thirteen, missed hearing the sordid tale. No doubt he suffered what was natural to his age, his nature and the event.

However, it was to set him upon the throne.

Soon after, Philip extended his power decisively southward. By invitation, he became Archon of Thessaly: leading chieftain, judge, war leader, virtual king. It genuinely benefitted the country with its long history of oppressive and warring barons; neither he nor his son ever had trouble in recruiting cavalry among the famed Thessalian horsemen. But Athens, with its democratic commitment and traditional hatred of monarchy, thought only of the growing menace from the north.

In fact, the last thing Philip wanted was war with Athens. He had larger and better plans. After the disastrous Peloponnesian War, the Spartans had propped their hated tyranny in south Greece by ceding to Persia the Greek colonies in Asia Minor, in return for Persian support. It had killed their prestige before their power declined. Since then all the city-states had agreed, in principle, that they had a sacred duty to liberate their Hellene kinsmen. Only, enmeshed in feuds many generations old, they could never combine to do it. To achieve it was Philip's dream.

Objective minds had long seen the necessity of a single high command. The nonagenarian political philosopher Isocrates, who remembered Socrates as a contemporary, had been urging it for decades, sometimes on rather unsuitable leaders; now he saw in Philip a really promising candidate, and wrote at some length to tell him so. Philip was indeed well qualified for the task. Had he not sired a genius, he would be remembered as the most brilliant general of antiquity next to Julius Caesar. He was neither a harsh ruler nor, by the time's standards, superfluously cruel in war. He respected culture, was at ease with statesman or peasant, and could undermine hostility with charm. His good balance is indeed surprising, seeing that his Theban captivity had not been his first: as a very small child he had had the shock of being sent as hostage to the wild Illyrians by the usurper Ptolemy, his mother's lover, whom his elder brother had to kill before he was ransomed back.

He could take a joke. After one of his victories he was supervising the routine business of selling his captives to the slave dealers, sprawling in his chair. "Spare me, Philip!" called a resourceful prisoner. "I was your father's friend!" Asked for details, he said they were confidential. Philip beckoned him up. "Pull down your cloak, sir," he whispered. "Your crotch is showing." With a grin Philip told the guards, "Yes, he's a good friend, let him go." To him is first credited the classic put-down to a chatty barber: "How do you like your hair cut, sir?" "In silence."

This robust humour was not passed on to his son. Alexander's recorded sayings have pith rather than wit; and the jokes which endeared him to his men were boyishly simple. Having thawed back to life a soldier dazed with cold in his own chair by the campfire, he said, "You're lucky it's not Darius's, *he'd* have had your head for it." This is a long way from Philip's pungent irony; perhaps the boy had felt its bite too young.

It was liked still less, however, by Philip's arch-enemy, the Athenian orator Demosthenes; a man entirely humourless, but with a notable gift for vituperation. He was the heir to a great ideal and its last defender. Inevitably, his name is touched with its grandeur, and with the aura of a lost cause. He was without doubt a patriot by belief as well as by profession; his faith in the free city-state was real—so long as the state was Athens. But only with effort does justice to Demosthenes survive a reading of his orations, well polished and published by himself. They were admired in eighteenth-century England when political scurrility was not impeded by libel laws. Their counterparts were the brutal cartoons of Gillray; Hogarth would have been too moral and Rowlandson too jolly. He catches no gleam from the brilliance of Athens' zenith, gives back no echo of Pericles' immortal affirmation that man's individuality is his right and his city's pride. Page after page is loaded with invective, against political or private enemies as often as against Macedon ("a country from which it was never yet possible to buy a decent slave"). No weapon is too mean for him; he will sneer at the poverty of an opponent's childhood, and he sticks at no lie he can get away with. He has all the skills of rhetoric; but his popularity is a dark comment on the Athens of his day. One cannot read him without feeling sure he would have spoken for the death of Socrates.

He led his city to ruin, not through treachery—even her

traitors could have done her better service—but from
inveterate hate and spite. No doubt he believed of Philip
exactly what he said of him, that he was a power-drunk
barbarian whose intent was to sack Athens and set up a
slave state there: Demosthenes had the envy which hopes
for evil in other men. His belief in the free city did not
pass his own city walls. He had no compunction in keeping up secret contacts with Persia, and got from King
Ochus huge sums for use in propaganda and bribery
against Macedon. Philip, of course, had his own fifth
column also; partly composed of merely venal agents, but
partly of men not without concern for their own cities,
who saw in Macedonian hegemony, as did Isocrates, an
end to the constant interstate wars, and a hope for the
Greek Asian cities. Philip, an unashamed practitioner of
realpolitik, was at least not sanctimonious.

The antagonists had met when Athens sent envoys to
Pella. (Alexander would have been about eight years
old.) Demosthenes, the star, had saved himself till the
last; but, face to face with Philip's formidable personality,
the orator "dried." Indulgently the King invited him to
start again from the beginning; but his nerve was gone.
He learned his speeches by heart, and now had lost the
thread. He could only stammer and sit down; and his
rivals, to whom he had boasted that he would leave Philip
without a word to say for himself, took care it was not
forgotten. By such events the fate of nations can be determined, as well as by the price of corn.

At the state dinner which followed, young Alexander,
still doing his music lessons, sang part songs with a friend.
Demosthenes on his return is said to have jeered at this
performance, and made some obscene pun or other. He
had had a hard youth, orphaned early and defrauded by
his trustees, and he shouldered the chip for life. In his
way he was as insecure as the boy whose lyre was soon

to be laid aside. But the metals behaved differently in the fire.

When Alexander was thirteen, a succession struggle in Epirus, Olympias' homeland, threatened feudal war. Philip intervened, setting on the throne her brother Alexandros (the Greek spelling will distinguish him from Alexander). It was a shrewd choice of a man who, in the Macedonian family disputes, could be trusted to see where his own interests lay; one of Philip's most successful diplomatic coups. Not faulty judgment, but the convergence of unseen forces, was to make it the engine of his fall.

In the same year, he took another decision equally momentous. Alexander was ready for higher education. Athens being now virtually an enemy country, he would have to get it at home. Philip looked about for a tutor.

There was a rush of applications. Isocrates, now running up to his century, showed some pique at being passed over. Speusippus, Plato's successor at the Academy, offered to resign and come; but Philip wanted the culture of Athens, not her politics. Only four years before, when Alexander was already nine years old, Plato had died, posing one of the great Ifs of history. His dream of the philosopher-king had not survived his own ruined hopes. By his teacher Socrates, and by him, the pattern of the silk purse had been devised. Ironic fate had handed a sow's ear to each, the brilliant unstable Alcibiades, the vain shallow Dionysius II; while in Macedon the silk was being spun for Aristotle.

Legend has Philip booking up the wisest man of the age on the day of Alexander's birth, like a peer putting his son down for Eton. In fact, even thirteen years later he did not know the value he was getting. Aristotle in his early forties was a scholar with a rising reputation, and the important asset of having studied some years with Plato, whom, it was said, he had hoped to succeed at the

Academy. But it is most unlikely that his academic status was decisive in Philip's choice. Aristotle was the son of his father's family doctor, a certain Nicomachus. He must have treated the childish ailments of Philip himself and his two dead elder brothers, who had probably known Aristotle himself as a boy. His native city, Stagira, in coastal Thrace, had been destroyed in the wars while he was studying in Athens; and, being homeless, he had formed connections of great use to Macedon.

After Plato's death he accepted the invitation of a former fellow student, Hermias, a eunuch governor who had seceded from Persian rule and established a despotate, albeit a benign one, in Atarneus, which commanded the strait between the mainland and Mytilene. He had gathered round him a little court of philosopher friends, conferring the hand of his niece and ward on Aristotle, who thus had influence in a state of great strategic value to Philip. By him the philosopher was welcomed with the courtesy he always showed to distinguished Greeks, and offered a country house where, away from court and family distractions, the prince was instructed with a chosen group of friends.

Aristotle's extant works date from later years when he had founded his own university, the Lyceum, in Athens. His Macedonian period must have been one of transition from Plato's teachings, and we have no firm evidence of what he taught there; but Alexander's later life provides many clues. Plato was a metaphysical philosopher whose work is suffused with the poetry he renounced for its sake in youth. His own mystical experience was one of the premises from which his logic constructed his universe. In him, Alexander's glowing imagination would have found an interpreter and a guide. Aristotle's whole temper was that of the inductive scientist. It is one of the great open questions of history, whether the gain balanced the loss.

He made an instant appeal to his pupil's practical and inquiring intellect, to his passion for exploration and discovery. Botany and zoology fascinated Alexander all his life. So did medicine. He concerned himself closely with his soldiers' wounds or sicknesses, and prescribed personally for his friends; and in this he must have been well taught, for all Greek doctors passed on their art to their sons. On campaign he studied the animal and plant life, having records kept and specimens sent to Aristotle; and is said to have released ringed stags to learn their life span (Plutarch romantically gives them gold collars, hardly an aid to their conservation). The Middle Ages had a whole collection of spurious epistles from him on these matters, chief source of the Romances' fantastic fauna; his real observations, which would have been a treasure to more than biology, have disappeared.

He also learned philosophy. In the Greek world, this was central to all adult studies. It had not then become an abstruse specialization, absorbed in the minutiae of its own grammatical inflections. Its language was comprehensible to the lay ear, and its subject was ultimate human value judgments. Its conclusions on these were brought to bear in debate upon law, statecraft, and personal ethics.

Aristotle's ethics were high principled, rather than profound. He would have agreed with Socrates that he who would be esteemed must buy it with reality whatever it costs to achieve; "be what you wish to seem." But the prayer Plato gives to Socrates is, "Make me to be beautiful within; and may outward things chime with the inward." Aristotle conceived the "great-souled man" as an image *first;* a superb role for which the man who would enact it must fit himself, below which he must never fall. Intellectual giant though he was, in giving this teaching to a man like Alexander he was a sorcerer's apprentice. Plato, in his middle years, might have been the sorcerer. Aristotle unleashed a force beyond his own conceiving.

Alexander's need for self-assurance was equal to his genius and strength of will. If he ever consciously resolved to be greatest among men, it was probably in his schooldays. As this dream became realized he would exult in it. And here it is vital not to think anachronistically. Modesty was not admired in the Greek world, but thought mean-spirited; the lying boast, only, was despised. That a man is entitled to his earned esteem is the kingpin on which the plot of the *Iliad* turns. The dying words of Euripides' Hippolytus, "Pray that your lawful sons may be like me," offended no Greek audience; he had earned the right. It was inevitable therefore that Alexander should in due course become one of the vainest men in human history. The secret of his magnetism, to those around him and to posterity, is that his vanity was redeemed by pride. To be truly what he wished to seem was his passion till his last breath. On the occasion when he sank below his own forgiveness, the shame of it almost killed him.

His course in law and civics was no doubt of use to him early in his campaigns, while he dealt with the old Greek colonies; he would have been taught the nature of Greek regimes: tyranny (then a technical term) through extreme and moderate oligarchy to democracy. The lessons would have taken for granted a homogeneous body of citizens (slaves, women and most immigrants being unenfranchised); all, at least by assimilation, Greek. Once outside such societies he would have to improvise. His tutor was explicit about the function of lesser breeds; Greeks were men, barbarians sub-men, created for men's use, like plants and animals. It was the conventional view of the time; and if Aristotle did not rise above it, he had some excuse. While he was in Macedon his friend and kinsman Hermias was lured by treachery into Ochus' hands, tortured to make him reveal his allies' plans (which he did not do) then crucified.

During one of the civics lessons, the students were given some hypothetical situation and asked how they would meet it. Alexander, who probably knew the "right" answer well enough, said that when it happened, he'd see. It was prophetic. He would do what he did by being flexible steel in an age of iron.

Among Aristotle's biological theories was that woman is an imperfect form of man. Himself a heterosexual, in the man's world of Greece he took for granted, no less than Plato, that a man's vital relationships would be with other men. Where Plato exalted love, he extolled friendship, wherein each should desire and promote the highest good in the other. Whatever reservations Alexander had about his civics course, to this precept he responded wholeheartedly. Whether they met in childhood or adolescence, by now he had the company of Hephaestion.

Like Ptolemy he was of local birth; they had probably met much earlier. At any rate Aristotle, who left Pella when Alexander was sixteen and never saw him or his friends again, wrote Hephaestion a whole book of letters. Lamentably, they are among his catalogued works no longer extant. Of still greater interest might have been Hephaestion's answers.

Had he outlived Alexander we would know much more of him. Had Alexander outlived him long enough to memorialize him, even that idealized portrait would have filled in some blanks. Probabilities suggest he may be one of the most underrated men in history. In his lifetime he must have aroused enormous envy; he left no one behind him with any interest in promoting his reputation,

and we have only the records of his rivals; that so little
is adduced against him is remarkable. The worst we ever
hear of him is that he was once slow to make up a private
quarrel in which, since its details are lost, he may have
had more provocation than we know. Starting his army
career simply as a Companion (that is, a member of the
king's own regiment of cavalry) he was steadily promoted,
obviously on merit, to the highest military and civil rank;
was never defeated in any of his very responsible independent assignments; carried out impeccably numerous
diplomatic missions of the first importance; and cor-
responded with two philosophers. His loss nearly unseated
Alexander's reason. Theories that this was some mere
bedmate or boon companion prized for his doglike devotion are hardly tenable.

He is described by Curtius as being taller than Alexander, and better looking, in which case he was certainly
handsome. No historian states plainly whether they were
physically lovers; but Plutarch says that on the site of
Troy, Alexander laid a wreath on Achilles' tomb, and
Hephaestion on Patroclus'. In spite of Homer's reticence,
classical Greece assumed the heroes' love to be sexual.
It would be characteristic of Alexander's passion for personal loyalties to make so public an avowal. Olympias,
at any rate, was wildly jealous of their attachment and
railed by letter at Hephaestion half across Asia. A fragmentary retort of his survives: "Stop quarrelling with
me; not that in any case I shall much care. You know
Alexander means more to me than anyone."

They had just under four years with Aristotle. When
Alexander was sixteen Philip, committed to a long elaborate siege in eastern Thrace, appointed his son Regent
of Macedon.

It is of course evident that he had already been at war.
No record of it remains; but the trust committed to him

was no sinecure. Though the experienced Antipater was left as his adviser, Philip cannot by this time have supposed he would not act on his own initiative if he thought fit. The border tribes, the still unsubdued Illyrians in particular, were a constant threat; so were the Athenians, who without declaration of war were using terrorist methods, seizing a Macedonian ship and selling the crew as slaves, capturing an envoy and demanding ransom; arresting in Athens a merchant shopping for Olympias, torturing him, on Demosthenes' orders, till he confessed to spying, and putting him to death. More urgently, there were the west Thracians, previously subdued, but, if they rose, a threat to Philip's communication line, now extended almost to the Hellespont.

Plutarch's note on this period is brief. Alexander, "not to sit idle, reduced the rebellious Maedi, and putting a colony of several peoples in their place called it after himself, Alexandropolis." The idea that he was seeking pastime is dispelled by a look at the map. Maedian country was in the wilds of today's Bulgarian frontier; raiders from there would descend into the cultivated Strymon valley, which intersected Philip's supply route. A successful revolt, triggering others, might have involved him in a major military disaster.

Alexander's first "colony" was doubtless a mere hill village. His father had founded his Thracian Philipopolis; only later days reveal the triumph the boy must have felt in this act of emulation. More significant is the fact that at sixteen he could call upon the standing army of Macedon, be followed unquestioningly into barbarian fastnesses and obeyed in a hard mountain campaign. It would be interesting to know where and how they had previously got to trust him.

After this he served under his father (Antipater now acting Regent), and was sent with the rank of general to subdue some rebel cities in south Thrace. At about this time he saved, as he claimed later, his father's life. It was probably during Philip's arduous siege of Perinthus, when he may have needed to hire extra troops. Even as Great King of Persia, Alexander still recalled it with resentment. Philip, he said,

> when a riot had broken out between Macedonian soldiers and Greek mercenaries, overcome by a wound he had got in the fracas, had fallen down and could do no more than sham dead; he himself had protected his body with his shield and killed with his own hand the men who were rushing at him. Which his father had never been man enough to admit, being unwilling to owe his son his life.

Unfortunately that is all we know of it.

Alexander's formal education was over, and Philip paid his school fee. It was a city. Aristotle's ruined birthplace, Stagira, was refounded, rebuilt, and repopulated, the people probably being bought out from slavery. This makes Alexander's education the most expensive on record. It was formative. He remembered always that the only self deserving of self-love is what would now be called the super-ego; the "intellectual soul" which must be trained to rule, like a king, over all lesser and baser appetites; to spurn the limits of mortality; to covet as riches only honour, nobility and glory. Leaving this spell behind him, the eminent apprentice of the dead sorcerer went home, to be taken aback by the subsequent thunder and lightning.

It is evident from Philip's confidence in his son that they were still getting on well together, as they normally did while in the field and well away from Olympias. Alexander now returned to resume his regency while Philip went on besieging the fortress ports, Perinthus and Byzantium. But Athens was now at open war, and with her commanding superiority in sea power supplied the beleaguered garrisons, forcing him to raise both sieges in the end. On his homeward march he defeated some hostile Scythians; but his army, slowed down with its spoil of cattle and slaves, was cut up by the northern tribe of Triballians, and the King himself was wounded too badly to be moved.

Meantime, the responsibilities of Alexander and Antipater were heavy. A complex politico-religious dispute about some sacred fields near Delphi had broken out in the southern states, promising a chance of Philip's favourite gambit, the solicited intervention of Macedon. (Time and again, the geography of Greece with its beautiful but barren mountains, its covetable farmlands, has determined its history. The long disastrous Peloponnesian War, the grave of Athenian greatness, had begun in a quarrel over sacred land in Megara.)

The Sacred League, a kind of religious United Nations, voted to punish the Amphissaeans, who had taken over the fields to farm. With the League Philip was in good standing, having evicted from Delphi some years earlier a Phocian force which had plundered Apollo's treasuries and temple. He had behaved both correctly and humanely, persuading his allies to fine the Phocians instead of throwing them off the cliffs; and had been put out by Demosthenes' propaganda representing them as oppressed martyrs and himself as a bloodstained tyrant. Now he sent word to the still-grateful League that his help, if asked for, would be forthcoming. The waiting time was crucial. Still laid up in Thrace, he ordered Alexander to mobilize the army; but lest Athens be alerted, he must give out that the campaign was to be against Illyria. He obeyed; before Philip could get back, rumour reached the Illyrians, who promptly rose in arms. For this risk

Alexander must have been prepared; he swept west to the border, repelled the invaders and pushed them back; his third independent operation, in rough terrain, this time against a more dangerous enemy. He was seventeen.

Philip returned, to await events in the south. During this interlude of peace, it seems, Alexander's parents found time to worry about his lack of sexual interests.

Perhaps he had turned down some marriage plan. Philip, a precocious womanizer if Ptolemy was his son, would be disconcerted to find a youth approaching eighteen, forward in all else, so backward here. The blood-stained and precarious royal succession made anxiety natural that he should beget an heir-presumptive in early life (and never was anxiety better justified by events). No more than other such parents in every age did these examine their own part in his reluctance. By now the very thought of marriage must have appålled him. Olympias nagged him, and is said to have hired a famous hetaira—one of those elegant "companions" who combined the skills of the geisha and the courtesan—to initiate him. She failed.

Aristotle taught neither asceticism nor Platonic sublimation. But his doctrine of the intellectual soul as king over the lower self offered a refuge to Alexander's pride for years. Never highly sexed, though with a deep need of affection, he had had his physical response to women frozen in childhood by his parents' mutual hate; it would be long in thawing. Meantime he had gathered a group of close and devoted friends, nearly all his elders. Hephaestion was evidently the only one of his age who could keep up with him; none of the rest got letters from Aristotle. Of the others none can have been a lover; nor, as events were soon to prove, did the inner ring contain sycophants drawn by rank. In these friends he invested his capital of emotion; his passionate generosity, his powerful magnetism, his compelling charm. Almost all were bound to him for life.

The Sacred League opened war upon the Amphissaeans; its scratch force proved ineffective. Demosthenes, foreseeing what must come, exhorted the unwilling Athenians to counter the menace of Philip by reaching accommodation with Thebes. The neighbours' quarrel was so old that, a century earlier, the Thebans had even thrown in their lot with the invading Xerxes. Their later overthrow of Spartan tyranny had aroused more envy than esteem. They had now a treaty with Macedon, and it was doubtful if they would denounce it.

When Philip had expelled the Phocians from the Delphic sanctuary in the earlier war, he had invited Athens, a League member, to send her own contingent. Demosthenes had secured a veto, mainly no doubt to prevent fraternization with the Macedonians, in whom fellow soldiers might discover fellow humans. When Philip's moderation had saved the Phocians' lives—they had to pay reparations and pull down their strongpoints—Demosthenes had denounced it as barbarity. As it now happened, the verdict against the Amphissaeans had just saved Athens herself, in the political infighting, from the dangers of a parallel charge of technical "impiety." But this diplomatic triumph had been achieved by Aeschines, Demosthenes' hated rival. Political commitment, and personal malice, now led him into a serious error. Next time the League met, he persuaded the Athenians to boycott it; and the meeting, unopposed by any Athenian delegate, accepted Philip's offered help.

His moment had come. His army was trained to a pitch unknown in Greece before. His cavalry, the aristocratic Companions, were augmented *en route* by the expert horsemen of Thessaly. The vital pass of Thermopylae was politely taken over from its Theban garrison. Philip marched on to Elatia on the Phocian border, about two days' march from Thebes and three from Attica.

Athens was in a panic. A beacon was built from the stalls and sheep pens of the marketplace to alert the suburbs. The citizens' Assembly was called by blast of trumpet. All moderates who dared to recall Philip's restraint after the Phocian War were denounced as traitors by Demosthenes' supporters. This time a Theban alliance got the vote; he headed the embassy sent to negotiate it.

Philip too sent envoys to Thebes. Both sides were heard at one session. Thebans' voting rights were confined to present and veteran soldier-citizens. The Macedonians cited their mutual treaty, recalled the hostile acts of Athens, and promised in return for alliance a fair share of victory gains. If the Thebans wished to be neutral, this would be granted them in return for right of passage.

Demosthenes then put up the offers of Athens. They consisted in shopping to Thebes two peoples protected by solemn Athenian pledges: the Boeotians of the neighbouring countryside, upheld against Theban rule in the sacred name of democracy; and, far worse, the Plataeans. This border tribe, Athens' sole ally in the heroic defence of Marathon, had been granted Athenian honorary citizenship in perpetuity. The Thebans were dubious. Demosthenes, who had never set foot upon a battlefield, taunted them with cowardice. This simple expedient met complete success. The Thebans tore up their treaty (or rather broke it up, for such things were carved on marble) and voted to ally with Athens.

Philip now knew where he stood. He had wanted no war with Athens. Though, his ascendancy once established, he would certainly have expected to direct her foreign policy—the pattern of Greek hegemonies since the days of Pericles—he proved innocent of any aim to enslave her people or destroy her culture. Probably he

nursed a secret wish to reincarnate Pericles in himself.
His repeated overtures had been blocked by Demosthenes'
inveterate hate and rebuffed with studied insults. Reared
in the traditions of Macedon, Philip took a simple and
comprehensive view of leaders who led from behind. His
belief that he had found one here was to prove correct.

Even now he did not march south. He first carried out
the League's commission. After a winter of manœuvring
about the Parnassan massif, he made by a ruse a lightning
march on Amphissa, captured the mercenaries sent there
by Demosthenes, and took the town's surrender. The
sacred fields were restored to the League. He and his son
were ceremonially thanked, honoured and crowned at the
Delphic sanctuary.

They did not go home. They got control of the
Corinthian Gulf without trouble, fortified their strongpoints, and moved back to Elatia. Even then, Philip sent
last offers of peace to Thebes and Athens. Demosthenes
had ensured refusal. Another great If of history had passed
its crossroads. In midsummer the forces of north and
south, about 30,000 men a side, met on the Boeotian
Plain of Chaeronea.

Philip commanded on the right, traditional station of
Macedonian kings. The notion that the weapon-holding
side is more "honourable" than the shield side is of immemorial age. It applied to the enemy as well; so Philip
knew from his days in Thebes who would be the élite
corps to meet the Macedonian left: the hitherto unbeaten
Sacred Band. This post he entrusted to the Companion
Cavalry, under Alexander.

Philip himself faced the Athenians, who had the advantage of rising ground. He lured them down from it with
a feigned retreat, entrapped and routed them. Among
those who fled the field was Demosthenes, getting his first
and last taste of war. The other troops thinned out their

line to fill the gap. Alexander had watched his moment. Now he hurled his horsemen against the Sacred Band, leading the charge.

By the standards of even the most courageous modern soldiering, Alexander exposed himself in battle as no responsible commander should. But ours were not the standards of Macedon, whose ethos was still Homeric. Not he alone, but his men, thought in terms of Sarpedon's words before the walls of Troy. Alexander probably knew them by heart.

> Glaukos, why is it you and I are honoured before others
> with pride of place, the choice meats and the filled
>   wine-cups
> in Lykia, and all men look on us as if we were immortals,
> and we are appointed a great piece of land by the banks
>   of Xanthos,
> good land, orchard and vineyard, and ploughland for the
>   planting of wheat?
> Therefore it is our duty in the forefront of the Lykians
> to take our stand, and bear our part in the blazing of
>   battle,
> so that a man of the close-armoured Lykians may say
>   of us,
> "Indeed, these are not ignoble men who are lords of
>   Lykia,
> these kings of ours, who feed upon the fat sheep
>   appointed
> and drink the exquisite sweet wine; since indeed there is
>   strength
> of valour in them, since they fight in the forefront of the
>   Lykians."

Philip's many wounds testify that he too, realistic expert as he was, took for granted this meaning of *noblesse oblige*.

It is true that throughout his career Alexander courted danger, though never without purpose, with almost re-

ligious fervour. He is often called fearless; but no man
with so powerful an imagination is immune to fear. He
had seen men die horribly in the field, in lingering agony
after. Perhaps this was why fear was always the first enemy
he had to kill.

In this first of his great battles, leading cavalry against
infantry (which did not give the advantage it would
acquire when stirrups were invented), after a fierce struggle he broke the Theban line. The Sacred Band, encircled,
refused surrender and died to the last man. The marble
lion which marked their common tomb is still to be seen
at Thebes.

Victory was complete; and Philip, whose efforts to
Hellenize himself had met with such bleak response,
reverted to Macedon. At the feast held that night upon
the field he proclaimed a Dionysiac "comus," and led its
tipsy, torchbearing procession over the battleground, singing a chant about Demosthenes. He was rebuked by an
aristocratic Athenian in the prisoners' pen; which sobered
him up at once. In all versions of this event, Alexander's
name is conspicuously absent. Philip had had to do with
bunglers and cowards, he with the brave; then and later
he did not exult over such enemies. His view of Athens,
however, was to remain that of a man who respects the
treasures of a great museum despite its philistine curators.

Philip's peace terms were conveyed to Athens by his
aristocratic captive, whom he had freed and asked to
supper. The despairing city had awaited only a barbaric
horde swarming through Attica to the sack, Demosthenes
having assured them that the Macedonian aim was "not
slavery but annihilation." All Philip in fact required was
that his hegemony be recognized. He did not propose even
to cross the border, and the prisoners could go home un-
ransomed.

While he waited the dead were burned. This labour,

carried out on pyres whose only fuel was wood, must have
called for strong stomachs in the soldiers of the ancient
world. Athenian casualties numbered more than a thousand. (Our age of firearms has forgotten the total de-
fencelessness of the retreating hoplite once he had turned
his back, and, his heavy shield discarded to help his
flight, could only run before the pursuing spears.) The
ashes were collected; to ask for the remains of one's dead
was the formal acknowledgment that the victor "possessed
the field." The Athenians asked; of course accepting
Philip's terms, which must have stunned them. He sent
them the ashes in a ceremonial cortège, under the escort
of Alexander.

He was eighteen. He would not pass that way again.
He was obsequiously received. Statues on the Acropolis
were decreed for his father and him, the head of the latter
still surviving. It would seem he visited Plato's Academy,
and took Hephaestion; to whom its principal, Xenocrates,
perhaps competing with Aristotle, wrote his own book of
letters.

Philip marched unopposed into the Peloponnese in a
show of strength. At Corinth he called a council, attended
by envoys of all the southern states but Sparta; they
voted him Supreme Commander of the Greek forces "for
defence" against the Persians. He returned at once to
Macedon to prepare his expedition.

Everything indicates that he and Alexander were now
on friendlier terms than at any other time of their lives.
Though it is likely that Philip's death had already been
determined and its authors awaited only opportunity, it
might have happened as a parting of father and son,
violent in circumstance like many in that age, but without
the violence of inner conflict which marked the son for
life. Fate decreed otherwise. Philip fell in love, and prepared for another wedding.

This time, the girl belonged to a noble Macedonian family. She was the niece and ward, her father being evidently dead, of that same Attalus who had avenged upon Pausanias the suicide of the King's young friend. Whether his rise to power preceded the betrothal or followed it, the sources do not make clear; but his rank was high, and this marriage must have been seen in Macedon as more significant than those of former legal concubines. Some historians have inferred that Philip had already resolved to divorce Olympias. Against this stands a massive piece of evidence. Alexander went to the wedding feast.

The outcome proves that it was not from fear of Philip. Olympias, in view of her rage at the event, must surely have opposed his giving it his countenance. He may have thought it would convey to others that her status was not in doubt, that it was a gesture he could afford. Or he may have done it in simple goodwill to his father, with whom he had served harmoniously through a long campaign, in an atmosphere of male camaraderie away from palace intrigues.

It was of course an ordeal. An adolescent so sexually fastidious, and with the homosexual preference which marked this phase of his life, would hardly attend for fun a drunken Macedonian wedding with the prospect of seeing his father put to bed, amid the usual bawdy jokes, beside a girl younger than himself. The added thought of his mother must have made him very tense indeed. However, for reasons sufficient to himself, he went, and stayed till the bride had retired and the toasts were called. Attalus proposed the health of the happy pair, coupled—whether in drink or calculation—with the hope that their union would produce a *legitimate* heir for Macedon.

Alexander's reaction was characteristically prompt. Shouting "What about me, you blackguard? A bastard, am I?" he hurled his goblet at Attalus' head. Noisy chaos broke out. Attalus threw his own goblet back. During the brawl, words passed between father and son which have not come down to us. Alexander's, whatever they were, caused Philip to draw his sword (he probably wore it for the ancient ritual of cutting the bride loaf) and lurch towards him. Lame from an old wound, and drunk, he fell sprawling. "Look, men," said Alexander coldly. "He's getting ready to cross from Europe to Asia, and he falls crossing from couch to couch." On this he walked out; from the house, and from the kingdom.

Clearly this crisis was unforeseen by all concerned, unless by Attalus. He had played his hand well, and was shrewd enough to count on Alexander's losing his temper; but even his insult may have been a drunken impulse. Philip cannot have had foreknowledge. He would not have accepted a generous gesture from the son who had shared his victories, to have him so affronted and rouse so predictable a fury. Philip was caught on the wrong foot while fuddled with wine; Alexander acted like Alexander; it was one of those situations where hidden fires, which the protagonists have been containing, are released by shock. Without more ado, Alexander told his mother to pack, and rode off with her over the rugged southwestern frontier to her brother's capital, Dodona in Epirus.

Nothing between father and son would ever be the same again. Alexander, and his mother, had received the deadliest insult of the ancient world and been offered no redress. What he had said to Philip to bring him to the verge of homicide remains an interesting speculation. It may have released a long-suppressed jealousy of his son's good looks, intellectual precocity, sensational popularity with his soldiers, and the tight loyal circle of "Alexander's friends."

Such a journey as the cross-country ride to Dodona

cannot have been undertaken guarding a woman without some kind of escort. It is likely these intimates provided one. Their allegiance was well known to Philip later.

With what feelings King Alexandros of Epirus, owing his throne to Philip, received his outraged sister is not recorded; nor whether Alexander felt welcome at Dodona, famed for hard winters, and for its oracle, the most ancient in the Greek world. Its centre was an oak of immemorial age housing doves whose murmur was significant, and ringed with bronze vessels which reverberated in wind. Its god was Zeus, who was questioned in writing, on a strip of lead; many examples have survived. The answer was drawn as a lottery by the barefoot priestess. No question from Alexander has rewarded the spade; yet this shrine was linked with that of Zeus-Ammon at Siwah, which later he consulted at the cost of trouble and danger, and with dramatic results. Being the man he was, it is hard to believe that at this crisis of his fortunes he did not visit a great centre of prophecy when he was on its doorstep. If so, he kept the secret of its answer. At Siwah he was to do the same.

Leaving his mother in the house where she was born, he rode north into Illyria. To this warlike land, less than two years before, he had thrust back its defeated army. That he could show himself there, and be received as a guest, speaks volumes for the decency with which his campaign had been waged, and the respect it must have commanded. What he meant to do there remains a mystery. For a time he was his mother's son, his judgment overwhelmed by his emotions. He may even have considered leading an Illyrian invasion, to seize his heritage by force, till his innate intelligence reasserted itself. He was, however, very capable of playing a war of nerves with Philip, who would certainly be reluctant to set out for Asia, leaving the home garrison depleted, with this dangerous and unpredictable presence in his rear. Never again would Alexander have to hold out in such harsh and humiliating conditions, conciliating uncouth hosts, wary of treachery, dossing down in primitive hill-forts after the grandeurs of Athens and Corinth where he had been fêted as a victor. Among the hardships whose endurance he used later to recall with pride, no word is ever quoted about his sojourn in Illyria. But it worked. A family guest-friend, Demaratus of Corinth, acted as a diplomatic go-between. Whether father or son put the first feeler out remains unknown.

Alexander returned to Macedon, most probably with his mother. The sources disagree, some leaving her in Epirus, but it is unlikely he would have accepted such terms; not only did her own good name hang on her reinstatement, but his legitimacy. Whatever the bargain struck between him and Philip their reconciliation was brittle. Soon it was strained enough to make him doubt his father's good faith about his succession.

He would not of course have returned without some kind of warranty. But he did not trust it. Most of Philip's offspring were girls, and the new wife had borne another; no viable heir but Alexander existed; his suspicions seem to have verged on the irrational. But the Attalid faction, the authors of his exile, were high in favour; many Macedonian heirs had been disinherited by treachery in the past; and to all this was added the emotional pressure of his mother, deeply affronted by the favours showered on the bride, which included the honorific royal name of Eurydice. His dependence on his friends' loyalty and affection increased; and they rallied to him with an openness which Philip began to suspect as treasonable. The atmosphere was explosive, and the first spark ignited it.

Arridaeus, Philip's retarded bastard, was of age to be

betrothed. The father of his affianced, the only important factor, was Pixodarus, satrap of Caria, a powerful semi-independent state in southern Asia Minor, of vital expedience in the coming war. Plutarch's account of what followed sheds a powerful light on Alexander's state of mind. His mother (by this account she was obviously in Macedon) and his friends kept bringing him false rumours, "as if Philip, through a brilliant match and a great connection, was trying to settle the kingdom upon Arridaeus." Alexander actually believed it. Almost crazily—and treasonably by any standards—he sent in secret a rival envoy to Caria, the tragic actor, Thettalus. Leading actors, who travelled widely, were often used in diplomacy; but to take on such a mission, Thettalus must have been a devoted personal friend. He was to dissuade the satrap from giving his daughter to "a fool and bastard," and offer Alexander's hand instead.

History is vague about the degree of Arridaeus' imbecility. He outlived his brother for some six years as a puppet king, able apparently to speak a few words in public, but taking no decision and never produced in battle. The wife he eventually married was a capable woman who acted for him, but the union was childless and probably unconsummated. It seems incredible that he would ever have been adopted as king by the Macedonian Assembly in preference to Alexander, even if their father in his lifetime had so decreed. Philip owed his own accession to the call for a fighting king; the direct heir, then passed over, was now in his early twenties, the obvious choice if the succession had to be changed. What blinded Alexander to all this?

Intellectually, he was outstandingly flexible and swift in his adjustments. Emotionally it was another matter. His demands on himself were such that though to his life's end he was equal to any physical hardship, pain or danger, under extreme psychological stress he would break rather than bend. This pattern appears in his story more than once.

The eagerness with which the satrap jumped at his offer must have opened his eyes; Pixodarus had clearly been promised no heir-apparent. But enlightenment came too late. Philip found out. And here the Plutarch manuscript has a tantalizing short gap. After the break, it says Philip went to Alexander's room, taking with him Philotas son of Parmenion, one of Alexander's close friends, and gave him a furious dressing down. He was probably confined to his room under house arrest. The presence of Philotas is unexplained, unless as a neutral witness, his father being Philip's oldest friend; but the young man's later record makes it not impossible that, unknown to Alexander, he had betrayed the plot.

Philip upbraided his son for being so unworthy of his rank as to seek an alliance with a mere Carian, the servitor of a barbarian king. In other words, he had been assured of his rank, and his doubts were as insulting as his action had been disastrous. For him the match was out of the question; and after Thettalus' revelations, Arridaeus was of course turned down. The diplomatic coup was ruined. For a man with Alexander's grasp of affairs it must have been a bitter moment. But worse was to come. The King, determined to show who was master and break up a subversive clique, banished from Macedon all Alexander's intimates. The one interesting exception was Hephaestion. There are several feasible reasons, the most obvious being that Philip, like Aristotle, thought him a good influence on Alexander; for whose conduct, too, he might be a useful hostage, especially if Philip knew them to be lovers. He was a shrewd judge of men. As it was, he gave a last crack of the trainer's whip; he had Thettalus, then in Corinth, arrested and brought to Pella in chains.

His professional status was that of an Irving or a Garrick. Even though only reprimanded—we hear nothing of any punishment beyond the gross humiliation of his fetters—it was an extreme step for Philip with his cultural aspirations. But he could have found no better way of flicking Alexander on the raw. His insistence on sharing every danger to which he exposed his men was almost an obsession. This time it had been impossible. The shame must have bitten deep; the resentment also. It is to his credit that he never pushed it out of his mind together with the friend concerned in it; Thettalus remained throughout his reign a welcome guest and favourite artist.

Meantime, the first phase of the Persian War had started. Parmenion and Attalus had taken an advance force across the Hellespont and secured a bridgehead. King Ochus had been poisoned the year before by his eunuch Grand Vizier, the king-maker Bagoas, whose power he had tried to curb; Arses his son was young and occupied with these internal dangers. The coastal satraps' resistance seems to have been disorganized and weak. Had Alexander's friendship with his father lasted, he himself would probably have held a command in the expedition. In his place went the hated Attalus.

Philip had one matter of home defence to see to before setting out himself: the conciliation of Epirus. Perhaps through Eurydice's persuasions, perhaps because Olympias had made herself intolerable, or because he blamed her for what her son had done, Philip had decided upon divorce. This would naturally affront his brother-in-law, King Alexandros. Evidently, however, the family honour was of more concern to Alexandros than his sister's feelings; for he readily accepted Philip's offered amends, the hand of her daughter Cleopatra. That he was her uncle was in those days no impediment.

It would be of great interest to know what plans Philip had made for Alexander in the coming war. He would not now be trusted as Regent. If left behind, he would have had to be imprisoned, and there is no sign at all of any such intention. The alternative would have been taking him along to Asia, and giving him a command under conditions where his pride and ambition would have guaranteed good performance. In the field together, away from Macedon, it is probable that once more the father and son would have become good comrades-in-arms.

The wedding plans were resplendent. High-ranking guests and state envoys were invited from all over Greece, as befitted Philip's status of pan-Hellenic war leader. Festival games in honour of the twelve Olympian gods were to be dedicated at a ceremony in the theatre at Aegae, near modern Edessa, the ancient capital. Their wooden images were paraded in gilded cars, to be set up in the round "orchestra" below the stage; each god with the lifelike colouring applied to all Greek sculpture, including its greatest marbles, bleached today only by time. A similar statue of Philip ended the pageant—making thirteen, a number already significant before the night of the Last Supper.

Ensured of publicity through the whole Greek world, Philip thought the time ideal for refuting Athenian propaganda about his "tyranny." Greek despots had traditionally gone about hedged with bodyguards. In planning the procession he arranged that, after all the notables had gone into the theatre (this must have included Alexander), his personal guard should be halted in the road outside, for him to make his entrance alone. The Captain of the Bodyguard, whom he thus instructed, was none other than Pausanias, promoted to this rank over the years.

The King's throne at such a ceremony would be on the

stage. He would enter through the *parodos,* the imposing side entrance to a Greek theatre's open wings. That the Captain of the Bodyguard should be standing there awaiting him must have seemed correct, or at any rate unsuspicious. As he came through the gateway, Pausanias thrust a dagger into his heart.

According to Diodorus, the only source to describe the scene in detail, the killer then ran away across a vineyard behind the theatre, towards horses standing by for his escape. He was ahead of his pursuers, when he caught his foot in a vine root. Before he could rise, he was cut down by the first men to overtake him.

The chiefs and nobles crowded to Alexander, unarmed at this sacred ceremony, and formed a bodyguard to take him to the citadel. His accession was not disputed. No other claimant was so much as named. He was King of Macedon.

The trial-by-historians of Alexander for his father's murder, more or less closed since Plutarch's day, has in modern times been reopened, despite a total lack of evidence for the prosecution. It would otherwise be a waste of space to re-examine it.

That he may have wished his father dead is neither here nor there. He had probably done so for at least a year. The world has been, and is, full of people visited by such wishes, who would be appalled at the thought of implementing them. Parricide was the most dreadful crime in Greek thought and religion, cursed by all the gods. That Alexander with his beliefs and temperament could not have borne this weight without going mad is obvious. However, this must not be taken as a decisive answer, in view of the possibility that Olympias had persuaded him he was not Philip's son.

The mating of gods in physical shape with mortals was

as sincere a belief with Greeks as is the Immaculate Conception to Catholics, with the difference that the former was not a unique event. Unlike the latter, it had never been attacked by science; Aristotle's genetic studies steered well clear of such hemlock-worthy blasphemies. Olympias in a Dionysiac trance may genuinely have imagined almost anything. The issue of parricide being inconclusive, we must proceed to more practical considerations of motive. Assuming Alexander morally prepared to kill, why do it now?

He was on display at a pan-Hellenic festival, with the precedence due to his rank; presented before the state envoys as heir apparent. The worst of his disgrace had blown over; ahead was the war with its great opportunities. He had lived under Philip's roof, and could surely have compassed his death when the incentive was far greater; for instance, just after the wedding speech of Attalus. It is true that Olympias' position had worsened as Alexander's had improved; but he did not later kill people at her demand, refusing even to remove a Regent she detested. There always remain, as credible human motives, sheer hate, and revenge; these must indeed have impelled the actual killer. But to Alexander the coming war would have offered many occasions of passing off a death as due to enemy action; this would surely have been the course of an intelligent man with devoted partisans. Why the public drama? Of all possible suspects, Alexander had least to gain by it.

Accomplices favoured by the prosecution are the three young men who struck down the murderer, allegedly to silence him; this on the grounds that two, Perdiccas and Leonnatus, later held commands under Alexander and were among his friends. The objection here is glaring. When Philip fell, says Diodorus, "immediately one group of the bodyguards hurried to the body of the King, while the rest poured out in pursuit of the assassin." Naturally they would. How could Alexander possibly have determined who would get there first? As our own age should know, no explanation is needed for their killing their man, beyond the violence engendered by a violent scene. Pausanias was making good his escape till the vine root tripped him, which does not suggest efficient pre-arrangements. Soldiers with quick reactions in a crisis do tend to get promoted; and had Alexander been cold to those who so zealously avenged his father, he would have been highly suspect to his own contemporaries.

Pausanias' accomplice with the horses must be borne in mind. That these were known to have been meant for the getaway suggests he was caught and interrogated. His evidence may have been of much importance in the subsequent trials.

The one item of "evidence" against Alexander in any ancient writer, indeed the only opinion, even, of the kind, occurs in Plutarch, that anecdotal holdall.

> . . . most of the blame was laid on Olympias, because she had added her exhortations to the young man's anger and urged him to the deed. But some slander [the Greek *diabole* means a false accusation] fell also on Alexander. For it is said that when Pausanias met him after the outrage and complained of it, Alexander quoted him the iambics from the *Medea* [Medea's revenge wiped out most of the other characters]: "The bride, the groom and the bride-giver."

It is perhaps sufficient to say that the last Illyrian frontier war at which Philip is known to have taken the field, and where his young friend presumably died, occurred when Alexander was twelve years old, and the "bride" about nine or ten.

Throughout his reign, Alexander never stands suspect of a surreptitious killing. When his power was vast, and he could have had anyone he chose put quietly out of the way, he suffered annoyance, frustration and downright insult from men he heartily disliked or distrusted; nothing happened to these people till he was ready to proceed against them openly. Whether on principle or from pride, he found furtiveness impossibly repugnant. Another constant trait was loyalty to his friends, and gratitude carried to extravagance towards those who had supported him when in disgrace with Philip. To believe he could have used Pausanias, sworn to protect him (which Pausanias as Captain of the Bodyguard would have known he could not do) and then shopped him with less compunction than a Mafia boss, calls for as much credulity as anything in the Romances.

As against all this, the incident is immemorially typical of a Greek blood-feud killing, where honour demands that revenge be taken, and be *seen* to be taken, by the wronged man himself or his next of kin. (The two such killings carried out in Athens while the present writer happened to be there were both public; one in front of a Plaka taverna, one in Omonia Square.) One editor of Diodorus notes with apparent scepticism that "Pausanias waited a long time for his revenge"; a startling observation in the context of ancient or, for that matter, modern Greece. It also ignores the recent rise of his enemy Attalus to high military rank and the status of royal father-in-law; favours which may well have seemed like rewards for the injury on which Pausanias had brooded for long obsessive years. He may even have been told so. That he was used, though not by Alexander, there is no need to doubt.

This was a time when most Athenian politicians were men on whose unsupported word one would not convict a dog. When, however, they remind their public of public events, we may start to listen. Some years after the mur-

der, Aeschines accused his enemy Demosthenes of having
ruined Athens through his blind hatred of Macedon. The
speech goes on:

> Now this was the man, fellow-citizens . . . who when
> informed through Charidemus' spies that Philip was
> dead, before anyone else had been told, made up a vision
> for himself and lied about the gods, pretending he had
> had the news not from Charidemus but from Zeus and
> Athene . . . who he says converse with him in the
> night and tell him of things to come.

The most authoritative comment on this "vision" remains that of the historian John Williams, written a
century and a half ago.

> The event was public and could not be concealed. The
> deputies of all Greece were assembled there, and no
> message from Charidemus to Demosthenes could have
> outstripped the speed with which the news of such an
> event passes from mouth to mouth in a populous coun-
> try. Not to mention that Charidemus would not have
> been the only deputy likely to despatch a messenger on
> such an occasion. Yet Demosthenes announced the
> death of Philip long before the news reached Athens
> from any other quarter. . . . The accuracy of his in-
> formation, and the falsehood respecting the alleged
> sources of his intelligence, almost indisputably prove
> that he was an accessory before the fact, and that he
> had previous notification of the very day on which the
> conspirators were to act.

The value of John Williams's comment rests not on his
erudition but his personal experience. He published his
life of Alexander in 1829, just after the Napoleonic Wars;
and his words about the flight of important news through
populous countries, written before telecommunications,
have the ring of certainty. The ancient world used for
long-distance signalling both the heliograph and the

beacon (the latter, in the *Agamemnon*, announces the fall of Troy). But since either called for a prearranged chain of signallers, their use would still be proof of complicity; for no verbal codes existed, and such signs could only confirm an expected fact.

Pausanias, the Captain of the Bodyguard, knew just where his men would be. He had had to form them up there. He can never have rated his chance of escape at more than even. However, he had horses ready, probably a ship too, and must have had some offered refuge. Demosthenes' speeches show again and again how utterly he had failed to take Alexander's measure. Even after the lightning victories which followed his accession, Demosthenes was mocking him as "Margites," the anti-hero of a burlesque epic. For him, in the "vision" of the demagogue, there had certainly been a role: the theatrical young paladin, the inept untried king who, his formidable father gone, could be swept aside without trouble.

Demosthenes' Persian paymaster had lately changed. The Vizier Bagoas, finding King Arses intractable, had poisoned him in turn, replacing him by a royal collateral, Darius III; one of whose first actions was to hand the Vizier a dose of his own medicine. The new Great King must have leaned greatly for the Greek intelligence on Demosthenes, who could have done him vital service in return for favours received, had he not been blinded by ingrained prejudice. Darius rested in false security; while Demosthenes broke off his mourning for his daughter's death, put on a festal wreath, and proposed a posthumous vote of thanks to Pausanias.

If the role he had promised himself was to emerge, as soon as it was absolutely safe to do so, and proclaim himself the author of the enterprise, to defer this moment was the wisest act of his life.

TROY

Alexander's reign began in 336 BC. He was a little over twenty.

"His physical looks are best portrayed in the statues Lysippus made of him. [Plutarch does not divulge which of Alexander's own contemporaries, if any, expressed this view.] And he approved being sculpted by him alone. [But he must have licensed a number of others.] For this artist has caught exactly those idiosyncrasies which many of his successors and friends later tried to imitate—the poise of his neck, tilted a little leftward, and his liquid eyes. Apelles' painting, 'The Thunder-Wielder,' did not get his complexion right, but made it too dark and tanned; for he was blond, they say, shading to ruddy on the breast and face."

His liquid eyes were grey. Their expressiveness altered Greek artistic convention. All important portrait heads feature a heavy bulge of the forehead above the brows (allowing for idealization, probably even more marked in life), caused perhaps by a development of the frontal lobes of the brain; and the loosely waving, heavy mane of hair, springing from a peak, its individual cut sloped down to the base of the neck when in south Greece the short curly crop was in fashion. Arrian, both of whose main sources were men who saw him often, says that he was very handsome.

Clean shaving, long general among young men in the south, did not reach Macedon till he introduced it. His looks must have been admired in childhood and boyhood; it was perhaps a sign of his ambisexual nature that he did not want to alter them with a beard. Once he had set the fashion, it was so widely followed that later legend had him ordering the whole Macedonian army to shave. He was quoted as saying that a beard gives the enemy a handhold in close combat. He may really have offered this reason to himself.

"In Aristoxenus' memoirs it is said that a very pleasant scent came from his skin, and that there was a fragrance in his breath and all his body which permeated the clothes he wore." His fondness for a daily bath, when he could get it, is evident from all the sources; but on campaign he must often have been unwashed, which makes the observation interesting. When not struck down by occasional local fevers, he was a very healthy man. In days before dentistry, a sweet breath testified to a good set of teeth, as well as a good digestion. He loved violently active exercise, hunting, running, ball games; but despised professional athletics, which in his century had grown degenerate, producing ugly specialized physiques, instead of the balanced beauty of classical sculpture. He was himself considered a runner of Olympic standard, but declined to enter for the Games "unless I had kings to run against." His pride would not tolerate even a suspicion that he had been given the race.

He loved music and theatre; artists braved immense hard journeys to appear before him, and were received as guests, not mere entertainers. He had himself by nature the actor's biological rhythm, liking when at leisure to sit up late and sleep on next morning; a pattern not necessarily associated with heavy drinking, as every man of the theatre knows.

He could not live without books, which he had sent out to him in the heart of Asia, adding to the favourites he carried along. Next after Homer, it seems the chief of these was Xenophon, whose influence shows unmistakably again and again. He heartened his men by reminding them of the *Anabasis* with its resolute Ten Thousand and its accompanying exposures of Persian inefficiency. The young Xenophon himself, who got out of bed on a night of despair to rally the army, because his seniors were dead and nobody else was doing it, must have been a man after Alexander's heart (and Shakespeare's, who transferred it to King Harry on the eve of Agincourt). No doubt the treatises on horsemanship and hunting were valued too; but above all Alexander, with his high sense of theatre, showed in the drama of his life where his chief debt lay: to *The Upbringing of Cyrus,* the author's sole work of fiction.

He must have read it first as history. Later when in Persia he would have learned of some discrepancies; but that the real Cyrus had died in battle, instead of in Socratic composure, probably endeared him all the more. The image of a conqueror brilliant, powerful and merciful, making friends of enemies, hailed as a father by the conquered, does not conflict with the fragmentary Persian records. Alexander had no need to discard his hero cult, as is seen from the devotion he lavished on Cyrus' tomb.

The military lore in the *Cyropaedia* he probably skipped as elementary; his own father had been a far more sophisticated teacher. But Xenophon claims to present not maxims for generals, but the pattern of an ideal ruler, governing his conquered peoples in a vast extended empire.

> He ruled over these nations, though they did not speak the same tongue as he, nor one nation the same as an-

other's; yet he was able to stretch the dread of him so far that all feared to withstand him; and he could rouse so eager a wish to please him that they all desired to be governed by his will.

. . . A ruler should not only be really better than his subjects; he should cast a kind of spell on them.

The astonishing corpus of the Alexander legends bears tribute to this last precept beyond anything dreamed of in Xenophon's philosophy.

Kindled by a spontaneous sense of affinity, admiration for Cyrus must have been a powerful antidote to Aristotle's insularity. Again and again Alexander's conduct displays his debt to what has been called the first historical novel of the Western world. The following excerpts could be taken for quotations from an Alexander history.

And on campaign, the general must show he can bear better than his men the heat of the sun in summer, the cold in winter, and hardship on a difficult march. All these things go to make him loved by those he leads.

When the rest went to dinner at the usual time, Cyrus stayed [among the wounded] with his aides and doctors, for he would not leave anyone uncared for.

The gods, like men, are more likely to incline to us if we pay them attention during our height of fortune, not just toady to them in adversity. And this too is the way to cherish one's friends.

He showed them always as much kindness as he could; for he held that just as it is hard to love people who seem to hate us, or have goodwill to those who are ill-wishing us, in the same way one who is affectionate and well disposed could not be hated by those aware of love. He tried to win the devotion of those around him by taking thought and trouble for them, showing glad-

ness in their prosperity and sympathy in their mis-
fortunes.

You [his men] possess in your souls what is fairest and
most soldierlike: you rejoice above all in being praised.
All men in love with praise feel constrained to endure
any hardships and any dangers.

Cyrus was most handsome in person, most generous
in his soul, most fond of learning, most in love with
honourable fame, so that he would bear all suffering
and all dangers for the sake of praise.

These last two extracts are central to an understanding
of Alexander. Moderns who have accused him of "an
unpleasant concern for his own glory" are thinking in
terms of another age. Greek literature up to, and on, its
very highest levels is permeated by the axiom that to
be fameworthy is the most honourable of aspirations, the
incentive of the best men to the best achievements. Socrates, Plato, Aristotle all accepted it. Its ethos outlasted
Greece and Rome. The last word of our single English
epic is *lofgeornost*—"most eager for fame." It closes the
lament of the warriors for the dead Beowulf.

Alexander III opened his reign in the traditional Macedonian way, by removing those who endangered his
succession.

Plutarch and Diodorus agree that he sought out and
punished the conspirators to his father's murder. Neither
describes the process of this inquiry. The purge was not
indiscriminate. Its most important victim was his cousin
Amyntas, Perdiccas III's son, who under more ordinary
succession laws would have been the reigning king. He
was a full-blooded Macedonian, unlike Alexander with his
unpopular Epirote mother. Philip must always have
seemed a usurper to Amyntas; he was the natural choice

had the coup succeeded, but whether he was killed on
evidence or suspicion is unknown. Alexander deserves the
benefit of the doubt, for in spite of his own humiliation
over the Carian marriage intrigue, he did nothing to his
half-brother Arridaeus, a harmless pawn on whom he
felt it demeaning to take revenge. He was a dangerous
pawn, however, to leave on the Macedonian chessboard.
Alexander simply attached him to his court and took him
on its travels. He must have been well cared for; he
was the longer-lived of the two.

Two princes of Lyncestis, a family of once-independent
kings in west Macedon, were executed. They may have
hoped to recover their former sovereignty. But the eldest,
another Alexandros, was let off because after the murder
he had at once hailed Alexander as king. At some stage
it seems to have emerged that the plot had been financed
with Persian gold. This was probably true, whether it was
supplied through Demosthenes or direct from Darius himself, who had good reason to dread Philip and no suspicion
of what he would get instead.

Attalus, a declared and dangerous enemy, presented a
special problem. He was on campaign in Asia Minor,
among his own troops, many of them bound to him by
tribal loyalties. He was believed, correctly, to be planning
treason. Alexander wanted him brought for trial according to Macedonian law, but could not risk his leading
his army over to the other side. An officer called Hecataeus
was therefore sent on a secret mission, to take him prisoner if possible; if not, to kill him. Attalus was already
in correspondence with Demosthenes with a view to
joining Athens; but, perhaps alarmed by Alexander's swift
initial successes—the sequence of events is uncertain—he
lost his nerve, and sent Demosthenes' letter to Macedon
with a plea for pardon. Hecataeus, however, had meantime decided he could afford to take no more chances,

and killed him out of hand. In these circumstances there were no complaints that the letter of the law had not been observed. Hecataeus would of course have been supplied with a royal warrant, which he could present before or after the deed to Attalus' officers and to the other general of the expeditionary force, Parmenion.

The case of Attalus is important. It offered Alexander a precedent, which would become crucial at a later crisis in his career.

Certainly at this moment he could afford no legal quibbles, nor can the decision have detained him long. He had not the time. At the news that the great Philip's imperium had passed to a youth of twenty, all his conquered lands rose up in instant revolt. Alexander was surrounded with more dangers than his father had faced at the death of Perdiccas III.

The most immediate was the defection of Thessaly, whose feudal lords had no notion of making the archonship hereditary to Macedon. They manned the impregnable pass between the massifs of Olympus and Ossa, the narrow river gorge of Tempe. Alexander saw at once that if they got away with it the whole south would rise, and he would face another Chaeronea. He marched swiftly down, surveyed the terrain, saw with his lightning strategic instinct where the pass could be turned by cutting steps on the Ossa flank; and appeared in the Thessalians' rear while his advance was still awaited. Stunned, they did homage without a fight, and offered him all Philip's former rights and tribute. (From the latter he exempted Phthia, because it had been the birthplace of Achilles.) At Thermopylae he summoned a conference of the Sacred League, which recognized him without a dissenting vote.

The panic at Athens was equal to that after Chaeronea. The vote of thanks to Philip's assassin was remembered with alarm; an embassy was dispatched to Alexander, to plead for pardon. He received it with courtesy, accusing no one. His march did not cross the Attic border. He did not, and never would, revisit the immortal museum of Western civilization. He called a conference at Corinth, as Philip had done before him, and was invested with Philip's commission as war leader against the Persians.

The passes and strongpoints commanding the south were manned. The magnificent Macedonian walls which crown the Acrocorinth had yet to rise, but its acropolis was garrisoned. Thebes, as in Philip's time, had its Cadmea (a man-made citadel of no great height) held by Macedonians. South Greece was secured, and none too soon considering the threat from the north. No expedition to Asia was possible before Thrace was controlled. Parmenion's expeditionary force was already in danger of having its communications cut.

In Macedon, Olympias had made good use of his absence. It is not credible that, as Justin says, she came galloping from Epirus to crown with gold the body of Pausanias, displayed on a traitor's cross. But she had enjoyed a far greater satisfaction; she had forced her young rival Eurydice to hang herself, presumably by threats of torture, after first watching the death of her newborn second infant. When Alexander came back he was angry, Plutarch says. He had spared Arridaeus, and this girl too had been a pawn of state.

Winter had come. Over its short span Alexander had to ready his newly inherited army for the urgent work of safeguarding the force already committed to Asia. In early spring, when Thracian war bands ceased to hibernate, he marched northeast with his usual cool-headed speed; his mind not only on immediate but future dangers. The military road to the Hellespont once secured, his objective was the hinterland of the still unsubdued Triballians. These were the tribesmen who had fallen on Philip during his return march from Byzantium, and given him his crippling wound. Their habitat was the riverland of the Ister (Danube) beyond the wild mountain range of Haemon, the Stara Planina of today's Bulgaria. When at sixteen he was left as Regent, his campaign against the Maedi had led him up that way; he would have pressed on then, had his father not recalled him "lest he should undertake too much." His strategic sense had been sound. He would now square the account, and protect the lifeline to Asia.

He had held no command since the battle of Chaeronea, the climax of a campaign directed by Philip throughout; he had not independently led an army since his repulse of the Illyrians when he was seventeen. He had been in exile, followed by disgrace; his status in Philip's planned expedition had been uncertain. Yet he had only to appear before the troops and lead them—and this into very difficult country, where Philip himself had been defeated— to be followed with élan and unquestioning trust. This fact, eclipsed in history by his later exploits, is perhaps as remarkable as any.

Beside his own Macedonians, he had a contingent of Agriani, a Thracian tribe whose young chieftain, Lambarus, he had already made a friend of, perhaps in his earlier wars, or because Lambarus had been sent to Pella, like some other noble Thracians, as hostage for his father's fealty. In any event he was devoted to Alexander. The warlike Thracians, who tattooed themselves blue and collected enemy heads as trophies, were considered rather backward even by the standards of rural Macedon. But Alexander throughout his life was concerned with the individual.

He showed from the outset of the campaign his characteristic swift adjustment to the unexpected. The defenders of the Haemon pass had walled themselves behind

a line of carts, which they started to bowl down on his
men with the lethal force of gravity. Throwing the phalanx
into open order, he told those who could not avoid a
cart to crouch under a roof of shields (thus anticipating
the Roman "tortoise"). The carts bounced over; not a
man was lost, the pass was carried. He advanced into the
river plain of the Triballians, a large force of whom
shortly cut off his rear. He turned round at once to meet
them; they withdrew into an impregnable gorge. He never
wasted his men's lives in atacking such positions; he sent
archers and slingers to harass from a distance; when the
enemy took the bait and came out in chase, he fell on them
with all his forces. Panicking, they were cut down with
the usual dire contrast of casualties between pursuer and
pursued. To soldiers of the ancient world there was a
force unknown today in what Alexander would say to his
men a decade later: "While I have led you, not one of you
has been killed in flight."

After this battle he marched north to the Ister. Not
only did he want to control the land it bounded; he had a
longing, says Arrian, to cross to the other side.

This is the first time of many in his life story where we
hear of such a craving—the Greek word is *pothos*. His
many-sided nature had a powerful strain of the explorer.
The Ister was the northern edge of the known Greek
world; all beyond was hearsay. But his dreams had always
their practical side; he did not aim to pass over the great
river only "because it was there." The tribes beyond were
known for fierce warriors and raiders; and he wanted before he left for Asia to make a lasting impression. If he
crossed to their side, they might later feel discouraged
from crossing to his.

The Danube in its lower course was such a stream as
neither he nor his men had ever before set eyes on. He

had had some war galleys sent up from Byzantium (now subdued) but they were only a squadron, with their rowers taking up room, and he had to embark an army. Here Xenophon came to his constant reader's aid; he has a passage about the inflated hide rafts used to cross the Euphrates. Hide was used also to make army tents (it must have made the baggage trains immensely cumbrous), and these Alexander had cobbled into rafts, stuffed with hay for buoyancy. He also commandeered the local dugout canoes. On this makeshift flotilla he crossed the Ister by night, with 4,000 foot and, astonishingly, 1,500 *cavalry*. The horses must have swum.

This whole campaign is described with the close detail of an eyewitness; presumably Ptolemy. He had not yet been promoted to high command; not till after Philip's death had Alexander been able to recall his banished friends. His present chief of staff was another friend of those days, Parmenion's son Philotas. Never having lost the royal favour, he had entered the new reign with higher rank.

However experienced the officers, this was a manœuvre quite new to the Macedonian army; its broad strategy and comprehensive grasp of detail must belong to Alexander. On the far bank the infantry advanced through high standing corn, flattening it by holding their sarissas sideways (they must have been extremely well drilled) to make a path for the cavalry. On open ground beyond, Alexander deployed his forces. But the local Getae were so shocked by this uncanny arrival in the dawn that they fled before the cavalry, first from their town, then on into the wilderness with such women and children as they could take on their horses' cruppers. The Macedonians took the town and "as much plunder as the Getae had left behind"; which, in fourth-century terms, would include any remaining women and children. For such victims, massacre or slavery were the universal alternatives. These were enslaved.

On the Ister shore, Alexander sacrificed to Zeus the Preserver, to Heracles, and to the spirit of the river for graciously granting them passage. Having got everyone back across without a single drowning, he sat down to await results. Soon respectful embassies arrived from the tribes along the river. Their reception must have gone on for some time; for the last arrivals were Celts, from some distant settlement near the Adriatic. Men whom even the Macedonians thought very tall, they towered over the rumoured conqueror they had come to placate. Either from vanity or curiosity, he asked them what thing on earth they dreaded most. They feared nothing, they said, unless that the sky should fall on them. Amused by this gasconading brag (one he never made for himself) he sent them home with a pact of friendship.

Still in the north, he got news that the formidable Illyrians had risen; and that an intermediate tribe, the Antariates, planned to fall on him as he marched to meet the danger. At this the young Lambarus, still at hand with the pick of his Thracian warriors, told him to forget the Antariates at any rate; they were worth nothing as fighters, he would invade them himself and keep them occupied. Moved as always by a spontaneous act of friendship, Alexander loaded him with gifts of honour, and promised to join them in kinship with the hand of Cynna, one of his bastard sisters. They never met again; Lambarus, after a devastating performance of his mission, went home, fell ill and died. Whether or not Cynna shared her brother's grief, the Agriani remained the most loyal of his auxiliaries.

Making haste over now familiar ground he reached the Illyrian frontier ranges. Cleitus, the Illyrians' chief war

lord, held the hill town of Pelium and the heights commanding it. The troops outside fled at sight of the Macedonians, leaving behind the freshly killed bodies of nine
victims just sacrificed for victory—three black rams, three
boys and three girls. (No wonder Alexander did not care
to dwell on his Illyrian exile.) He invested the town;
just avoided being encircled by a large relieving force;
led out a troop to rescue Philotas, who was commanding
a guard over the draught animals; but after doing so was
himself dangerously trapped in a narrow pass between
hills and river. This situation he met with sheer bravura.
He had guessed from the Illyrians' earlier flight that his
name had run before him—in those parts he had been
known for years—and he threw what troops he had into
a polished display of aggressive drill. Their expertise and
unknown intentions so dismayed the tribesmen that they
started falling back. He ordered his men to yell and beat
on their shields. The enemy abandoned their vantage
points and bolted for the fort.

Still in difficult country, and harassed as he crossed a
river, he got his archers firing from midstream, and set up
his light catapults—a very smart operation, since they
were taken apart for mule transport. His men were ex-
tricated in a fighting withdrawal, never once presenting
their defenceless backs. Shortly after, taking advantage
of the Illyrians' indiscipline, which he must have known
well, he put on a night attack and routed them out of the
town. The west was settled; but he was to have no respite.
A still more serious danger now threatened from the
south.

Word of the risings had spread. The new King of
Macedon, after a brief appearance at Corinth, had vanished into the wilds whence no news came. After no long
delay, Demosthenes emerged and, contacting Darius and
his leading satraps, offered, if they would finance him, to

keep Alexander tied down in Greece. The Greek cities of Asia were tacitly written off to bondage; Demosthenes' democratic principles were strictly parochial. So eagerly did Darius respond that his account rolls, when captured later in Sardis, showed disbursements to his ally of 300 talents.

Presently it was learned that the Thebans had admitted some anti-Macedonians whose lives Philip had spared after Chaeronea on condition of their exile, murdered two Macedonian commanders who in peacetime laxity had gone outside the citadel, and proceeded to invest the garrison within it. Elated by this news, and well supplied with funds, Demosthenes sent Thebes a large consignment of arms. Continuing to assure the Athenians that Alexander was a strutting boy, he urged them to join the war. They voted to do so, and started to prepare. Still no word came from the hinterland Then rumour announced that Alexander was dead.

No sickness or wound had caused a genuine error. Demosthenes produced a man who swore to having seen him fall. On the strength of this, the Thebans openly proclaimed alliance with Persia against Macedon. When, within a week, they heard that an army led by Alexander was coming down through Thessaly, they refused at first to credit it. At all events, it could not conceivably be *that* Alexander. It would be Alexandros of Lyncestis. (They must have supposed him the new king.)

They were swiftly disillusioned. Alexander had brought his forces down from Pelium, through a series of mountain passes, a distance even by air of a hundred miles, in a six-day march. Scarcely pausing to pick up his allied troops from central Greece, in another six he was already in Boeotia. He appeared before Thebes next day.

Had he in fact been dead, it would have cancelled the

Thebans' treaty. His early forbearance may have come
from knowledge of the rumour. For reasons which may
have been emotional or religious, he encamped by the
precinct of the hero Iolaus, Heracles' charioteer and beloved companion, at whose shrine the couples of the
Sacred Band used to take their vows. He sent an envoy
to the city, offering to accept their surrender on terms if
they would give up the anti-Macedonians who were there
illegally. The Thebans refused, with a mocking counter-
demand for Philotas and Antipater. They made a sortie
against Alexander's pickets, some of whom they killed.
He now moved to a strategic position, near the gate that
faced towards Attica and gave him the nearest approach
to the beleaguered Macedonian garrison.

It was also the approach route from Athens, of whose
intentions he would by now have heard. But in that respect
his vigilance was needless. No troops from the south appeared. The alarming speed of his march had brought
painful second thoughts. Without protest from Demosthenes the Athenians closed their gates, leaving the
Thebans to weather the storm alone.

It did not yet break. Alexander still awaited a parley.
He had collected on his southward march contingents
of troops from Macedonian satellites, chiefly Phocians
and Plataeans. The latter, it will be remembered, were
the descendants of the Marathon heroes, inheritors of
their perpetual Athenian citizenship, whom Demosthenes
had traded to the Thebans on the eve of Chaeronea.

Alexander kept close to the Theban siege lines, at their
nearest point of approach to the Macedonian garrison,
trapped inside the Cadmea. This, as can still be seen, was
no acropolis perched on natural rock; it relied for defence
on its massive walls. For the next sequence of events,
which Arrian gives in vivid detail, he expressly says that

his source is Ptolemy, who must have taken part. He claimed that Perdiccas, still at that time holding only a small command, was posted next the siege works. For some reason, without awaiting orders, he rushed his men to the palisade and started to tear it down.

For justice towards Perdiccas we shall look in vain to Ptolemy, who had been his mortal enemy many years before he wrote his History, and has probably suppressed a good reason for this apparent breach of discipline, such as a signal from the garrison of some weakness in the enemy dispositions which needed quick action. Perdiccas was the man for it, as he had shown at Philip's death. He broke through and got in. A fellow officer, seeing this, led up his men in support. Alexander, not far off, perceived they were all in danger of being cut off inside; he sent reinforcements, still reserving his main army. Assaulting the inner palisade, Perdiccas fell badly wounded. The rest pressed on; then the Thebans, rallying, got them on the run. This was decisive for Alexander; he charged at once, thrusting back the Thebans with such force that the city gates, which had been opened to let them in again, were jammed and let in their pursuers too.

It was the end. As the Macedonians flooded in, "with Alexander appearing everywhere," the Theban cavalry pelted off across the plain, the infantry fled as they could; and the ancient city was given up to sack. The Phocians and the Plataeans, Arrian says, were the chief agents of a massacre that spared neither age nor sex, nor even suppliants hauled out of the temples. It has been said that Alexander could have stopped it if he had liked. This would possibly have been true in Thrace or in Illyria; it would certainly have been true after he crossed to Asia, when his authority was absolute over all his forces. His position at Thebes was unique. The allied troops were

men to most of whom, till they joined his forced march
a week before, he had been unknown except by name,
simply the awe-inspiring Philip's twenty-one-year-old son;
while the Thebans were familiar enemies, against whom
generations of hatred had been stored. Before Philip's
intervention, the Phocian War had been marked with
hideous savageries. The atrocities of the lately betrayed
Plataeans, if anyone's fault but their own, may most
fairly be blamed upon Demosthenes.

Arrian says the "best" of the Theban citizens (a term
often, but not always, meaning the upper classes) had
wanted to ask for terms, but had been prevented by the
extremists. Alexander's genius for command included an
unerring instinct for rare moments when commands will
be disregarded with consequent loss of face; but for the
rest of his life, he seldom refused the petition of a Theban;
if he found one serving as a Persian mercenary, he pardoned him because he had no home. Even during the
shambles, he saved where he could find them—it must
have been hit or miss—priests, old guest-friends of Macedonians (probably the hosts of his father's youth), and
the descendants of Pindar, along with the poet's house.
By general vote of the allies, most of the city was razed.

After the sack, the Thracian troops dragged before
Alexander a woman whom they charged with killing one
of their officers. She admitted it freely. He had broken into
her house, raped her, and demanded to know where her
valuables were hidden. In the well, she had told him,
leading him up the garden to it and, when he craned over,
pushing him in. When his men arrived she had finished
him off with stones. She added, defiantly, that she was the
sister of Theagenes, who had fallen at Chaeronea, leading
the Sacred Band. He pardoned her at once and freed her
with her children. This well-known Plutarch anecdote

upholds Ptolemy's apportionment of the blame for the massacre. Its most significant fact is that the woman was brought before Alexander. These Thracians were not newly joined allies but his regular troops. If they had been let loose to sack the city, he could not have given a judgment which implied that their officer had got what he deserved; and in any case, they would have taken their own revenge.

Meantime the Athenians were celebrating the Eleusinian Mysteries, the most solemn rite of the Attic year, when the first Theban fugitives galloped up with the news. For the third time panic reigned in Athens. The Mysteries were abandoned. Villagers with their household goods crowded within the walls. A peace embassy was chosen to sue for mercy: some pro-Macedonians, and trustfully, the city's eloquent champion, Demosthenes. He rode with the rest as far as the Attic frontier; where his reflections grew so disturbing that he excused himself and retired.

The miserable remnant brought the victor abject congratulations on his safe return from the north and recent victory. Civilly he accepted Athens' submission, and agreed to spare her if the most virulent anti-Macedonians were given up. Even this he was talked out of by the tactful Demades, the same man Philip had used as his envoy after Chaeronea. Antipater in Macedon, getting the news that Demosthenes had been spared, must have thought the young King had taken leave of his senses. He was quick to correct the error after Alexander was dead. To Alexander himself, his own standards being what they were, it must have seemed unthinkable that Demosthenes could lift his head again. Here he failed to get the measure of fourth-century Athens. None the less, in withholding from that head a martyr's crown, he proved wiser than old Antipater.

His work in the south was over. Greece was secured. He

returned to Macedon, to prepare for the enterprise which was to fill the remaining third of his life.

In Macedon, Alexander performed the traditional sacrifices at the feast of Olympian Zeus, and held, besides the usual Games, contests for artists "in honour of the Muses." During this time he got news that a famous statue of Orpheus, enshrined in south Macedon, had started to sweat profusely. The seers, pondering the omen, decided that the new King's exploits would give the poets work.

He never had, as he must have hoped to have, his epic. Both he and posterity have been better served by the memoirs of a soldier, a sailor and an engineer. His best poetic epigraph was coined a good deal later by the Cavalier Montrose, thrown away in the middle of a love lyric.

> I will like Alexander reign,
>   And I will reign alone;
> My spirit ever did disdain
>   A rival near my throne.
> He either fears his fate too much,
>   Or his deserts are small,
> Who will not put it to the touch
>   To win or lose it all.

It is briefer than he would have wished; but it distils his essence.

Meantime Darius, whose troops had been waging local defensive war against Parmenion's bridgehead, disturbed by the news from Greece, had hired, also from Greece, some 50,000 mercenaries. Their general was Memnon, a veteran of Ochus' reign. He had been involved in the satraps' revolt and spent his exile in Macedon, where he had studied his hosts' tactics before being recalled. Alexander, who never thought the worse of old Artabazus for taking the field against him in the service of a Persian king, felt no such tolerance towards Greeks who did so. The army raised by Memnon had but few hard-up soldiers hiring their swords for bread; mostly it was of southerners continuing the war against Macedon after their cities had signed peace treaties. These Alexander resented as he did not the Persians who were only doing their duty.

He prepared to set out in spring. During the winter, he was urged by all those nearest him to marry and beget an heir before he left, lest he should be killed.

Antipater is said to have been insistent; loyal advice, for he was to be left as Regent, and if the King died childless would be well placed to seize the throne. But he had no more success than Philip and Olympias before him. Alexander impatiently replied that this was no time to sit at home "holding marriage feasts and awaiting the birth of children." To have done the first need not have entailed the second. If offspring did not appear after his departure, he could have summoned his bride to Asia and tried again. Clearly he still found the whole idea repugnant. He may have reflected, too, that a child reared in Macedon in his absence would be wholly dominated by Olympias.

Had he taken Antipater's advice, he might have been survived by a successor eleven years old; had he taken his parents', one of perhaps fourteen; and the whole course of Hellenistic history would have been altered. It is said that when asked how he had contrived to subdue Greece so swiftly, he answered, "By never putting off anything till tomorrow." This one thing he put off; and set in train a generation of wars.

At least it saved him expense. A much more pressing problem just then was money. It was said of Philip that at his accession his most valuable asset was a cup of thin gold, which he kept at night in the bed box under his pillow. Later he amassed much wealth, but he had also spent it: on his army, on buying support in Greece, on civilizing Macedon, and on preparing for the war. Alexander was to say later, "I inherited from my father a few gold and silver cups, less than sixty talents in the treasury; and debts of five hundred that he owed. When I had borrowed another eight hundred, I set out." In spite of this, or because of it, he realized all his personal estate, and gave it away to friends and loyal supporters. Some would take nothing, like Perdiccas; whose inclusion suggests, in spite of Ptolemy, that he did the right thing at Thebes. "What are you keeping for yourself?" he asked. "Hope," said Alexander, to which Perdiccas' prophetic answer was, "That I'll share."

In early spring, Alexander marched east with 30,000 infantry, partly light-armed skirmishers and archers, and about 5,000 cavalry: scarcely more than the Macedonian numbers at Chaeronea, to invade an empire which, if marshalled by an enemy of a calibre anywhere near his own, could have put a million in the field. Tarn has well said that he embarked upon the war at first because "he never thought of not doing it; it was his inheritance." It was in what the war engendered that his unique genius appeared.

He marched to the Hellespont alongside his fleet; but the far superior Persian navy did not attack. At the crossing of the straits he took the helm of his own flagship; probably as a boy he had sailed on the now-vanished Pella lagoon. Having sacrificed in midstream to Poseidon, on the further shore he cast his spear before him as an omen, and was the first to wade to land. He had no backward look for Europe, which he was never to see again.

Typically, before doing anything else he made straight for Troy—ruined, but traceable on its site of natural rock

—made offerings to its patroness Athene, and dedicated at her shrine his whole panoply of arms; taking for himself, as of right, his choice of her ancient, allegedly Homeric trophies, including a shield which would later save his life. Here he and Hephaestion paid their tribute to the immortal friends; Plutarch says also that Alexander and his comrades stripped and ran a ceremonial race round Achilles' gravemound. All sources agree that he sacrificed to the hero. Some enterprising tourist tout offered him the authentic lyre of Paris (whose other name was Alexandros); he crisply rejected this relic of an effete hedonist, saying he would prefer the instrument to which Achilles sang about the deeds of heroes. The truth is perhaps that lyres and singing were still a sore subject, even after eight or ten years.

After this romantic dedication of his adventure, he marshalled his forces for the conquest of transpontine Greece, his only present objective. He marched north, then east along the coast of the Dardanelles, where the Persian force awaited him.

It was not yet led by Darius, who put nothing off till tomorrow if next week or next month would do. Its most expert commander was the mercenary general Memnon, leading 15,000 of his Greeks. He was, however, outranked by half a dozen aristocratic Persians. When he advised scorching the countryside and starving out the Macedonians, who could not live very long on what they brought, the local satrap indignantly refused and carried the others with him. They then decided to hold the eastern bank of the River Granicus, just inshore from its mouth; a reasonable alternative in view of their (much-disputed) numbers, which seem to have been inferior to the invaders'. Alexander would have to tackle them before he advanced inland, and the high river banks gave them a needed advantage.

As Alexander neared the river, his scouts reported the Persians' position. Since his landing he had been joined by Parmenion, who had replaced his son Philotas as second-in-command. If Parmenion did advise Alexander against pitched battle and propose a dawn surprise—another disputed matter in view of later events—it was probably on the assumption that the enemy would adopt the obviously sensible tactic of posting their firm-stanced infantry on the top of the bank, to prod back with their spears the insecure and slithering horsemen as they scrambled up. Instead it was held by cavalry. General Fuller is surely right in seeing here another example of aristocratic *noblesse oblige* and racial pride. The mere infantry were foreign hirelings—no gentleman should shelter himself behind them.

Medieval knights, on big horses, anchored by stirrups into their massive saddles and holding their huge spears in rests, would have offered an impregnable defense line. But the Persians, with the insecure seat of the ancient horseman, were also handicapped by having not even small spears as combat hand weapons, but missile javelins, of which each man is unlikely to have carried more than two. The Macedonians had strong battle lances of cornel wood. Depending though they did on the rider's arm movements, since using his horse's forward impetus would have pushed him off, they were still superior armament. The armies were near enough for Alexander to be aware of this.

Drawing up his forces to front the river, he gave the left wing to Parmenion, himself taking up the time-honoured royal station on the right; his brigade commander here was Philotas. Arrian gives the name of all section leaders; and it is interesting to see the great future generals, Craterus and Perdiccas, still only phalanx commanders. Ptolemy and Hephaestion had as yet no commands at all.

A true professional, Alexander had no favourites in the field.

The fact that he himself was so resplendently armed as to be recognizable as far as he could be seen, deplorable by modern standards, was professional too throughout all ages of war but ours. That practical soldier Xenophon relates approvingly of Cyrus that his arms shone like a mirror and his helmet had a white plume. Alexander put up two of them, one each side.

Having launched his first shock-troops into the river, he returned to the right wing, gave his war yell, and, riding in front, drove straight into the massive formation drawn up on purpose to receive him. He directed his thrust towards the Persian high command, traditionally in the centre, rescuing some of his own centre assault troops who were hard pressed. The scrimmage on the steep churned-up bank was for some time indecisive, the Macedonians being faced with hand-to-hand combat whenever they reached the top; the Persians, their javelins expended, now using side arms. In this hacking and shoving Alexander's spear was broken; he got another from one of his squires, a Demaratus of Corinth, probably the grandson of the Demaratus who had negotiated his return from exile. With this he dashed at a conspicuous Persian general, killed him, and was at once involved in a mêlée, getting a blow on the helmet which removed one of its plumes. While he was accounting for this assailant, another raised his scimitar to bring it down on him; the brother of his childhood nurse Hellanice, Cleitus "the Black," was in time to cut through the second attacker's arm.

Resolution, discipline, and the strong cornel-wood lances carried the day. The Persians fell into confusion, then into flight. Alexander let them go; he concentrated his assault upon the mercenaries, whom he regarded as traitors to Greece. Here there was a savage slaughter. Some must have escaped, but he only took about 2,000 prisoners, whom he did not re-employ but sent to hard labour in Macedon. Memnon himself got away to fight again. The Persian satrap Arsames, who had overruled his advice before the battle, also escaped, but killed himself.

Macedonian casualties were light. To the twenty-five Companions who had fallen in the first assault Alexander gave special funeral honours with tax remission to their families, and had their statues cast in bronze. After the battle he went to see the wounded, Arrian says: "looking at their wounds, asking how they got them, encouraging each to tell about his deeds and even brag of them." Glimpses like this explain the extraordinary relationship that was to evolve between him and his army in ensuing years.

He buried the Persian generals with the honours of war, and gave the dead Greek mercenaries a proper Greek funeral. To fourth-century men there was much more in this than a gesture; it was the rite of peaceful passage to the land of shades. What to modern man may seem cynical seemed to contemporaries generous and unusual; his effect on them will be better understood if this is borne in mind. Of a piece with it is his pardoning of local people who, unlike the mercenaries, had been serving the Persians under conscription.

He now marched south to Sardis, a formidable inland fortress on high rock, which surrendered without a fight. In Asia Minor he would be dealing mostly with cities where only the garrison and officials felt loyalty to Persia; these Lydians were the people of King Croesus, conquered in Cyrus' day. The treasury of Sardis, if not quite up to Croesus' legend, was well filled, and came just when he needed it. He built a temple to Olympian Zeus on the old site of the royal palace under the divine direction of a lightning bolt, garrisoned the acropolis, and allowed the people their traditional customs and laws. Olympian Zeus, the patron god of Macedon, is on the reverse of nearly all his silver coinage, enthroned, after Phidias' famous statue at Olympia. The obverse has Heracles with his lion-mask hood. As the mints go east, the Zeus, carved by non-Greek craftsmen, grows increasingly vague, the Heracles more and more like Alexander.

The Greek coastal city of Ephesus opened its gates to him, disclosing a society seething with hate and vendetta. Greek oligarch collaborators had ruled it for the Persians. On the news of Alexander's victory, these people had been lynched by the democrats, or dragged from temple sanctuary and stoned to death with their children. He restored the democracy, but strictly forbade any more reprisals, "knowing that once they got leave, the people would kill some men unjustly, from mere hate, or to get hold of their wealth, along with those who deserved it." Arrian says his popularity soared after this decree.

He sacrificed there to Artemis (Saint Paul's Diana of the Ephesians) and held a brilliant victory parade. Greek cities now fell to him like ripe fruit. In each he evicted pro-Persian quislings and established Greek-style democracies. This, he told them, was what he had come to do; and he may not yet have been looking further.

Fifty miles south he was in Caria, and gazed for the first time on that state so calamitous in his past. The satrap Pixodarus had been some time dead, succeeded by a kinsman devoted to Persian interests. Had Alexander's intrigue come off, it would probably have brought him nothing but a redundant Carian wife. He got instead a Carian mother.

Pixodarus was a usurper. His predecessors had been a brother and sister, married (as in Egypt) by royal custom. On her husband's death, Ada the wife had the right to rule alone, but had been expelled by Pixodarus. Retiring in good order, she had established herself in the strong harbour fortress of Alinda. This she now surrendered to Alexander, offering him allegiance if he restored her rights. Diplomatic courtesies soon turned to maternal adoration, indulgently and affectionately received. She cosseted and spoiled him; shocked by his plain diet, she plied him with *cordon bleu* till he was driven to polite excuses. Before long, she formally adopted him as her son. By now the irony may have amused him.

Unlike many men whose childhood has been mother dominated, Alexander was never drawn sexually to older women. He preferred the filial role. Later he was to assume it with much deeper involvement; and to a third such bond, seemingly the most casual and incongruous, he was to owe his life.

He marched to Miletus, a port in the usurper's territory. Its garrison commander began to treat for surrender, got wind of seaborne reinforcements and changed his mind. Alexander's small fleet of 160 ships slipped swiftly into the strategic harbour of Lade across the narrow strait; the Persians, forced to take second best, beached their belated 400 vessels northward up the coast.

Parmenion is said to have urged a sea fight, presumably because of the better Macedonian position. An eagle had been propitiously seen on shore at their ships' sterns. Alexander preferred to let the Persians alone, because, he said, their ships were crewed by more experienced seamen, and a victory would give a fillip to their morale. The eagle had perched on *land,* pointing out where fortune lay. Finally, "he would not risk sacrificing the skill and courage of his Macedonians."[2] Reckless with his own life, he was never wasteful of theirs, a fact well known to them and never undervalued.

He breached and stormed the Miletus walls, his ships

closing the harbour mouth against Persian aid. Some of the garrison escaped by sea, rafted with their wooden shields, to an offshore islet. He sailed after them, but, "seeing the men on the island would fight to the last, he pitied them as high-minded and faithful soldiers." The Milesians he let go free; the mercenaries were Greek, but he hired them in his own service.

The powerful Persian fleet, denied the harbour, was still beached with all its soldiers. Warships of the ancient world could never carry stores enough to feed for long their rowers, their seamen and the troops they carried. They had constantly to put in for water and supplies; hence the importance of supporting land troops. This fleet had none. Alexander sent out Philotas to occupy the surrounding coast and virtually besiege them by cutting them off from provisions. On land they were vastly outnumbered; after one vain attempt to provoke a sea fight, their stores were exhausted and they had to go. The complete success of this minor operation suggested to Alexander's logical mind a major long-term strategy. Why not refuse to the Persian navy *all* its ports of call?

"He interpreted the eagle to mean that he should conquer the ships by land." Alexander's impetuosity in battle went with a surprising readiness to form a long-term objective and to wait. His plan meant mastering the whole east Mediterranean seaboard before he struck inland; but it would secure both the liberated cities and his own communications. He laid a heavy stake on it by disbanding, except a couple of transports for his siege engines, all his own ships; which, despite his haul at Sardis, he could still not well afford to maintain. It would leave him cut off if he were defeated; but defeat, like fear, he presumed not to exist.

His next objective was Halicarnassus, the late Pixodarus' capital. A commanding fortress rebuilt in later ages by Seljuks and Crusaders, it was a tougher proposition than Miletus and needed a full-scale siege. One of its two commanders was the expert Memnon. Arrian describes in detail the filling of its great moat to bring up the siege towers, the sorties from the fort to burn them, the final breach of the wall. When the city was clearly at his mercy, Alexander broke off the action and withdrew, offering a parley to discuss terms next day. He was roused at midnight to see the town in flames; Memnon and his men had fired it and a wind was spreading the blaze. He stormed inside, ordering all fire raisers caught in the act to be killed, but citizens spared. Memnon and his staff had got away.

Alexander was now master of Caria. He garrisoned its fortresses, and restored Queen Ada to the satrap's throne.

His next action was to give Parmenion his separate command. If the young King's rejection of his advice was stressed in later chronicles for expedient reasons, this is no proof that such incidents were fictitious. They suggest a familiar human pattern. Parmenion was now in his middle sixties. He had been Philip's intimate friend for more than twenty years. He now found himself working with a high command mostly a full generation younger, under a leader in his early twenties. If he had adjusted with ease from Philip's mental processes to Alexander's, it would have been little short of a miracle. Shakespeare's Antony complains that Octavius' tutelary genius daunts his own, and Parmenion may have felt this perennial situation. On Alexander's side, a man who had been so close to his father, who had married a daughter of Attalus when he was in power and Alexander in disgrace, must always have created some sense of tension. At all events, he now detached Parmenion to command the communication lines over the conquered territory. A tendency to repeat this policy was to have terrible results for both of them.

Alexander now gave home leave to all Macedonian soldiers newly married before setting out; a wildly popular directive, and thoughtful for future Macedonian manpower. He next moved against the mountain hill tribes, everywhere in the world intractable; midwinter had driven them down into the valleys, easing the task of subjugation. During this time, Parmenion intercepted a message from Darius to Alexandros of Lyncestis—whose two brothers had been executed for complicity in Philip's murder—offering him the throne of Macedon if he would procure Alexander's death. This prince had now been promoted to command of the Thracian cavalry. As a possible successor should Alexander die childless, he had always been a source of danger; his survival represented a notable departure from Macedonian royal precedent. Even now, however, Alexander, lacking proof that the Persian offer had been solicited, did not charge him with treason, but kept him under precautionary arrest. It was remembered that during the recent siege, a swallow had entered the royal tent, and fluttered over its sleeping occupant. Half waking, Alexander had gently brushed it away, but it had returned and perched on his head. The seers divined that the warnings of this domestic bird meant domestic danger. However, Alexander still held his hand.

The winter was spent in reducing coastal strongholds, working south and down round Asia Minor's eastward curve. With the spring he struck inland as far as Gordium, locale of the famous knot. It was a leather thong, intricately wound about the shaft of an ancient vehicle on which their most famous king, the legendary Midas, was supposed to have arrived. Plutarch says, most probably by hindsight, that the man who could undo it was destined to rule the world. Arrian says that by some accounts Alexander cut it with his sword in proverbial manner; by others, he tugged out the shaft it was wound round, and discovered the hidden end. "I shall not try," writes Arrian conscientiously, "to say exactly how Alexander dealt with this knot." It is agreed he dealt with it. There were thunderings and lightnings, to clinch the matter.

Further south, he approached the almost impregnable pass of the Cilician Gates, but had not to force it. Its holding force fled as soon as they heard he was there in person. At Tarsus, he nearly killed himself by jumping into the Cydnus (the stream that carried Cleopatra's barge to Antony) while tired, hot and sweating. It was snow water; he got cramp and a bad chill, and his life was thought in danger. Here he made one of his impassioned testimonies to friendship. His doctor, Philip, was about to dose him, when a letter arrived from Parmenion, assuring him that Darius had bribed the man to poison him. In view of the offer to Alexandros of Lyncestis, this cannot have seemed trivial. It may even have been tried on Philip, though ignored. Alexander handed him the letter and, while he read it, tossed the medicine down. Philip, looking up in horror, saw Alexander smiling and holding the empty cup. The potion was a strong purge. He endured without loss of trust this benighted treatment, though it must have delayed his recovery, which took some weeks.

Darius meantime, stirred at last to action, had marched west from Babylon with an enormous army, and made camp on level ground where he had plenty of room to deploy it, barring the Macedonians' southward march, somewhere near modern Aleppo. Unaware that Alexander was ill—his convalescence probably prolonged by two years' incessant labour—Darius thought he was hanging back from fear, and was much encouraged.

The Great King, who stood six and a half feet tall, is

said by Diodorus to have won renown during Ochus' reign by killing in single combat a Cilician champion whom no other warrior would face. He was now about fifty; the duel, if it ever took place, may have been fought a quarter century before. It may have been propaganda to support his accession, which needed support; power and luxury may have changed him; or his courage may have been, as courage can be, specific rather than general. It would seem at any rate that since the news from the Granicus he had been a frightened man. The recent death of Memnon, from illness while on campaign, had further disconcerted him.

Alexander, when on his feet again, conducted methodical mopping-up operations to safeguard his flanks and communications. Darius, much cheered by this further delay, began to think of offensive action. Arrian blames flattering courtiers for this overconfidence; it is also possible that keener soldiers simply wanted to push him into the field.

With a formidable battle now ahead, Alexander set up a field hospital by the inlet bay of Issus, left there his sick and wounded, and marched southward to meet Darius; unaware that Darius, by a different inland route, was marching north. Hidden from each other the armies passed. Darius arrived at Issus in Alexander's rear. The only Macedonians he found were the patients in the hospital. Whether or not by his orders, they were cut up alive. This atrocity was never repaid in kind by Alexander; a restraint seldom practised in the ancient world or, indeed, in some parts of the modern one.

The news that Darius had left his first-class position in the plain, and marched to Issus where he had no room to manœuvre, seemed so incredible to Alexander that he sent a scout ship to make sure. The bay was reported swarming with Persians. He assembled his officers for briefing.

Arrian says he told them how Xenophon and his Ten Thousand, a body of isolated, unsupported infantry, had successfully fought their way from Babylon to the sea. He recalled their own ordeals successfully overcome together, "and whatever else at such a time in the face of danger a brave general would say to hearten brave men" —a thing he was very good at. The fact that they were cut off if they lost was unworthy even of mention. At the end they crowded round him, grasping his hands and begging him to lead them on. Latter-day clichés about the stiff upper lip, derived from Roman tradition, tend to obscure the highly emotional bond between Alexander and his men, which was to last his lifetime.

As at the Granicus, the Persians formed up behind a steep-banked river. Their front stretched from the sea to the near hills; a host which could have encircled the Macedonians with ease, had the terrain given them room. As it was, a great mass of reserves stood uselessly in the rear.

Ptolemy's reckoning of the Persian force at 600,000 is thought by modern historians much exaggerated. To the Macedonians, outnumbered even on conservative estimates at eight or ten to one, it must have looked like it at the time. Darius' Greek mercenaries alone are still thought to have been 12,000; the 5,000 Macedonian horse were a squadron compared with the heavily mailed Persian cavalry. Its commander was the distinguished general Nabarzanes, for whom the battle would be the prologue to a sombre drama.

Alexander took the intervening passes unhurriedly, keeping his men fresh. When, on the edge of the bay, he formed them in battle order, he made no speeches. He rode about the line, having a word with the officers, singling out men who had done well before and speaking of their exploits. The fact that he must have known several thousand men by name was one of Alexander's secret weapons. Xenophon speaks highly of this gift in a commander.

To Parmenion, who had rejoined him on the march, he gave the important left-wing posting next the sea. The centre was mainly infantry. He himself with the household cavalry and the Companions led on the right.

Arrian describes the battle in detail. The Persians massed their cavalry against Parmenion's vulnerable flank on the beach. Alexander sent reinforcements, riding low behind the tall sarissas of the infantry, to attempt surprise; but Nabarzanes fought on undaunted. Towards the right the tough Agriani, legacy of the dead prince Lambarus, dashed out at opposing Persian skirmishers and made them run. In the centre, where the phalanx faced the Greek mercenaries, the contest was stubborn, the Macedonians fighting for their pride, the Greeks to humble it. Pride, discipline, morale and the long sarissa carried the phalanx slowly forward. Alexander, watching his time, hurled himself with the Companion Cavalry across the river, smashing the enemy left, and turned the flank of the Greeks. Leaving the phalanx to finish a now easy task, he made for the target he had all along had his eye on: the royal Persian guard, the "Immortals," in whose midst stood the Great King, conspicuous in his ornate chariot by his height and royal robe. Mounted upon the ageing but still spirited Bucephalas (who probably owed his long life to the light weight of his rider) Alexander raised the battle paean, and led the yelling cavalry, already exalted by success, in a thundering relentless charge.

As it neared, perhaps when in the dust cloud Alexander could be clearly seen, Darius' nerve broke. He turned his chariot and fled. In wild confusion the Persian centre followed him. The whole front crumbled. The huge army poured off into the narrow passes. Thousands of men who had never been used in battle were trampled to death or jostled over precipices, by fugitives themselves being ridden down by the Macedonians. Nabarzanes, still resolutely fighting an indecisive action against Parmenion, saw débâcle and heard that the King had fled. He then disengaged his men as best he could, with feelings that time was to reveal.

Had the royal chariot been occupied by Darius' younger brother, Oxathres, it is unlikely the fight would have been so prompt. He put up a good fight beside the King till it was too late; a fact not lost on Alexander when next they met.

Eager to pursue Darius, he waited to be sure that victory was secure; the prize was great, but he was a professional. Then he changed horses for the chase; to find, some miles along, the royal chariot, the royal weapons and robe, of which Darius had disencumbered himself before hastening his flight on horseback. Alexander, returning with these trophies, found them the least of what the Great King had left behind.

His tent stood intact, with the appointments of a palace; toilet and table ware in gold and silver, inlaid furniture, a divan, a sumptuous bath, a throne. Alexander, looking around at a setting which must have made his father's famous palace seem almost ascetic, is said to have exclaimed, "So *this* is what it means to be a king."

Dining that night with his chief officers, in the tent, off the gold and silver, the stains of battle washed off in the royal bath, he heard women wailing not far off, and asked what was going on. He was told it came from the harem. Darius had left behind him his wife, reputed the fairest woman in Asia; their two young daughters; his heir, a boy of five or six; and his mother. Learning that his chariot and robe had been brought back with the spoils, they were lamenting his death, and the fate they foresaw for themselves.

Other eminent Persians had left their women in what then seemed safety at Damascus. Darius, self-indulgent and too confident, had brought his household along. To Alexander this in itself must have seemed highly unprofessional; the sequel of their abandonment—and to troops who owed vengeance for the hospital atrocity— came as a revelation. The ladies had so far been unmolested. They were, of course, the perquisites reserved for him.

He sent an officer at once to reassure them; Darius still lived, they would be protected. The Queen Mother, Sisygambis, would receive the names of noble fallen Persians, with his leave to direct their funeral rites. Next day, having seen the wounded—he had a sword cut on the thigh himself—he visited the family. Arrian admits that the event has accumulated legend. There is, however, no conflict of the evidence. He, Curtius and Plutarch vary only slightly, and all to the same effect.

Alexander brought Hephaestion with him. They walked in together, both simply dressed. Hephaestion's looks and presence first struck the women, used to associate height with royalty, and the venerable Sisygambis began to prostrate herself before him. He drew back; the harem eunuchs made warning signs; in distress she began again with the King. He stepped forward and raised her up. "Never mind, Mother. You made no mistake, he too is Alexander." Mystifying as this may have seemed when passed through an interpreter, she thanked him with regal dignity.

The Queen, Stateira, was Darius' sister. Dynastic incest was common in the East, but this marriage predated his accession. Since, however, an accredited beauty of that day must have been well under thirty, she would be a legitimate half-sister by a younger wife of their father. Her two daughters, barely out of childhood, were old enough for the captive's usual fate. Alexander promised them all his safeguard. He bent to the youngest child, the little boy, who fearlessly hugged his neck. Turning to Hephaestion—not to the interpreter—he said that Sisygambis' grandchild shared her nature; a pity it had missed her son.

The family was given the dignity, seclusion and safety of a royal harem. To Sisygambis he had been drawn at once. Her age exempted her from strict purdah, and he called again on her.

She had never been the wife of a king, only the mother, and that late in life. But to the old aristocrat who had bewailed her son's heroic death, the truth of his survival may have been a greater blow. She and Alexander seem to have found much in common, despite all gulfs of culture and language, and even the gaffe with which his next visit opened. Recalling his mother and sister doing fancy work at the loom, he arrived with a gift of choice coloured wools. Sisygambis had never seen such stuff but in the hands of servants; she felt bitterly what seemed a reminder of her new condition. He read her face, got to the bottom of the trouble, and begged pardon gracefully. Their friendship prospered.

The young Queen he never saw again; from self-mastery, Plutarch says; in any case, resolved that scandal should have no straw to catch at. In flattery or joke, friends urged him to claim his *droit du seigneur;* he forbade them to name her in his presence. Though the abstinence itself may have cost him little, the thought for the women's pride and self-respect, the maintenance of their little court and accustomed service, came from natural generosity. A fact needing more explanation is that, with the troublesome train of their furniture, ladies and household eunuchs, he took them along on his march. It may have been to enjoy the company of Sisygambis —only at his death did the depth of their bond appear— it may have been to be sure they were not molested. Yet he had captured strongholds where he could have established them in safety. There is another possible motive, which would have been very like him.

The most picturesque subplot of Xenophon's *Cyropaedia* is the story (quite fictional, as far as anyone knows) of Cyrus and the Lady of Susa. After his great victory over the Assyrian confederation, she was reserved for him as the best of the booty, along with her wealthy household. Her beloved husband, away in distant parts, had missed the battle. The Persian officers, who had glimpsed her beauty as she tore her robe in lamentation, reported her "the loveliest woman of mortal birth in Asia." They had assured her by way of comfort that she was destined for the finest among men; now they urged him to view his prize. No, he answered, by God he would not, especially if her beauty was so great. He might gaze on her too long, and forget his duties; love, when all was said, was a kind of slavery. He confided her protection to a trusted follower; when this man fell in love with her, for her safety he was sent away. Moved by so much chivalry, she offered to send her husband word of it, and beg him to ally with Cyrus. Trustingly he arrived. "They embraced each other with joy, as well they might when they had had no hope of ever meeting again." She told him of Cyrus' compassion and self-command, and begged it should be repaid with loyalty. Gratefully he took the King's right hand; and remained faithful until death.

Alexander had not only a powerful sense of theatre; he had learned from Aristotle how the great-souled man chooses his role and lives it through. He had also a real delight in giving pleasure to others, whose sincerity is attested by many human anecdotes. It is tempting to guess that he had hopes of surpassing Xenophon's drama. Darius had not shown himself in the light of an implacable foe who would fight while life was in him. The reunion with wife, mother and children, presided over by a gracious victor, would indeed have made one of history's great set Alexander-pieces, to whose possibilities no one was more alive than Alexander. His determination to make such dreams come true was attended by much success. If he was disappointed of this one, fate rather than impracticability was to blame.

The Lady's story had another aspect. Her husband become Cyrus' vassal.

There is no moment in Alexander's career of which it can be said with certainty that this was when he decided he need not stop short with his father's aim of freeing the Greek cities; that he could, and would, be Great King of Persia. But the likeliest time is surely after Issus, when he saw what imperial splendours had enshrined a man of straw.

Darius fled through the night on relays of horses, with a handful of his suite. At daybreak he was joined by some 4,000 scattered fugitives. About 8,000 of his Greeks escaped home by sea. The King himself scarcely drew rein till he was across the Euphrates.

Alexander, his road swept clear before him, marched due south towards Judaea and the coastal cities of the Phoenicians. His Greek obligations were all fulfilled; he was now embarked on a war of conquest.

It is as foolish to apply anachronistic moral standards to this as it would be to condemn Hippocrates for not teaching aseptic surgery. In the long evolution of human thought (so generally in advance of human conduct) the notion that war was wrong had not yet entered the world. Socrates himself, who regarded his life work as a search for the good, said proudly at his trial, "It would be strange, Athenians, if I who stood my ground in the battle-line, facing death at my commander's order, should desert the station where God posted me." Aristotle warmly supported wars of Hellenizing conquest so long as "barbarians" were not treated as men. A century later, a handful of Stoics began to question war's morality, but were little heeded. Rome's soldier Christians went to martyrdom sooner than worship the Divine Caesar or the Eagles of their legion; not for refusing to fight. In our own generation, what has been tolerated, and even approved, by the same opinion formers who condemn Alexander, shows a discrepancy of standards so bizarre that one might suppose it is his better qualities, rather than his worse, that arouse resentment. The words of that underrated philosopher the Earl of Chesterfield are as true today as in 1748: "The things which happen in our own times, and which we see ourselves, do not surprise us near so much as things which we read of in times past though not in the least more extraordinary."

From some camp in Mesopotamia Darius wrote to Alexander, requiring terms for the ransom of his family. His note was a general manifesto, accusing Philip as first aggressor, and Alexander for breaking an old alliance— an unwise reminder, to a man in a position of strength, of Macedonian humiliation in Xerxes' war. He, Darius, had taken up arms against these injuries; but "the battle had gone as some god willed it."

This almost invited Alexander to say, as he promptly did, that he held the land "by the gift of heaven." The rest of his reply was an uncompromising challenge. He had been elected to avenge the wrong to Greece by Xerxes.

Ochus had invaded the domain of his father Philip; Darius himself had procured Philip's death, and "boasted of it in letters before all the world" (captured perhaps at Sardis?). Also, Darius was a usurper who had conspired to murder his predecessor (true or false, a suspicion natural to any king of Macedon). The royal family would be freely returned whenever he cared to come and ask in person. (The failure to blackmail him by threatening their safety makes a melancholy contrast with modern times.)

Later legends contain innumerable, and often interminable, spurious challenges of Alexander's. The peroration of this one, probably from the royal archives, has an authentic ring.

> . . . And in future when you send to me, send to the lord of Asia; and do not write to me what to do, but ask me, as master of all you own, for anything you need. Or I shall judge you an offender. If you claim your kingdom, take your stand and fight for it, and do not run; for I shall make my way wherever you may be.

Soon after, a force under Parmenion took the surrender of Damascus. The Governor had proposed it secretly; Parmenion, wary of treachery, would not lead his men inside, but told him to come out with his treasure under pretence of taking flight. He was followed, therefore, by a panic crowd, including the harems of the Persian nobles engaged at Issus.

These ladies, not being royal game, were not so strictly preserved. One has a role in Alexander's legend, another in his history. Only Plutarch says that he took for himself Barsine, Memnon's widow and Artabazus' daughter; for the staggering reason that Parmenion—of all people! —told him she would be good for him. The dubiety of the story lies not only in this, but in the powerful motive for inventing it. No record at all exists of such a woman accompanying his march; nor of any claim by her, or her powerful kin, that she had borne him offspring. Yet twelve years after his death a boy was produced, seventeen years old, born therefore five years after Damascus, her alleged son "brought up in Pergamon"; a claimant and shortlived pawn in the succession wars, chosen probably for a physical resemblance to Alexander. That he actually did marry another Barsine must have helped both to launch and preserve the story; but no source reports any notice whatever taken by him of a child who, Roxane's being posthumous, would have been during his lifetime his only son, by a near-royal mother. In a man who named cities after his horse and dog, this strains credulity.

A more convincing character is a Macedonian beauty, perhaps a high-class hetaira, who fell to Philotas' lot. He found her worth impressing, and kept her entertained with his own and his family's distinguished exploits. She listened most politely. It was to turn out, however, that he had overrated his own charm.

Alexander's real booty from Damascus was a vast haul of treasure, the Great King's war chest and the private coffers of the nobles, relieving him at last of all worries about financing his campaign. He also captured four Greek envoys; two from Thebes, whom he released at once, accepting their Persianizing as natural; one from Sparta, imprisoned for a time and then let go; and an elderly Athenian, son of the famous general, Iphicrates, the guest-friend of his grandparents. This last he charmed into joining his suite, where he remained for life, his ashes being sent scrupulously back to his kin in Athens.

Sidon gladly opened its gates, turning out a pro-Persian governor. This had an interesting sequel: Hephaestion's first independent mission. Before its conquest by Persia some generations back, Sidon had been a monarchy. Alexander directed Hephaestion to choose a king.

It was a graceful mark of honour, implying that Hephaestion himself was worthy of the office, if he could have been spared; but Alexander was realistic about such missions, and this called for both integrity and skill. Hephaestion was at once surrounded with sycophancy and intrigue. His own host, a leading citizen, perhaps fearful of hostile factions, declined with the excuse that he was not of the royal blood. At this, Hephaestion asked if any actual scion of the line survived; to get the unexpected reply that one did, but, born into peasant poverty, he was working as a daily gardener. Hephaestion took up his references and found them excellent; too tactful to intrude on him at his lowly job, he sent him emissaries with a royal robe in which he could arrive with dignity. They found him busy with the watering. The Sidonians, astounded by this choice of the one candidate who could not have produced a bribe, settled down to it pretty well. The carefulness of his own honour, and his friend's, which such a choice implies, along with its success, tell us much about Hephaestion.

King Abdalonymus remained a good worker, respectable and honest. It is pleasant to record an instance of human gratitude. After Hephaestion's death, while his grandiose memorials stood unfinished because Alexander too was gone, and jealous rivals were paring to the bone —as Ptolemy surely did—this brilliant officer's record, Abdalonymus was designing his own sarcophagus. A fine Hellenistic frieze of tinted marble shows a battle scene, with Alexander in heroic action. But the central figure, a handsome cavalryman hewing down a Persian foe, is generally accepted as Hephaestion's one surviving likeness.

From Sidon Alexander marched on southward towards the formidable obstacle of Tyre. This massive Phoenician fortress port was an island, separated by a deep channel from the shore. It had its own large merchant and war fleet, and a harbour open to Persian ships. On his approach it sent him envoys, offering to be at his orders. He tested them by asking to perform a state sacrifice at the temple of Melkart, the Tyrian Heracles. This brought a refusal to open their gates to Macedonians, with a claim that they would shut out Persians too, an undertaking they were unlikely to honour once he had passed by.

Alexander called a war council, aware of the huge task ahead. If they left Tyre two-faced in their rear, he said, the Persians could use it as an invasion base against Greece, where Sparta was now in open revolt against his Regent Antipater, and Athens awaiting her chance. Ahead lay Egypt, a rich objective, eager to receive him; the brutality and sacrilege of Ochus' reconquest had never been forgiven there. The coast once secured, and all Asia this side of Euphrates in their power, they could march for Babylon.

This realistic assessment convinced his staff. He made a last attempt to avoid such a costly siege, by sending envoys with an ultimatum. The Tyrians, violating the immemorial sanctity of heralds, brought them out on the walls for him to view their murder, and threw their bodies in the sea. After this, Alexander announced that he had had a dream, in which Heracles stood on the Tyrian walls, with hand outstretched to lead him into the city.

These walls, made of dressed and mortared stone, were 150 feet high on the landward side. Stratagem and surprise were out; he settled down at once to business, and began to run a mole out from the mainland.

Out of missile range, the first stretch went quickly. He stood over the work, giving out prizes for zeal. But the channel deepened, the fill took more stones and time; they came into bowshot of the walls; Tyrian ships now had draught to approach and harry them. He had two moving towers built, mounted with catapults, armoured with hide and with a hide screen stretched between them. Dragged along as the work advanced, it could shelter the carriers till at the last moment they dashed out to tip their loads. When the wind was high, the Tyrians launched a blazing fireship, its tall yards hung with cauldrons of flaming pitch. The towers burned out, their crews leaping off or perishing inside. Alexander ordered new towers, and went off to Sidon to raise a war fleet.

This took a couple of weeks, during which he discharged his restless energy in a ten-day expedition to subdue the neighbouring tribes. With him, for company, went the now elderly Lysimachus, the obscure Macedonian gentleman who had beguiled his childhood with tales from Homer. When he went scouting in the hills, Lysimachus begged to come along, recalling this old game and declaring himself no older than his examplar Phoenix, Achilles' guardian. Plutarch continues,

> But when, leaving their horses, they began to walk into the hills, the rest of the soldiers went a good way ahead, so that night approaching and the enemy near, Alexander lingered behind so long, to hearten and help the lagging tired old man, that before he knew it he was left in the rear a long way from his soldiers, with a small company, on a bitter night in the dark, and in a very bad place; till seeing many scattered fires of the enemy some way off, and trusting to his swiftness . . . he ran straight to one of the nearest fires, and killing with his dagger two of the barbarians who sat by it, snatched up a burning brand, and returned with it to his own people. They at once made a great fire, which so scared the enemy that most of them fled, and those who attacked

them were soon routed; and thus they rested securely
for what was left of the night.

After this tribute to friendship he went back to Sidon,
where 120 Cypriot ships awaited him; the island rulers
had thrown off the Persian yoke and joined his cause.
In all he raised about 200 sail; and led them over to the
attack. His own flagship took the post of danger nearest
the city walls. But the Tyrians, startled by his numbers,
merely closed their harbour with a boom of ships, as he
had done himself at Miletus. He could not tempt them out.

His operations were now enormous, using engineers
from Cyprus and the whole Phoenician littoral, besides
the expert Greeks he had brought along. He mounted
catapults on shipboard, and began to bombard the walls
with heavy stones. The Tyrians cast rocks into the sea to
obstruct the ships. Doggedly he had the rocks fished for
and hauled up. For this his ships had to anchor; the
Tyrians sent armoured ships to cut their cables. He
brought up support ships. The enemy sent divers to cut
the cables under water. He replaced the cables with
anchor chains. At length the channel allowed his ships
alongside the walls, which the mole was also nearing.

The inventive Tyrians, men in advance of their time,
produced their most modern weapon. They heated sand
red hot, and projected it at the foremost Macedonians.
Diodorus says, "It sifted down under their corselets and
their clothes, searing the flesh with intense heat . . .
they screamed entreaties like men under torture, and none
could help them, but with the excruciating pain they went
mad and died." Many threw themselves in the sea. Unaware that it was to become a commonplace of civilized
warfare, Alexander considered it an atrocity. In view
of his fondness for leading the van, only chance must have
saved him from being flayed alive himself.

Half a year had passed in these labours. In the end it was by ships, supported from the mole though this ran short of the walls, that Tyre was stormed. Master now of the landward channel, he could bring round his assault craft under the weaker seaward walls. His torsion catapults could hurl heavy stones and crack ashlar masonry; the bow type were giant versions of the medieval crossbow, their pointed bronze bolts could pierce armour. His landing craft bore portable towers, a feature of his siege train which carted them in sections. On the day of the final assault he boarded a tower himself. One may picture a broad-beamed galley, with two or three oar banks to give it speed, the weird top-heavy-looking structure amidships crowned with armed men behind the glittering figure of Alexander who directed the pilot here and there on the lookout for a breach; the gangway lolling like a giant tongue, ready to be stuck out when one appeared. Meantime he watched, says Arrian, for brave deeds deserving of honour.

He saw one when the Captain of the Bodyguard, Admetus, leaped straight into the first good breach that opened, cheering on his men, and died there. By that time Alexander's ship had raced up in support; he ran out across his gangplank and led the party through. Meantime his ships had forced the harbour boom. The Tyrians, knowing all was lost, fled from the walls.

The Macedonians pursued them, cutting down all they could overtake. Alexander forbade them to drag anyone out of temple sanctuary. (In one temple a famous statue of Apollo, Carthaginian loot from Sicily, was found chained to its base, the god having informed some Tyrian seer in a dream that he was leaving to join Alexander.) Arrian does not give the number of the slain, but reckons the captives enslaved at 30,000, obviously the large majority even in a populous merchant port. Curtius says

6,000 armed men were killed. Both he and Diodorus say
that 2,000 were crucified. These may have been corpses;
the Macedonians displayed the bodies of executed criminals in this way, though without the mutilations later
practised in England. Curtius, never trustworthy with
atrocity stories, infers they were alive. It would be wrong
to exclude this entirely, because of the red-hot sand; but
on Alexander's general record, coupled with his concern
at this stage of his career for Hellenic standards, the
balance of probability is against it.

At some time during the siege he had another embassy
from Darius, who now offered not only the large sum
of 10,000 talents for his family, but also peace terms:
all Asia Minor west of the Euphrates, a treaty of alliance,
and his daughter's hand in marriage. This was the occasion of the famous bit of dialogue with Parmenion: "I'd
take it, Alexander, if I were you." "If I were you, so
would I. But I'm Alexander." His answer was that he had
no need of money, nor of being offered half the land,
which he already held, instead of the whole. He would
marry, if he liked, Darius' daughter with or without his
leave; and if he wanted an alliance let him come and
ask. Leaving him to take any steps which this reply suggested to him, Alexander marched towards Egypt.

As Wilcken has pointed out in a masterly analysis, this
moment of decision by Alexander is one of history's great
proofs that individuals, not mere economic forces, can
change the destinies of mankind. Had he listened to
Parmenion, Greek civilization would have been more
solidly established in Asia Minor but would never have
touched the East; the balance of power with Persia would
have remained precarious, and the emergence of a
stronger king there might have reversed the defeat of
Xerxes in future years.

Hephaestion, getting promotion, was now put in charge

of the fleet to patrol the coast. Alexander marched south to Gaza, the last point of coastal resistance. It was held by a eunuch general, Betis, who thought its high steep site impregnable. It was not a port; but if Alexander by-passed it, Darius would be encouraged to come down in his rear. His two-month siege included raising a high earthwork to bring his engines in range. While he was up there, some bird of prey dropped a stone on his head; perhaps mistaking his helmet for a tortoise whose shell it wished to crack, like the bald head of the poet Aeschylus, who died from the similar misjudgment of an eagle. Though unharmed Alexander asked the seer Aristander to read the omen. He pronounced that Alexander would take the city, but he must watch his safety today.

On this advice he kept out of range for some time during which nothing much was happening. Then a sally in strength from the fort began to drive his men off the ring wall; on which he at once dashed to their help at the head of his troop. Soon he was nearly killed by a man who, after surrendering to him and being spared, whipped out a dagger; with his quick reflexes he dodged the blow, and struck home. Whether thinking the omen now ful-filled, or defying it, or just carried away by enthusiasm, he kept in action, till a heavy bolt from a crossbow catapult sank deep into his shoulder. His doctor pulled it out, causing a good deal of haemorrhage, and put on a field dressing which, since Alexander went straight back into the battle, soon slipped off. He fought on, pouring blood under his armour, till he fainted. The wound was serious and kept him out of action for some time, but he directed operations until the city fell.

All good historians have rejected Curtius' story that the brave Betis was brought before him wounded, refused to bow the knee, and was thereon dragged round the city at his chariot tail. Anyone unconvinced by his constant generosity to brave enemies, in which he took some pride, may here safely trust his vanity. Achilles, before thus mistreating Hector, had personally killed him in the climactic duel of the epic. Alexander's wound had kept him from fighting in the final assault at all; he was the last man in the world to put on such an unpleasantly inferior display. The tale is interesting as a typical piece of Athenian propaganda, written by someone who had learned of his Homeric aspirations but knew nothing of his nature at first hand, or was too "committed" to care.

In Egypt he had no campaigning, only a triumphal progress.

Hephaestion with the fleet awaited him at the Delta. The Persian satrap Mazaces, long aware of the Issus débâcle and with no adequate Persian garrison, put a good face on necessity and welcomed Alexander in. Leaving the harbour of Pelusium manned, he marched up the Nile, alongside his fleet, to Memphis.

There can be scarcely a European today not furnished with some visual image of ancient Egypt however trite. It takes an effort of imagination to conceive the pristine impact on Alexander and his men, most of whom had never seen even Athens, of this fabled civilization, a legend since their childhood, as they followed the great river which was its sustainer, arterial road and sacred way; when they reached the towering temples of Memphis, the Pyramids with sides of geometric smoothness, the still unravaged smile of the huge Sphinx. It must have changed the whole scale of their human vision.

Hailed everywhere as deliverer by the Egyptians, he was enthroned as Pharaoh, with the double crown and uraeus, the crossed sceptres of the crook and flail, symbols of the shepherd and the judge. Cartouches survive of "Horus, the strong prince, he who laid hands on the lands of the foreigners, beloved of Ammon and selected of Ra, son of Ra, Alexandros." In respect of Egypt and its peoples, by immemorial tradition he was now a god.

He was also the King, by free choice of his subjects. His first action was to sacrifice to the bull god Apis, in the temple where Ochus had speared to death (and, it was said, ordered roast for dinner) the sacred beast which was the divine incarnation. Alexander reverenced all their gods; quite sincerely, for in the tolerant Hellenic way he identified each with some Greek god whose attributes seemed to fit. There was constant traffic between Greece and Egypt, and the priests could probably converse without interpreters.

He did not neglect the Greek world, but held ceremonial games, not only for athletes but—probably with more personal enjoyment—for the performing arts. Crowds of competitors flocked from the Greek cities. This was his first taste of real magnificence; he did not reach the palace of Persia as a raw provincial.

From Memphis he returned down river to the coast, where he had business to transact about his conquests in Asia Minor. Cruising across the Delta, he beached near Lake Mareotis. The spot looked to him just the place for a city; good harbourage, good land, good air, good access to the Nile. So keen was he to get the work begun that he walked over the site, trailing after him architects and engineers, pointing out positions for the marketplace, the temples of Greek and Egyptian gods, the sacred way. Being short of marker white, he accepted some meal from someone resourceful. Birds came to feed on it, from which the seers forecast that the city would prosper, and nourish many strangers; a prediction that Alexandria continues to fulfil. At some time in his eager progress, he must have crossed the site of his own tomb.

"After this," says Arrian, "he was seized with a longing

to visit Ammon in Siwah." Though this oracular shrine was renowned throughout the Greek world, it had neither political nor strategic value. No Pharaoh, we are told, had ever been there before. In Persia, Darius was mobilizing; and, Egypt now secure, the sooner he .was met the better. Yet on this pilgrimage Alexander was determined. He may have heard things from the priests at Memphis which made it indispensable to him; it is equally likely that he had heard something at Dodona.

Various reasons are offered on his behalf; that Perseus, a maternal forebear, and Heracles, a paternal one, had both sought before great labours the advice of Zeus-Ammon. He was their common ancestor, and therefore Alexander's. But Arrian adds that he went "hoping to know more truly about himself, or at any rate to say he did."

He turned from the coast to the dangerous inland route, where, if a dust storm rose, it could engulf an army, and was said once to have done so. As they toiled through the sand, water ran short, but rain came to save them. Ptolemy (here proprietorial) averred that two serpents guided them, speaking with human voices. Before calling him a charlatan it should be remembered that desert sands can emit uncanny sounds. At all events, they reached the green shady oasis of Siwah. The High Priest, used to Greek pilgrims and probably speaking some Greek, hailed Alexander as "Son of Ammon." This formal address, which by now must have been familiar to him, was noted by his friends, who were admitted to the forecourt after ritual purifications. The divine Pharaoh, whose person could bring only sanctity, went in as he was, and entered the holy of holies quite alone.

The oracle worked on a peculiar principle: that of planchette on an immensely impressive scale. Originating in the Ammon temple at Thebes, its antiquity was immemorial. The symbol of the god, a round navel-shaped object, was carried in a kind of boat hung with precious vessels; long carrying poles rested on the shoulders of many priests. Under the god's direction they would turn, halt or bow; from these movements the seer would read the god's response. (A similar ritual is still carried out in Alexandria by a Muslim sect, though of course without the idol; the devotees say that divine guidance comes as pressure on their shoulders.) This strange procession may have been visible from the courtyard. Its meaning, however, was revealed to Alexander only, within the shrine. If he had indeed intended, as Arrian said, to declare what he had learned about himself, the solemn experience changed his mind. His sole comment was that he had had the answer his soul desired. He never told what the question was.

He is said to have written to Olympias that he would tell her in private when he got back to Macedon. Anything he would tell her, he probably told Hephaestion; if so, he was as silent as the grave to which he took the secret.

If the letter was written, Alexander's main question must have concerned his origins. From this time, his sense of destiny acquired a daimonic force. Scientific rationalism is here anachronistic. Greeks (including philosophers) saw in all outstanding qualities a touch of the divine. He had excelled all other men again and again in leadership, courage, contrivance, endurance; and what he already felt in himself had been confirmed. He continued to acknowledge Philip as his human father, assuming perhaps a kind of dual fatherhood of seed and soul; a matter he must often have pondered without imparting his thoughts to anyone. But that he did henceforward regard himself as in some sort Ammon's son is certain, and was commonly known. It was not irreconcilable with the mortality witnessed by his battle scars; god-begotten men died, but were received into the heavens.

No one, of course, in his lifetime supposed he could have been begotten by the pharaoh Nectanebo. This freak of later legend stems solely from his high prestige in Egypt. Folklore, which can be neither enforced nor bought, should never be ignored.

Alexander returned to Memphis by the ordinary and safer pilgrim route. Here he received Greek embassies graciously, sacrificed to Zeus, held a parade, and more contests for athletes and poets, the latter being at little loss for a theme. Getting down to the business of government, he gave as usual the civil posts to native governors, the garrison commands to officers of his own, and restored all rites and customs which the Persians had suppressed.

At some time in Egypt, Philotas was accused to him, by persons unknown, of some unknown disloyalty. This may have been when his fair captive from Damascus, Antigone, began to talk. Philotas, she widely revealed, was forever bragging that he and Parmenion his father had done all the real work of conquest, though its credit went to The Boy. Such careless gossip hardly suggests devotion; and it cannot have amazed her when the loyal Craterus brought her for a private interview with Alexander. He did nothing about it—it must have struck him as just Philotas' usual style—merely telling her to warn him of anything serious. She returned to Philotas, in whom she did not confide.

His younger brother, Hector, to whom Alexander had been much attached, had lately lost his life when a crowded ferry foundered in which he was trying to catch up the royal barge. Alexander had given him a splendid funeral. Perhaps there had been a love affair, of which

Philotas had not much approved; and after his bereavement it would be a time for tact.

From Egypt Alexander marched to Tyre, now refortified for Macedon. The Persian fleet, without a base in the Mediterranean, already mostly captured or dispersed, was no further threat. It was time to turn east. He sacrificed to Melkart-Heracles—he had Herculean labours ahead—and held more games. The theatre was splendidly represented, two of its sponsors being tributary kings. One lavish production starred the now famous Thettalus, Alexander's devoted envoy to Caria. Keeping his eager partisanship to himself, he was bitterly disappointed when the judges, whom he had scrupulously refrained from nudging, gave someone else the award. Only later in private did he confess he would have given half 'he had to see Thettalus win the crown.

It was in the same spirit, and at about this time, that he made one of his few bad misjudgments of men. Among his friends exiled by Philip had been one Harpalus, a Macedonian aristocrat; whose attachment can only have been genuine, for Alexander could then offer no material return. Those days were over; Harpalus, recalled at the accession, and prevented by lameness from serving in war, was put straight into a treasury appointment. He had probably never had his hands on money before. During the Issus phase of the campaign he had got into some unspecified scrape, presumably financial, and gone off to Greece with an obscure accomplice. Alexander, loyal and grateful, apparently convinced he had been led astray, sent a "come back, all is forgiven" message. He reappeared; he must have had considerable address, was a cultivated person on whom Alexander relied to send him books, and may really have been touched and penitent. To prove that all was indeed forgiven, Alexander returned this luxury-loving man to the temptations which had lately overset him, and put him in charge of the whole army chest. For a time he accompanied the expedition. Lack of opportunity, and the old easy charm, confirmed Alexander's misplaced confidence. Disillusion would be long delayed.

Western Asia, Egypt, and all his communications with Macedon were now secure. He turned east to meet Darius; leaving forever the Greek world, except what he took with him.

PERSIA

From this time on, Alexander's chroniclers record outstanding events, between which weeks will have passed, occupied in the mere conveyance of a huge court, administration and army from place to place, or planning and populating a new city, or resting his men after a hard campaign. Over the vast and varied landscapes of Asia, amid the excitements of exploration and war, he evolved a kind of daily life which he pursued when nothing interfered with it. Plutarch has most to say of it, probably drawing on the vanished memoirs of Chares, the court chamberlain.

Alexander's day began with public prayers. His priesthood, unlike his privilege of divinity, was a function of his human kingship. His personal celebrations were for great events; but regularly as a matter of course he recommended his people to the gods. Almost to the day of his death, when so ill he had to be carried in a litter to the shrine, he made the morning libation.

After this he "took breakfast sitting" (in a chair, not on a dining couch); then spent the day in "hunting, administering justice, managing army business, or reading." He was a keen hunter, intrigued by changes of country and its game; while the army lumbered along at foot pace he would pass his time at the chase. He lived close to the long ages of man in which wild animals were vital sources of food, and dangerous enemies; as Xenophon recognized when he called the sport "the image of war."

"Administering justice" was already an enormous task. First there were the affairs of Macedon. Antipater was firm and capable, but Olympias detested him; her complaints, accusations and intrigues followed Alexander everywhere. She was jealous of his friends; furiously jealous of Hephaestion. Alexander, who wrote to her faithfully and sent her a stream of lavish gifts, occasionally came to the end of his patience, and is quoted as once remarking that she charged pretty high rent for the nine months' lodging she had given him. He even allowed himself to be seen in public sharing one of her letters with Hephaestion; which, considering how it would have enraged her, betrays some exasperation.

There was also mainland Greece with its restless "subject-allies." Sparta was in revolt till crushed by Antipater in 331. The danger from the south necessitated a standing army in Macedon, and garrisons in all those strongpoints whose magnificent ashlar walls can be seen today. Had Alexander not been able to attract foreign troops, continue paying them, and keep their loyalty, his forces would have stretched to breaking point. Antipater would deal with home emergencies; but all important policy decisions came to the King.

Far outweighing all this was the complex administration of the conquered lands. In the liberated city-states he had restored Greek forms of government; where Persian satrapies were indigenous he had appointed satraps, native ones if possible; to old kingdoms he had given kings. He was Pharaoh of Egypt, and founder of Alexandria, an enormous project employing swarms of experts. During the growing pains of all these communities, a constant traffic of problems and arbitrations followed his march.

"Managing army business" meant, to him, much more than making staff appointments and directing grand strategy. He never thought himself above the concerns of a regimental officer. Without doubt the love of the army was the breath of life to him; but never in his life did he try to get it cheap. It was not just a matter of being first into danger and last to take comforts when conditions were rough. Before a battle he could greet men by name instead of making speeches. To have one's exploits remembered by him was in itself an award, though his material rewards were generous. He was constantly interested in the common soldier's predicaments, however remote from his own. When a man with a good record was found malingering to stay near his mistress, Alexander, having gone into the matter, said that being a free courtesan she could not be compelled, but perhaps could be persuaded to follow her man. If he was hard up, Alexander probably furnished the persuasion. Whether in the field or routine fatigues, he watched out for merit. A soldier in the treasure train, who shouldered a heavy pack when the mule in his charge gave out, was told just to get it as far as his own tent, and keep the contents. Like Xenophon's Cyrus, Alexander aroused an eager wish to please him. He never needed, for troops under his command, the brutal punishments of the Roman army. No regiment of his was ever "decimated"—numbered off in tens and every tenth man killed. Yet his discipline was meticulous. Once when his troops were drawn up in battle formation, he noticed a single soldier fixing belatedly the throwing strap of his javelin and, walking up to him, pushed him out of the phalanx, saying he had no use for slovens. From him, as the survival of the story shows, this must have been as traumatic as a flogging from Julius Caesar.

He could take the surrender of wealthy cities, and hold

back his troops from sacking them. One of his rare impositions of the death sentence was on two of his Macedonians who had raped the wives of two foreign auxiliaries; his men were his men wherever they came from. This close attention to their affairs must often have taken up nearly as much time as the administration of his empire.

Never described in detail, but evident from results, are innumerable personal conversations with the men he regarded, and treated, as his friends: Macedonian generals, actors, musicians; in due course Persian lords and at least one Persian eunuch; an Indian sage; old Sisygambis; all people he individually knew. From time to time he must have looked in on his poor imbecile half-brother Arridaeus, who disappears from history till Alexander's death, when he is discovered close at hand in the royal palace.

Seeing that routine business was constantly falling into arrears during periods of violent action, it is astonishing that he found time to read; not only history and civics, but classical tragedy and modern poetry. At the supper parties which closed his day and relaxed its tensions, "no prince's conversation was ever so agreeable"; so says Plutarch, adding that this applied as long as he was sober.

About Alexander's drinking habits much nonsense has been written which can be corrected by the most elementary medical knowledge combined with the evidence of his life. Aristobulus, cited by Plutarch, says he liked to sit up late over the wine, not drinking heavily but for the sake of the talk. It seems incredible that this should arouse scepticism when any night of the year in London, Paris, New York, Athens or Rome, hundreds of people whose constitution it suits will be found doing precisely this. In Alexander's case, the mere record of his dynamic energy (he took exercise on the march by jumping off and on a moving chariot) and his astonishing powers of recuperation makes the idea of habitual drunkenness absurd. On the other hand, male Macedonian social life embraced, traditionally, the deliberate heavy drinking bout in honour of this or that; and in these he certainly did not hold back, getting disastrously drunk on two occasions at least. There is no doubt that he and his generals made up a pretty hard-drinking mess; but it is abundantly clear from the overall picture that he usually behaved as Aristobulus says he did, though sometimes he made a night of it.

In vino veritas, and he was no exception. When he took too much, the insecurities of his boyhood surfaced in an insatiable craving for reassurance. He loved being told of his achievements, and if he did not get enough he asked for more. No doubt hostile propagandists made the most of it; but it would be foolish to reject Plutarch's statement which, though citing no good source, has so much psychological consistency. Probably he could irritate his dearest friends, even though, we are told, he only claimed what was true. But the kind of affection he inspired throughout his lifetime supports Aristobulus' words about his more habitual charm.

In July 331, about the time of his twenty-fifth birthday, Alexander marched east to Mesopotamia, where beyond the Tigris Darius was awaiting him.

A great mobilization had been held of the forces from the still unconquered eastern empire. The valuable stiffening of Greek mercenaries had been lost, all but about 4,000. But beside the élite troops of Persia, there were the less disciplined but fierce and tough levies of Bactria and Sogdiana under Bessus, the powerful satrap of Bactria and cousin of the King; also auxiliaries of many tributary races from the Caucasus to the Indian frontier. All were

now based on Babylon, where the Persian commanders
had worked hard on improving weaponry. After the lesson
of Issus, javelins had been replaced with spears; and there
was a squadron of the fearsome scythed chariots, with
their spearheaded yoke poles and multi-bladed wheels.
Nothing, unfortunately, could be done about the continuing liability of Darius as commander-in-chief.

The cavalry under Nabarzanes was of high calibre;
born horsemen, and far better mounted than the Greeks.
Beside the tall Nisaeans, probably as big as modern
chargers, Bucephalas must have looked like a thickset
pony. For such troops to wear down the Greeks with
harrying tactics promised better results than a pitched
battle, even without Darius' known record. But either
he was resolved to redeem the honour lost at Issus, or
had been made to feel he ought. He marched his huge
host towards the ancient town of Arbela, between the
Tigris and the hills.

A cavalry detachment was sent west to the Euphrates,
to locate and oppose Alexander's crossing. But his advance engineers ran out their double bridge on piles
from their own side till Alexander came up; the Persians,
commanded by Mazaeus, satrap of Babylon, made off
without opposing him. Babylon, the heart of ancient conquered Assyria, was not the most loyal part of the Persian
empire.

The Tigris, whose name means Arrow, was too swift
to bridge and had to be forded. Alexander got his infantry
across between two columns of cavalry, one to break the
current for them, the other to catch any men swept
away. He headed the infantry himself, and then stood on
the bank pointing out the shallower places. Not a man
was lost.

No other commander of unmechanized forces could
ever move as fast as Alexander. He also knew when to

take his time. Instead of striking across the hot river plain, where the retreating Mazaeus had burned the crops, he skirted it by the northern uplands, cooler and well watered. Too late to catch him as he struggled across the Tigris, Darius improved the time by sending an army of slaves to level the intervening plain of Gaugamela. He had been told that Issus had been lost because he had not had room to deploy his forces; and the chariots would need smooth ground.

As Alexander marched south towards him east of the Tigris, there was an eclipse of the moon, one of the most alarming phenomena of the ancient world. Thanks to Aristotle, Alexander understood its cause; not for him the fatal delay of the superstitious Nicias which, in the previous century, had lost the whole Athenian force in Sicily and with it the Peloponnesian War. Alexander did not, however, bother his anxious soldiers with astronomy, but summoned the seers to cheer them up by identifying the darkened moon with Persia. He sacrificed punctiliously to the powers involved, the Sun, Moon and Earth; his knowing what they were doing did not affect his belief that they were gods.

A Persian moon had indeed been eclipsed for ever. Stateira, wife of Darius, the most beautiful woman of mortal birth in Asia, had fallen sick and died. Plutarch says, without hint of scandal, that she died in childbirth, in which case it must have been much earlier. In any event, Alexander had held up his march for a day to perform her funeral rites, assuming the duties of a kinsman, including a day-long fast.

He may well have reproached himself, if he had sacrificed her to his sense of theatre. The splendid set piece from Xenophon would never be enacted now. Even in cushioned wagons, journeys over earth roads on hard wheels must have been a tiring business, with exposure to local infections. He must have wished he had been content with a less spectacular piece of generosity, which —since he had never attempted to use the women as hostages—he could have afforded. He had now to witness the grief of the children and Sisygambis; and though her continuing affection shows that she never blamed him, there need be no doubt that his mourning was sincere.

Curtius has a story here, with important later implications. Alexander sent one of the Queen's attendant eunuchs, who is actually named, to inform Darius of her death and assure him that she had had the customary Persian funeral honours. The scene moves to Darius' tent, where Darius cries out that such honours must be the tribute to a mistress. The eunuch reassures him, and he then expresses respect for his enemy's conduct. This episode is the prologue to much inside information from Darius' headquarters. In Curtius, it has every indication of having been first supplied by an eyewitness; a vivid and lively raconteur with a courtier's sense of tact. More will be heard before long of such a person.

Darius now sent out scouts to report on the approach of Alexander. He caught a few, and learned where the Persians were. He then gave his men a four-day rest, trusting Darius not to move from his swept and garnished battleground. He also had his own base camp fortified, no doubt remembering the Issus massacre; and left in it all noncombatants, including Queen Sisygambis. He then led his troops towards the plain of Gaugamela. From the low hills that fringed it he saw the vast Persian host, of which the most conservative estimate is 200,000 infantry and 40,000 cavalry. His own numbers were 40,000 infantry and 7,000 horse.

He convened a war council in the style of Macedon, whose kings conferred with their chiefs as *primi inter pares*. Several commanders were for bringing the rested troops straight into action; which, in view of Persian numbers, says a good deal for their confidence in Alexander. The experienced Parmenion pointed out that this was a field prepared for them by Darius, who might have hidden pit traps and caltrops in their way. Alexander agreed, made camp and rode out to reconnoitre, probably glad of the excuse to pause and calculate, without seeming overimpressed by Persian strength. He took a good look, in full view of their outposts. After noting their immense superiority in cavalry, the arm on which his own tactics most relied, he rode back to think.

Parmenion, who had evidently gone with him, advised him to try a night attack. He answered that he would not "steal a victory"—referring to Xenophon, original coiner of the phrase "to steal a march." To flourish bravura over shrewdness was part of the Alexander touch. Night operations had endless possibilities of confusion and error; a night pursuit would give routed enemies the chance to re-form and retrieve morale. Darius had been allowed a year in which to collect his remaining assets and put them on the table. Now Alexander meant to beat him at his own game on his chosen pitch, and pick up the stake entire, with unarguable finality. It was the crux of his own destiny, and of much more, and this he knew. He ordered his men a good dinner and told them to get some sleep; they were to set out before dawn. He himself sat up late, thinking and planning.

Darius had been thinking too. As Alexander had hoped, he had been thinking like Parmenion. The Greeks were hopelessly outnumbered; what would they do but try to snatch advantage from a night surprise? Orders went out, not just to the outposts but to the whole huge host, to stand by all night, the men in arms and the horses bridled. To hear was to obey. Night passed, the men grew tired. In Alexander's tent the lamp went out. Decisions taken, the outcome laid on the gods, he fell into deep sleep. When it was time for the men to be roused and fed, his officers found him sleeping like a child. They gave the necessary orders and came back. Finally Parmenion had to shake him. When asked how he could be so calm, he said he had had far more to worry about when the Persians were burning the crops ahead of him. Now, he had been given his heart's desire.

It was a bad day for history when Quintus Curtius enrolled at a Roman school of rhetoric. With access to priceless sources now destroyed by fire or sack, of which he gives us tempting glimpses, he makes every major speech in his History a showpiece of his own, which seekers of fact can safely discard unread. In this spirit of academic exercise he furnishes Darius and Alexander with long pre-battle orations, which need not detain us. More interestingly, since it comes from a first-hand source, Arrian describes Alexander's briefing of his officers. He told them they did not need speeches to inspire them; their own courage and pride in it would do that; just let each encourage the men under his command. They were not fighting now for Asia Minor, or for Egypt, but for the sovereignty of all Asia. Let each keep strict discipline in time of danger; observe complete silence when ordered to advance silently; raise a terrifying battle yell when the right moment came; be alert for orders, and swiftly pass them on. He was thinking ahead to the blinding dust which would prevent all visual signals. He needed to keep his plan flexible, and wanted swift response to any change of tactics.

The instruction to make the war yell terrifying may not be unrelated to the fact that, according to Plutarch, before the battle he sacrificed to Fear. Greeks readily personified any natural force; but there is no other record of his ever honouring this deity. It would seem that since

Issus he thought of Fear as Darius' familiar spirit. All these preparations attended to, he marched his men from the low hills down to the plain, as dawn light revealed the hosts to one another.

The Persian front, with plenty of room to manœuvre, and outnumbering the Macedonians by about five to one, was so much longer that if things went amiss they stood to be not only outflanked but encircled. Alexander deepened his flanks with reverses which in case of an enveloping movement could turn outward to form a square. Parmenion as usual led the left wing, where he was opposed by the brave and able Mazaeus, whose withdrawal at the Euphrates had certainly not been caused by cowardice. Darius took the royal station in the centre; but had in front of him his Greek mercenaries and other strong contingents; also fifteen elephants and fifty scythed chariots. Alexander led the Macedonian right. Confronting him was the massive army of Bactria, led by its satrap, Bessus. So far did its line overlap his own, that he started the battle nearly opposite Darius.

He began, however, edging out to his right, as if to escape the Persian overlap. Darius ordered a corresponding movement to keep his overlap extended; he still committed no troops to action, trying to divine what Alexander meant to do. He kept moving right, till he was approaching the edge of Darius' carefully flattened arena. On the rougher ground beyond, scythed chariots would not run and cavalry would be hampered. It was a trial of nerve. Darius, falling to the bluff, ordered Bessus' men to oppose further rightward movement. Persian troops were now engaged. Alexander, by a series of precisely timed manœuvres, caused more and more of them to be involved. He himself, at the head of the Companion Cavalry, meticulously bided his time.

He had been located, and Darius ordered the scythed

chariots to charge him. But he had been permitted a
leisurely reconnaissance beforehand and his arrangements
for them were made. They were attacked with missiles
by the Agriani; some of the daring tribesmen leaped head
on at the horses, dragging them to a halt and pulling
down the charioteers. Those that got through met wide
lanes in the well-drilled infantry, shot harmlessly past and
were disposed of at leisure in the rear.

Meantime, Darius' left wing was becoming increasingly
committed, while Parmenion's forces still pinned down
his right. The centre was thinning. Despite Alexander's
fewer numbers, he had ingeniously contrived that his apex
of strength should meet an area of Persian weakness just
where he wanted it to be.

It was time to change horses. A squire had been holding ready the veteran Bucephalas, now twenty-four, keeping him fresh for this moment, the climax of his active
service. Alexander rode to the head of the royal squadron.
Forming it into column, with a tapering point of which he
was the apex, he raised the war yell, and hurtled towards
Darius, now in the front line. The cavalry had not forgotten their orders to make a terrifying noise; they thun-
dered after, offering their tributes to Fear.

Fear was their friend. As, unimpeded by the fifteen
elephants, they rolled up the Persian front and approached
the royal chariot, Darius wheeled it round, snatching the
reins dropped by its wounded driver, and was the first
to fly. The fall of the charioteer had been seen by neighbouring Persians; the chariot's flight convinced them that
it was the King who had fallen and died. The centre dis-
integrated; a signal for general rout. Alexander and his
cavalry crashed on, hewing their way in pursuit, and
intent on catching Darius.

A message then arrived from Parmenion that his sector
was still heavily engaged. Alexander was no Rupert of the

Rhine; once the messenger had located him in the dust
and confusion, he abandoned the tempting chase to support his men and consolidate his victory. While reaching
the threatened point he fought a fierce engagement in
which sixty Companions died and Hephaestion was
wounded. Much dispute has raged over this message,
and on whether it was later stressed by Alexander's
chroniclers to discredit Parmenion. Its propaganda value
seems very doubtful, considering that Parmenion's was a
holding operation, competently fulfilled, and the message
saved Alexander from the grave danger of leaving a
doubtful field. He was no doubt anxious to tell the world
why he had let Darius slip through his fingers, and to
receive proper credit for rescuing his left wing (whose
danger was over by the time he got there); but this is a
long way from finding scapegoats, and Parmenion emerges
from the account without discredit.

As it was, Alexander's forward dash had left a small
gap in the line, not of strategic size, but big enough for a
small task force detailed by Darius to attempt the rescue
of his family. This troop of Royal Guards and Indians got
through, and penetrated as far as the base camp, where
they wasted valuable time in looting, and in killing noncombatants, before they reached their objective. Diodorus
relates that many Persian captives joined forces with their
countrymen and prepared for an escape; but that the
Queen Mother Sisygambis, when the women called to her
to hurry, sat silent and immobile in her chair. Soon afterwards the Persian troop was beaten off.

Meantime the satrap Mazaeus had learned of Darius'
flight. Like Nabarzanes at Issus, who had also held down
the redoubtable Parmenion and been similarly left in the
lurch, he decided his obligations were at an end. He ex-
tricated as many of his men as he could, and went racing
back to Babylon. Though he and Nabarzanes had reached

the same conclusion, they were different men; each would act as his nature prompted him.

Alexander, finding Parmenion's force already out of trouble, dashed off with the Companions, still hoping to catch Darius on his way to his base at Arbela. So furious was the race that a thousand horses foundered. (Not Bucephalas. Alexander had taken time to have him cared for. The old horse, never used again in battle, was to be cherished for six more years.) At Arbela it was proved that the horses had died in vain; once more the Great King's chariot was found abandoned, along with whatever could not be carried away in the headlong Persian flight; this must have included a good many women. Alexander paused, to rest his men and consider his objective. Hitherto, he had accorded Darius much the same military importance as himself. At Arbela he decided that the capture was, after all, a very low priority. So completely did he discard the pursuit in favour of other aims, so open was his contempt for Darius as an enemy, that it would have been inconsistent to put much importance on Parmenion's responsibility, if any, for letting him slip away.

The military historian E. W. Marsden, concluding his analysis of the battle, puts down the victory partly to the Macedonians' superior morale and closer ties with their commander, partly to Alexander's remarkably detailed understanding of the art of war. He sums up,

> It is difficult to re-create the chaos characteristic of full-scale engagements at certain stages, the confusion caused by noise, movement and dust, the atmosphere of doubt and uncertainty, the horrible carnage. . . . It must be extraordinarily difficult for modern generals to remain calm and detached when controlling operations in a command-post some miles from the scene of the fighting. How much harder it would be for Alexander and Darius who were stationed in the line of battle itself! Darius

appears not to have possessed that rare ability to sift
conflicting reports, to make correct observations, and,
remaining cool and unflurried, to issue swift and well-
considered orders in such circumstances. Alexander had
this ability in a pronounced degree. That was the third
decisive factor at Gaugamela.

Darius and a ragged remnant struggled southeast over
the mountain passes towards Ecbatana (Hamadan), the
summer resort of the Persian kings. The Royal Road
south, to Babylon, Susa and Persepolis, the rich heart of
the empire, was left open to Alexander. The choice of objective did not take him long. By now he must have talked
through his interpreters with captive Persians, and formed
his own estimate of Darius' value to morale.

Curtius, drawing again it seems on the Persian inform-
ant to whom some earlier chronicler had access, says that
Darius abandoned the great cities to keep Alexander from
following his trail. Certainly if his objective was to rally
Persia to arms, his remaining months of life give little sign
of it. Though his son was a captive, he had an effective
heir in his warrior brother Oxathres. Had he succeeded a
Great King fallen inspiringly in battle against the invader,
the course of the war might have been much altered.

As it was, its next phase was mere swanning for Alexander. He may not yet have guessed it while nearing the
huge brick-and-bitumen walls of Babylon. Herodotus,
who went there a century before, says they enclosed 60
square miles, in which food crops could be grown during
a siege. Even the old fortifications of Nebuchadnezzar,
now an inner ring, were vast. The outer ones were 180
feet thick and 400 high, a monument to the Assyrian
builders with their hordes of expendable slaves. Cyrus had
taken it without a fight; but Alexander must have known
Xenophon's livelier version. Its mass was visible for miles
across the plain, promising a siege at least as colossal as

that of Tyre. But there was no need even to reconnoitre it. Alexander was met on the road by Mazaeus its satrap, fresh from his tussle with Parmenion. Now, bringing his children as hostages, he invited Alexander in.

It was not much more than a century since Babylon had last tried to revolt from Persia, and been crushed by Xerxes with severity. Its luxury-loving people were disaffected or indifferent; its garrison was disillusioned; its commander had no sentiment for a beaten fugitive king. It remained only to placate the victor. Alexander, naturally wary of a trap when this astonishing gift was offered him, still advanced in battle order, leading the van. But the walls were undefended, the hundred gates wide open, the drawbridges down. He entered as King of Babylon, in a state chariot plated with gold, among splendours never to be surpassed in the triumphs of the Caesars. The city treasurer, eager to outdo Mazaeus, had had the route strewn with flowers and censed with perfume. Rare and exotic gifts, choice horses, cars bearing caged lions and leopards, were led in the procession; magi and priests attended, royal praise singers chanted, Mazaeus' cavalry paraded. As always with Alexander, one Roman adornment was lacking: the spectacle of captives humiliated in chains.

After viewing the ancient splendours of the palace, he visited its treasury. Of this vast hoard no assessment remains. He paid out lavish bounties to all his men; his mercenaries got two months' extra pay. These included many Greeks who, given leave to go home when the Greek cities had all been fired, had chosen to stay on. All could now afford the luxuries of a city they had not been let loose to sack. Here in Babylon was the real beginning of his extravagant generosities which henceforth would flow out to all around him. This first donative was good

policy and fair dealing. But to give pleasure, to be surrounded with gratitude and liking, met a deep need in his
nature. In his childhood, his tutor Leonidas had made him
live poor in the midst of plenty; he loved profusion as
only those can who have been pinched. He loved display;
it went with his sense of theatre. All these cravings were
fed in Babylon; as the money came in, he would develop
his personal style.

From the throne he granted Babylon the status it had
had before Xerxes crushed it and threw down the ziggurat
of Bel. The priests of the god were now given much gold
to rebuild his sanctuary. (It would have fateful consequences later.) Mazaeus was at once confirmed in his
rank of satrap. The gift of this great office to a Persian,
gratifying to Iranians, can hardly have been as popular
with Macedonians; to emphasize his good performance
at Gaugamela would be natural, and Parmenion's reputation could not be damaged by tributes to the strength of
his opponent. The posts of garrison commander and
treasurer of course went to Macedonians. Alexander was
a month in Babylon, giving his men a holiday. He was
busy himself, though it is not likely that the pomps of the
court were irksome. When ready to march, he put his now
impressive treasure train in the charge of Harpalus; the
loyal friend of boyhood was to know himself thoroughly
forgiven.

The soldiers were broken in gently after the demoraliz-
ing joys of the city; marched into pleasant country where
games were held. There was an important novelty: prizes
were offered for valour on campaign. Typically of the extraordinary rapport between this army and its leader, all
ranks were invited to offer the judges their views by accla-
mation. There were eight awards. They consisted not of
the usual gold wreath or money, but of command appoint-

ments, each over a thousand men. Up till now Alexander had kept his staff within the tribal hierarchies of the homeland; now, with sound dramatic flair and canny assurance that choices would be popular, he introduced real promotion on merit.

Susa lay ahead, but required no haste. It had capitulated directly after the battle to the envoys he had sent ahead. News of Darius' flight would have outstripped them, for the Royal Road had the world's fastest post relay, with fresh horses and men stationed all along it. Darius himself may have ordered surrender in the hope of saving the city from sack. It was spared; with the ironic result that it survives today only as a mound. (The impressive fortress which crowns it was built not by Alexander, but by nineteenth-century archaeologists as a necessary refuge from the local tribesmen.) However, it was then the administrative capital of the empire and chief royal seat, built in an out-thrust of the Mesopotamian plain on the threshold of the Iranian plateau. Fragments from the palace suggest bright glowing surfaces of glazed ceramics, mostly blue and yellow moulded in relief. In its treasury, Alexander found the enormous sum—not counting jewels, which were never even approximately valued—of 40,000 talents in silver, and 9,000 darics in gold. Reckoned by Wilcken in 1931 as somewhere near £14,000,000, it could only be thought of today in terms of Fort Knox.

The house of the king-making eunuch vizier, Bagoas, forfeit at his death to Darius, was found to contain a thousand talents' worth of rich robes alone. Plutarch says that the house and all its contents were presented to Parmenion. Among the palace treasures, a specially precious casket was taken by Alexander to house his copy of the *Iliad,* edited for him by Aristotle when he was a boy. It still lived in the bed box under his pillow. The dagger must have been kept in quicker reach. There would be more times than one when he would be close to needing it.

The gold and silver was mostly in solid ingots, which had been issued for coining a few at a time. Alexander had larger ideas. The metals poured into his mints, the hand-punched money poured out of them, wearing out the moulds whose many variants can still be seen. Olympian Zeus soon has around him on the obverse the symbols of the lion, and the royal *kyrbasia* or peaked cap, circled with the *mitra,* the purple ribbon. It would be a fair guess that in the privacy of his bedroom, Alexander had already tried it on.

He kept giving money away, delighted to be asked for it, which he took as a sign of friendship. Told that some modest sum would be quite enough, he said, "For you to ask, but not for me to give." But magnificence did not make him pompous. An independent young man among the friends he used to play ball with had obstinately refused to cadge, and heard rumours that Alexander was not pleased with him. At the next game, whenever he got the ball he shied it past the King, who finally called, "What about me?" "You didn't ask," he called back; on which, says Plutarch, Alexander laughed and gave him many presents.

Given or spent, the wealth of Susa began to influence history. For centuries it had lain sterile as if still unmined; now it would flow in the track of Alexander and his spendthrift armies. The busy trade routes it created began to Hellenize his empire before he set his hand to the work.

It was at Susa that, mounting the throne of the six-foot-odd Darius, he found his feet would not touch the ground. Someone shoved a low table under them. An old palace eunuch wept; it had been his master's wine table. Touched

by such loyal grief, Alexander began to pick his feet up;
but Philotas pointed out the good omen, and he changed
his mind.

Among his loot was the ancient spoil of Xerxes carried back from Athens; including the archaic bronze statue
group of Harmodius and Aristogiton, the tyrannicide
lovers, from the Acropolis. This precious monument he
later returned to Athens, where it still stood in Arrian's
day. He held victory sacrifices and a torch relay race.
Fresh troops joined him from Macedon.

The Persian satrap was reinstated again, with a garrison
under Macedonian command. Here, at Susa, he installed
Sisygambis and her grandchildren in the harem from
which Darius had carried them out to war. The great
scene would never now be played; and he had a rough
road ahead, up the mountain passes into Persis.

Here he met his first resistance since Gaugamela. The
Uxian hill people sent to say the kings always paid them
road toll to use their passes. Confident banditry now
ceased to pay. Susian guides showed him a back stair to
their fastness, and he trapped them in. He considered ex-
pelling the whole tribe from its strategic habitat; but the
chief, a kinsman of Sisygambis, smuggled a messenger
through to Susa, begging her to intercede. After some
hesitation she wrote to Alexander. It was the first favour
she had ever asked of him; he at once issued a general
pardon, and, for good measure, tax exemption as well.

Between him and Persepolis, the impregnable pass of
the Persian Gates was defended by the satrap of Persis,
who had closed its gorge with a wall. From the cliffs
above, his men flung boulders; it was a death trap and
Alexander soon withdrew his troops. By one of history's
revenges the story of Thermopylae was now acted in reverse. A local shepherd among the prisoners offered to
show a route round the pass. Alexander promised a rich

reward, and followed. The track, far longer and more dangerous than that over which Ephialtes led Xerxes' men, was under deep snow as well; but he and his small force scrambled briskly along it. When he surprised the advance guard of the Persians, they behaved just like the Phocians of Leonidas; escaped as best they could into the hills, without warning their commander, who was taken quite unawares. The main Macedonian army then forced the pass without trouble. Persepolis lay open.

Here no one was in a position to offer formal surrender. Instead Alexander got a panic message from its treasurer that the city was in anarchy, and that unless they made haste, the treasure (for which he evidently feared to be held responsible) would be looted.

The fate of Persepolis, thus tilting in the scales, was probably decided by an encounter on the road. In the confusion thousands of Greek slaves (presumably from Greek Asia Minor) escaped and came to meet Alexander's army. Some were elderly men, who must have been in slavery since Ochus' wars. It was a macabre and hideous embassy. Diodorus says,

> All had been mutilated. Some lacked hands, some feet, some ears and noses. They were men who had learned skills and crafts and done well in training; after which their other extremities had been cut off and they were left only with those on which their work depended.

Curtius says they had been branded too. Both sources agree that Alexander wept for them.

He offered to give them transport home and provide for their remaining lives. Conferring, they decided that to return to their cities as repulsive freaks would be unendurable. By now they would be forgotten there. (Ancient Greece was not notable for compassion; Alexander's was felt as rather eccentric.) Some had slave wives who had borne them children. They asked for a grant of land where they could live together. He allowed that they were right; gave them money, seed grain and livestock, good clothes for themselves and for their women; and appointed them their sad village.

Next day he marched upon Persepolis. His soldiers got what they had been straining at the leash for ever since Gaugemela—a wealthy city to sack.

It was the ceremonial capital of the empire; the opulent counterpart of little Aegae in Macedon. The King and his chief nobles had seats there; a rich merchant class must have supplied them. Curtius says that many citizens were casually killed because the loot-sated troops could not be bothered with ransoms. It is difficult today, yet some attempt should be made, to imagine the orgiastic pleasure of a sack to men of the ancient world who after hardship and danger felt it to be their due; where power, aggression, greed, lust, rivalry, the instincts of the hunter and the gambler, could be roused and fed in one vertiginous stream of action. No one, perhaps, but Alexander could have held them back at Babylon and Susa. Now he gave them a day at it. Even so he issued orders that the women should not be stripped of the jewels they wore.

The treasurer was promoted to governor. He had saved the palace strongrooms intact. Their contents amounted to three times as much as had been taken at Susa.

Darius wintered at Ecbatana, watched by Alexander's intelligence for signs of life. There being none, Alexander wintered in Persepolis. It must have been at this time that he made his long-awaited pilgrimage to the tomb of Cyrus the Great at neighbouring Pasargadae, his ancient capital in what had once been Elam; a small Persian Macedon from which he too had conquered an empire. Here, as the sequel shows, Alexander paid him honour. If he had

earned it, so had Xenophon; but the rewards of history
are capricious. Between them, Persian and Athenian,
they had impressed on an eager mind, when no one else
was doing it, that all men are God's children, and that
anywhere among them may be found the excellent ones
whom, said Alexander, he makes more his own than the
rest.

He returned to the palace of Persepolis, with its tall
lotus-topped columns and endless reliefs of tribute bear-
ers bringing offerings to its builder, Darius the Great. We
hear of no such regal ceremonies as had marked his stay
at Babylon or Susa; perhaps only because winter had
made access difficult. When spring came, and it was time
to march, he burned the palace down.

This action is known today by people who know virtually nothing else about him (and who remain more impressed by this outrage to an empty building than by the
living holocausts of Coventry and Dresden); fit retribution, if he deserved it, for a man who cared intensely
about his good name. The sources are not unanimous
(though nor are they irreconcilable) as to why he did it,
and historians debate the matter still.

Arrian, whose source, Ptolemy, must certainly have
been present, simply says he did it against the advice of
Parmenion, who pointed out that it would be looked on
as the act of a conqueror rather than a king. Diodorus,
Curtius and Plutarch all agree that Alexander gave a
drinking party to which were invited a number of flute
girls and hetairas; among them Thais, the Athenian courtesan, mistress of Ptolemy the future king; that at the
height of the revelry she recalled Xerxes' ravaging of the
Acropolis, and urged Alexander to let an Athenian girl
pay it back in kind; that thereon he proclaimed a Dionysiac comus, which he led with wreath on head and torch

in hand; that he threw the first torch himself and let her throw the next one. Plutarch says he had second thoughts after a while, and ordered the fire put out. If so he was too late; the layer of ash was found by archaeologists to cover everything.

No one was hurt; when it got too hot inside, they came out to watch the spectacle. There is no doubt that a really first-class fire, when no fear for human life intrudes, is one of the great atavistic joys still known to man. Today it is very shocking to think of archaeological treasures burning; to Macedonians and still more to Greeks, the significance of Persepolis was rather different.

Tarn has preferred to reject the party entirely, and have the palace burned "as a manifesto." True, there is no party in Arrian. It does, however, seem likely that Ptolemy, a venerable King and grandfather when he wrote, may have thought fit to suppress such details of his riotous youth as the exuberant Thais. Parmenion's objections are no doubt historically true. He may even have been reminding Alexander of intentions which he himself had expressed at soberer moments. He did wish to be a king rather than a conqueror; and the burning of the kings' ceremonial seat must certainly have been held against him by the Persians. On the whole, it is hard not to conclude that, like so many happenings at very successful parties, it seemed a good idea at the time.

As to the archaeological treasures, they were left so wholly to the lion, the lizard and the shifting sands that Persepolis is today the best preserved of all monuments of the Achaemenian era.

The troops outside, seeing the bonfire and knowing that the cream of Persian wealth had been skimmed, took it as a sign their labours were over and that they could now march home with their loot. They were soon undeceived; Alexander had merely paused before a final reckoning with Darius. They were now to be led into hard unknown country, with a strictly military objective. Yet without protest they followed their commander.

Too little has been made, too much taken for granted, of the extraordinary magnetism which this implies. The army of Macedon was steeped in an archaic, feudal democracy. Its forebears had made and unmade and murdered kings. He had grown up among these men; he accepted their traditional freedom of speech, unparalleled in the annals of emperors. Save for foreign auxiliaries, he was all alone with them in hostile country; if they mutinied he was wholly at their mercy. He kept no secret police to intimidate or spy on them; two later plots against his life were both revealed to him at the last moment by ordinary people. He had created a relationship of unique intimacy and trust, and inspired a possessiveness which was to create unforeseen complications. Their dependence on him grew almost superstitious, as their reaction to his wounds and sickness shows. When spring had melted the mountain snows, they followed him north towards Ecbatana.

When he reached it, Darius had gone. He took possession of the summer palace. In its strongrooms he deposited the enormous reserves of treasure which were left when he had filled his war chest. As treasurer and governor he left his old friend Harpalus.

Darius had left, as usual, the initiative to the enemy. At the news of Alexander's advance he moved northward, sending the women ahead for safety. He himself paused *en route* to meet promised reinforcements. But they had smelled disaster, and did not keep the rendezvous.

Alexander came on, taking time to secure his communications. In Media he was met by a certain Bistanes; a surviving son of King Ochus, eager to tell which way Darius had fled.

This incident underlines a factor of great importance in Alexander's story, the power of blood feud in the ancient world. By standards of modern nationalism Bistanes was a traitor; by those of his day, he fulfilled a religious duty in avenging his poisoned father and brother, to whose murder he believed (rightly or wrongly) that Darius had been a party. Had he been a Greek, this obligation would similarly have cancelled other loyalties.

Darius was making north towards the pass of the Caspian Gates, hoping to reach Bactria. For the rest of his story, Curtius has a detailed narrative, unique to himself. It is entirely without propaganda value; almost free from rhetoric; and returns us, this time at some length, to the account suggestive of an eloquent eyewitness, soon to appear upon the scene.

Darius had gathered up from the ruins of Gaugamela about 30,000 infantry and 4,000 skirmishers. Among the former were some 3,000 Greek mercenaries, the faithful core of Memnon's 50,000. Even if some were exiles who dared not go home, most of them could have deserted to the Macedonians. Their courage and loyalty were exemplary.

The 3,000 cavalry and many foot soldiers were Bactrians, under the command of their satrap, Bessus. Other commands were held by the capable cavalry general, Nabarzanes; and by the ancient Artabazus, the friend of Alexander's childhood, now in his nineties but still alert and spry.

The Great King's household was pathetically depleted. His coffers held only 7,000 talents; his concubines had gone; his personal attendants were down to a handful of court eunuchs; the senior an Egyptian, Bubaces, the

youngest a boy called Bagoas, an accomplished singer
and dancer. A favourite of the King, he had been cas-
trated to preserve his exceptional beauty.

When the reinforcements failed to appear, Darius made
camp and held a war council. Curtius has written him an
oration; his own may have been little better. The rest of
the speeches sound much more authentic. Old Artabazus
reaffirmed his loyalty and that of his Persian troops. Nabarzanes then came forward. Pointing out that bad luck
seemed to be dogging them, he inferred that the gods had
at present forsaken Darius, and proposed that Bessus, his
cousin, should for a time assume the throne, retiring when
the enemy was vanquished.

It sounds as if the formal meaning was that Bessus
should stand in for the King as royal scapegoat, to shoulder his bad luck. But Darius had no doubt of the real intent. He drew his sword, and made for Nabarzanes. He
was politely restrained with gestures of pleading for mercy,
and the two leaders got away. A vivid account follows of
their efforts to subvert the loyal Persians during the
night, opposed by the indomitable Artabazus. He had
withstood the dangerous tyrant Ochus, but now kept faith
with a weak king who had not wronged him, though sure
of a free pardon from Alexander.

Nabarzanes' priorities were different. Since the flight at
Issus, he had seen that the only hope of effective Persian
resistance was to get rid of Darius. His plan had been to
hand him over to Alexander, make peace to get a breathing space, proclaim Bessus King in Bactria, and from
there renew the war. But the Greeks and Persians would
not come in. In the morning, therefore, the two professed
repentance and loyalty, and rejoined the march.

Darius trustingly believed them; not so the Greeks,
who knew of the night's activities. Their commander,
Patron, made his way during that day's march to the royal

chariot, beckoned to Bubaces the chief eunuch, and asked to speak with the King, who had some knowledge of Greek, without interpreter; a needed precaution, since Bessus was riding near by. Darius listened to his warning, and dismissed him with a kindly word. If Patron was right, his own position was hopeless; and it is to his credit that he did not clutch at straws at the cost of faithful lives.

At the next halt, on the Caspian side of the Elburz Mountains, Artabazus begged the King to seek safety among Patron's Greeks. This counsel of despair Darius rejected with dignity, veiling his face as the old man was led out in tears. When the Persians went off to forage for provisions, all the Bactrians stayed. At nightfall the body-guard round the tent, drawn from the renowned Immortals, slipped silently away. Darius, abandoning hope, lay down upon the ground.

"Hence there was a great solitude in the tent, except for a few eunuchs who stood about the King, because they had nowhere to withdraw to." This intimate touch pins down, effectively, our first-hand witness.

Presently Darius called Bubaces to him, and ordered the eunuchs to save themselves. At his wail of distress, the others ran up and added their lamentations. Bessus and Nabarzanes, thinking the King had killed himself, came running in. On hearing from the eunuchs that he was alive they held back no longer, but seized and bound him, and carried him off in a common transport cart.

The loyal troops were too much outnumbered to attempt resistance. Darius had not won the kind of loyalty by which forlorn hopes are inspired. Two Persian lords rode back over the pass to guide Alexander and throw their master on his mercy. It was the best choice for the unhappy man, but made too late. Alexander with his best-mounted cavalry made a breakneck dash to the rescue, fell on the rear of the straggling Bactrians whose discipline had already gone to pieces, and began hewing their way towards the prisoner. The conspirators untied him and told him to mount a horse. He replied that he would rather deal with Alexander. At this Bessus and a certain Barsaentes, with or without Nabarzanes, stabbed him with their javelins, crippled the draught mules of the cart, and took to flight. Nabarzanes, who may have opposed their action, went off separately with six hundred riders of his own.

The dying King was found by a Macedonian soldier, who heard him groaning for water. Here Curtius ends, the manuscript being damaged. Plutarch says that Darius was given a drink, expressed his thanks, commended Alexander's chivalry and wished him luck as his successor; propaganda or romance perhaps, though he would certainly have preferred him to Bessus. But the two kings, the fortunate and the luckless, were not to meet in life. Alexander had had a long fruitless search among the covered carts; when he reached the right one, Darius had breathed his last. Alexander laid his own cloak over him —the last gesture left to make—and ordered his body sent to Sisygambis for a royal burial at Persepolis.

On the Hyrcanian Plain bordering the Caspian Sea, he took the surrender of Nabarzanes. Having rejected Bessus for reasons nowhere explained, he sent to ask for safe conduct, which he would never have got had Alexander not thought he deserved a hearing. His war record, and whatever he had to say at his audience, must have made a good impression; though he never got any office or command, his share in regicide was pardoned. He left behind him the customary gifts of honour, and one unusual one —the young dancer, Bagoas. "He had been loved by

Darius, and was soon to be loved by Alexander." Seeing that this attachment seems to have been lifelong, the source of the Curtius narrative is not far to seek.

Plutarch states circumstantially that Alexander had twice refused, and taken as an insult, proffered gifts of Greek slave-boy beauties. So, although Curtius typically infers that the young Persian was presented as a mere gift or bribe, probability suggests a more substantial motive: namely that he had been an eyewitness of Darius' murder, and could testify that Nabarzanes had opposed it.

Nabarzanes had been a brave, and till near the end a loyal soldier. Though ready in desperation to get rid of a hopelessly bad commander by putting him into the hands of a chivalrous enemy, he may yet have drawn the line at regicide—an appalling crime in Zoroastrian belief, as Alexander well knew later, when he had Bessos tried by a Persian court.

As for Bagoas, he must have known ever since the arrival of the Queen's eunuch to announce her death that the captive ladies had been allowed to keep their own attendants. Besides any loyalty he felt to his master—whose memory he seems to have handled kindly—he had little to lose by following him, and no future among the rebels. The murder was a panic action, unforeseen by everyone, including the killers themselves.

A whole train of circumstance falls into place with this assumption: the departure from the other conspirators of Nabarzanes and his men immediately after the murder; Bagoas' flight in his company; and the statement of Curtius himself that "it was mostly through the boy's pleadings that he [Alexander] was moved to pardon Nabarzanes." The testimony of the dead King's own favourite was solid evidence; a far more likely influence upon Alexander than the mere wheedlings of an attractive youth. Clearly, though, it was without any reluctance that he kept

Bagoas at court to give the chroniclers his valuable account. Supposing that his Persian-learned Greek was unequal to so sustained a narrative, we may amuse ourselves by conjecturing that Alexander dictated the final form himself.*

In any case, Bagoas stayed on. We hear of him from Curtius, Plutarch and Athenaeus, more doubtfully from Arrian; Ptolemy is far more likely to have blue-pencilled Alexander's Persian boy than his own Athenian mistress, not because he was a boy, a matter of indifference in the Greek world, but because he was a "barbarian" eunuch. Alexander's view that "all men are God's children" was shared by few of his countrymen.

To race-conscious Macedonians, Bagoas was a little eccentricity of Alexander's about which the less said the better. But the story of Darius' end—and who else can have supplied it?—tells us much of him, and indirectly of Alexander. Besides the vivid detail, the talent for evoking a scene, there are the loyalty and perceptive good taste which do not attempt crude flattery of a royal lover at the expense of the dead; the pathos of Darius' last night, the insistence that "he nothing common did or mean"; his graceful tributes to his victor which, whether or not he ever uttered them, could not hurt his memory and would give such pleasure now. Sensitivity, self-respect, charm without sycophancy, and beauty for good measure; no wonder that Alexander's fastidious sexual standards were met for once.

Besides the scenes which only the eunuchs witnessed, part of the story must have been related by Artabazus, who came in soon after Nabarzanes and was received with

---

* In a fictional account of this incident (*The Persian Boy*) a different explanation of Bagoas' arrival was given. Later reflection, however, has persuaded me that the one above is more consistent with the evidence. M.R.

the warmest pleasure by Alexander, being at once reinstated in his rank. After years in Macedon his Greek must
have been fluent. Last arrived the Greek mercenaries,
from their hideout in the hills.

They had sent to ask for terms; but Alexander, with
his usual animus against Greeks fighting for Persia, demanded unconditional surrender. Some straggled off;
one man, an Athenian with a virulent anti-Macedonian
record, killed himself; about 1,500 came in. By then
Alexander would have heard of their fidelity from Artabazus and Bagoas. No one was punished; those who had
been hired before he declared war he let go free; the rest
he reprimanded, and conscripted into his army at their
usual rate of pay. The account of Patron's attempt to
warn Darius against his murderers may come from Patron himself.

On his record, Alexander would have treated Darius'
body with respect in any case; but the royal funeral now
accorded him was also a manifesto; it was the duty of a
Great King to his predecessor. There was a pretender in
the field. Bessus in the east had put on the *kyrbasia* with
upstanding peak (the prerogative of royalty; satraps had
to wear theirs flattened) and called himself Artaxerxes.

Whether patriotism or ambition moved him is uncertain. It was already becoming evident that he had two
disabilities never known to Alexander: he could not discipline his men, nor attach their loyalty. In any case, Alexander now claimed the right to proceed against him for
rebellion, regicide, and treason against two kings running.
To enhance this claim, an important act of allegiance now
took place. Oxathres, Darius' fighting brother, arrived
voluntarily to accept Alexander as King. Again the blood
feud was paramount; the enemy of his brother's killer was
a natural ally. Alexander, who seems to have formed a
high opinion of him, recruited him at once into the Com-

panions. His adherence was of the highest propaganda value; its only price was revenge on Bessus.

Alexander had now to break the news to his men that even Darius' death had not ended the war. He assembled the Macedonians and convinced them with "effective arguments" which must have come down to sheer personality, there being no question of force. Even the Greek auxiliaries, offered free choice and their expenses home, did not all depart. Those who signed on again got three talents each; gifts to the Macedonians were on the same dazzling scale. Such occasions were among the major pleasures of Alexander's life.

He was now to march into the unknown wilds of central Asia with the vast accretions of his court and army, which the Persian Romance remembers. "A moving world was his camp . . . the market that followed him was like a capital city's; anything could be bought there, were it as rare as bird's milk." There were the secretariat, the engineers, craftsmen, stewards and doctors and grooms and slaves and architects and armourers in his actual employ; a horde of independent speculators who lived off the well-paid troops; the womenfolk of soldiers and civilians who with their children were almost a second army. His lines of communication would be indefinitely extended; there was no knowing what supplies the country would provide. The holding force he must leave behind would be vital to them all as a diver's airpipe. This command he gave to Parmenion. He was now about seventy; rough campaigning lay ahead; the appointment, honourable and suited to his years, also probably solved for Alexander a long-standing problem. The old general was given his own army, partly of mercenaries (including perhaps the new Greek conscripts) and access to the Ecbatana treasure for his own needs, and those of Alexander's commissariat.

When still in Hyrcania, Alexander had mounted a

small operation against the Mardians of the mountain forests, notable only for Bucephalas' penultimate appearance in history. While being led through the woods by the royal squires, whose charge the King's horses were, he and the rest of the string were carried off by local raiders. He was now twenty-five, and his likely fate all too obvious. The old horse had probably saved the life of his master, boy and man, half a dozen times; the thought of his ending his days as a broken-down beast of burden so appalled Alexander that he sent out heralds to threaten general devastation if he were not returned. The effect was prompt; the friends were reunited; in his relief, Alexander even gave the robbers a reward.

The royal squires, among whose services to the King was that of bringing him his spare horses in battle, were the teen-aged sons of Macedonian aristocrats. In earlier troubled reigns they had been hostages for their fathers; now their duties were something between those of page and esquire in a medieval castle, except that there was no special body-squire for the King. There were enough of them—perhaps something near fifty—to take their watches in rota, and they guarded the royal room or tent at night. When fresh troops came out from Macedon to Hyrcania, new squires probably came too, for the batch Alexander had brought out with him would be grown men. The cherished Bucephalas' ordeal may have started some of the newcomers off with a bad mark, and begun momentous events.

Unlike medieval princes, who trained their esquires only in war and manners, Alexander had his educated, even when on campaign. Their schooling was the charge of Callisthenes, a figure of some importance in Alexander's history. He was a great-nephew of Aristotle, who had recommended him for the post of royal archivist.

(Hence the use of his name by the Pseudo-Callisthenes author.) He was a literary dilettante, who had written a history of Greece up to the time of Philip's accession, and is quoted by later writers for antiquarian notes, especially on the Homeric sites. Alexander, like his contemporaries, treated the *Iliad* as history; he probably delighted in visiting the reputed scenes of the heroes' birth or exploits in Greek Asia. Many ancient writers accuse Callisthenes of flattery without defining it, and no direct quotation from his work survives. Probably he stressed Alexander's descent from the paladins of both sides in the Trojan War, and likened his deeds to theirs. If the flattery consisted in a florid presentation of substantially real achievements, it did him a disservice which he may have perceived as his mind matured.

Meantime, Callisthenes had remained in close touch with the Lyceum, though henceforth correspondence would take much longer on the road. It does not appear that his sycophancy was rebuked by Aristotle, who had many ties with Macedon, especially a close friendship with Antipater which as yet involved him in no conflict of loyalties. He is quoted as having said of Callisthenes that he had a good intelligence but not wisdom; and on another, probably later, occasion that he was not likely to live long; a deduction, perhaps, from indiscretions in his private letters. Certainly he believed, like Aristotle and his school, that Persians were destructive, corrupt barbarians, and that Alexander's proper mission should be of conquest and revenge. Uneasiness must have crept in when old Artabazus was received as a guest of honour; when a Persian prince appeared in the Companion Cavalry; when satraps were reappointed after surrender; when Darius' favourite castrato, a being regarded by conventional Greeks as less than human, found his way into the royal bed. The demeanour of a Greek conqueror ought to have been an ostentatious display of Greek superiority, a proper sense of contrast.

Instead of this a further shock awaited him. Alexander began to experiment with Persian dress.

What he wore is rather vague, as is also what he adapted it from. His own version was more "modest" than the Persian, more "stately" than the Median. The dignitaries in the Persepolis reliefs date from more than a century earlier, and the fashion cannot have been quite static. The Medes wear coats and trousers, the Persians long robes (court dress no doubt) and fluted top hats. Nobody wears the "Persian sash" adopted by Alexander. Persians, like Medes, wore trousers in daily life, but Plutarch assures us that Alexander refrained from the barbarism of encasing either his upper or his lower limbs. He wore some kind of long robe, with a sash, and probably a cape over the arms, in the royal colours later used by the Roman Caesars, purple and white. He also wore the *mitra,* which strictly speaking was a headband in these colours. But since the fillet by itself was such common headwear among Greeks that it cannot have been controversial, he must on state occasions have worn it tied around the *kyrbasia,* like other Persian kings. The upright point of this helmet-shaped bonnet was an important symbol of royalty.

Herodotus remarks of Persian dress that the shoes allow for something to be slipped inside them, to make the wearer look taller. This may have had influence too.

Alexander used this outfit at first for audiences with Persians; then for private parties; then he started to go out in it; riding, Plutarch says; presumably in a chariot. The Macedonians did not like it much, but thought it a pardonable fad, like Bagoas, for which he had earned indulgence. No one complained aloud.

Towards Persians it was good policy; but policy was never the whole story with Alexander, who was complex, emotional, and much affected by human contacts. If Persians had repelled him on acquaintance, he was incapable of sycophancy to them, and would soon have resumed with emphasis the conquering Greek. Clearly they had attracted him. Their sense of style, their dignity and good looks, the courage so cruelly wasted by their king, the integrity of old Artabazus, Bagoas' delicate tact, had made their mark. He wanted to come before them as an aristocrat in their own terms; and guidance was easily had. Oxathres and Artabazus knew all the ceremonial; and trifles they could not be asked about without some loss of dignity could be learned in relaxed intimacy from Bagoas, versed in every detail of the royal day and night. Bagoas' influence is one of history's imponderables. It did not grow less as he passed out of adolescence; but this, like the talent of Hephaestion, is a thing Ptolemy can be relied upon to ignore.

From this time begin the tensions between the concepts of king and conqueror. In the latter the Macedonians had invested their racial pride; and, as important, the prospect of going home, leaving behind a colony to supply tribute and slaves. On the Persian side feelings were divided. The legitimate Ochus and his heir had both been murdered; the makeshift Darius had been an unmitigated disaster; Bessus was for some a hero, for others a regicide beside whom this foreign conqueror was no great change for the worse since he seemed willing to grow civilized. Though they had never known democracy they valued justice, and thought him just.

Bactria, still loyal to its satrap, would give him some hard fighting. The days of pitched battles were over till he got to India. For the next two years he would be campaigning in rough country, against tribesmen familiar with it, and often established in precipitous strongholds. Sometimes a satrap who had sworn him fealty and been his guest would revolt when his back was turned; the chivalric code of honour he had brought from home was to suffer rude disillusions. If he began to trust his experiences before his hopes, it was not illogical. He was dealing with one of the most serious of these rebellions when an act of greater treachery, much nearer home, produced a major crisis of his life.

While quartered in the royal stronghold of Drangiana, he learned that a plot to murder him had been connived at, if no worse, by his boyhood friend Philotas.

Alexander had taken no steps about the earlier warnings. He assessed the loyalty of his friends by his own to them. (One cause of this optimism had no doubt been the bedrock constancy of Hephaestion, a certainty since boyhood.) Philotas, losing no position of trust, had assumed a good deal of pomp and luxury, with a *nouveau-riche* flamboyance that had made him enemies. He was now the only survivor of Parmenion's three sons, the second having lately died of sickness. Parmenion's posting in the rear, considering his age, was no just cause for resentment; but it did diminish the family power at court.

Little is known of the plot to kill Alexander, nothing of the means designed. Its known instigator was an obscure Dymnus, elsewhere unmentioned, apparently on the fringe of Alexander's personal circle, who complained of some unspecified slight. He tried to recruit a youth called Nicomachus, whose lover he was but who, horrified at what he heard, at once told his elder brother. The two, impatient to discharge their perilous knowledge and clear themselves, went to Philotas as someone close to the King. All sources agree he did not report it. Diodorus, Plutarch and Curtius say he promised to do so two days running, and excused himself on the ground that Alexander had been too busy, though in fact he had talked with him freely. The brothers were growing desperate, and suspicious. The elder now went direct to the royal rooms, and informed the squire in charge of Alexander's weapons. He, unlike Philotas, burst straight in upon Alexander during his bath. He questioned the brother, learned there had been delay, and was told the reason.

Reacting with customary speed, before doing anything else he had the whole camp cordoned round to keep news from leaving it. Then he sent a squad to arrest Dymnus, who certified his guilt by killing himself before he could be seized. He had apparently disclosed to Nicomachus the names of some other conspirators, one of them in the Royal Bodyguard; which certainly would suggest something more than the personal anger of a private man. Philotas' known conduct had been clearly treasonable. All sources agree that he admitted having been told of the plot; his defence was that he had not believed in it. (Some historians, in periods more peaceful than ours, have even accepted this; it can now be agreed that honest men, warned of a bomb upon a plane, do not take chances.) Though Nicomachus would not have approached him had he known him to be involved, Dymnus may only have told as much as he dared.

Till the camp had been enclosed, Alexander was forced to keep up a normal manner with Philotas, much against his nature. He then had all the accused arrested. Arrian, citing both his sources, says Philotas had a public trial before the Macedonian Assembly, Alexander himself speaking for the prosecution—he was a material witness, as having been available when Philotas said he was not. Philotas spoke in his own defence (Curtius' florid artifice makes his version useless). The Assembly judged him worthy of death. Arrian says nothing of his interrogation by torture, to which Diodorus, Plutarch and Curtius all refer.

Before deciding that Ptolemy was whitewashing, we must ask as always whether he would have seen a need for it. Almost certainly not, in an ordinary treason trial, as he shows elsewhere. Torture in such cases was general throughout Greece, with one exception. The democratic Athenians, exempting their own citizens, let them offer their slaves instead: if torture produced no evidence, it was taken that they had witnessed nothing amiss; accused citizens who did not make use of this facility were highly suspect. In Philotas' case, his high rank and his war record may have caused Ptolemy to keep quiet, and the question remains open.

There were several more trials, some ending in acquittals. Among those condemned, "lacking words to defend himself," was the long-suspect Alexandros of Lyncestis. Of royal descent, he had probably been chosen, whether or not he knew it, as a suitable puppet king. The Macedonians traditionally executed in public those they had condemned; in this case it was done with javelins. There was no arbitrary purge. But Alexander was now faced with a dreadful choice.

Whether plotter or callous opportunist, Philotas had been a traitor. No army in hostile country could afford to let him live. Still less could it now afford to carry, on its lifeline of communications, a father on whom had devolved the archaic duties of the blood feud.

Prince Oxathres had joined a foreign invader to avenge his brother; Prince Bistanes to avenge his father. There could be no surety that Parmenion, whether or not his son's accomplice, would not change sides when his death was known. This had been Alexander's first thought when he threw his ring round the camp. The ancient laws of Macedon provided that the close male relatives of any

traitor should share his death. It was not mere fright-
fulness; it did not presume their collusion; it simply recognized the blood feud, which would make all who survived
into enemies of the King.

It would be strange if at this moment Alexander did
not remember Attalus. A proven traitor, he had been
secure from arrest among his own tribal levies. The
practical problem here was just the same. Two factors
only were altered: on the one hand, Parmenion's guilt
was not established; on the other, he was infinitely more
dangerous.

Till now the young conqueror had known only the
rewards of power; glory, homage, splendour, limitless
wealth and the pleasures of generosity; admiration, love.
They had cost him only the hardships and dangers which
were his pride. For the first time he learned power's
terrible necessities. He knew them when he saw them; yet
it is possible he kept a last option open.

Three agents on racing dromedaries were sent out on
the guarded road. They carried such a royal warrant as
had protected the slayer of Attalus. This they gave to
Parmenion's senior officers at Ecbatana. In the private
park of the palace where he had his residence, one envoy
whom he knew offered him first a letter from the King,
then one forged in Philotas' name. He was reading the
second "joyfully, as could be seen from his countenance,"
when they struck him down.

This letter, mentioned by Curtius without comment,
explanation or drama, deserves very serious attention.
Why bother with either letter, when Parmenion was already defenceless among his killers? Etiquette demanded
that the royal dispatch be read before anything else; it
had to be there to authenticate the one that mattered, the
Philotas forgery. It was when Parmenion showed evident
pleasure at its contents, and not before, that he was killed.

If he had shown puzzlement, irritation, vague disapproval, anger, fear, would the daggers have been drawn? Curtius in one of his unreliable purple passages states that Philotas incriminated his father. One of the conspirators may have done so, truly or falsely. It would seem that Alexander, rather than accept such testimony unsupported, took a last chance by working into the forged letter some sign, extracted during the interrogations, which would convey only to a man with guilty knowledge that the plot was going well. It would be hit and miss, open to tragic misunderstandings, but the only feasible test remaining.

Arrian says of Alexander that, unlike other kings, he repented when he knew he had done wrong. We read of such regrets; even of bitter shame; but never of his repenting Parmenion's death. It had been done not in passion but in considered decision; and by his decision he stood.

The appalling risk it had involved of causing Parmenion's troops to mutiny—a contingency he had no power whatever to prevent—could only have been run in the firm belief that a still worse danger threatened. (Only the other day, modern Europe has seen the mere dismissal of a popular general followed at once by an army revolt.) Alexander had had to stake everything on the loyalty of troops hundreds of miles away from him, whom he could neither persuade nor coerce when they were forced to choose between him and their own commander. The implications of this have been too little considered.

There was no mutiny. His own army took it quietly; men of Macedon, their folk memory stored with grim tales of its dynastic struggles, and fully satisfied of Philotas' guilt, they were unlikely to acquit his powerful father. A temporary, *ad hoc* censors' board examined home letters for signs of disaffection. Resentful men were segregated into a special corps—receiving, apparently, no punishment but the slur of unreliability—and challenged to redeem themselves by good performance in action. This they did, even with keenness, probably after an address from Alexander himself.

He now knew that a man who wished him dead had held command of his finest striking force, the Companion Cavalry. Hephaestion had proved himself in command, and it would probably have been Alexander's choice to put the whole corps under a man in whom he had perfect trust. But he was identified with the new controversial policies, a tactful and well-liked diplomat among the Persians, whose customs, and probably speech, he had taken the trouble to learn. To avoid an open snub to the conservatives at this touchy time, Alexander divided the Companions between him and Cleitus "the Black," his nurse's brother who had saved his life in the scrimmage at the Granicus. The family was related to the royal house, and had had no need to treat little princes with deference. Probably Alexander had known Cleitus since his infancy and through much of his stormy childhood, with subconscious associations of which he himself was unaware.

Bessus was still in control of Bactria. The two-year resistance of this province has been described as a national rising, but this is true in no modern sense. Its bonds of unity were tribal and familial, and its ancient feuds were never laid aside.

Alexander wintered among a peaceful tribe whom Cyrus, provisioned by them at a time of crisis, had named "The Benefactors," and whom Alexander took to his heart. With the spring he moved on into the wilds. Through this whole phase of campaigning, rugged country meant well-defined routes however rough; and at strategic points along these ancient trails—some reaching to India, some as far as China whose existence he never guessed— he would mark his passage by founding another city.

Modern archaeology is only now beginning to learn how real and solid were his efforts to implant centres of civilization in the wilderness. The garrison was there for protection as well as for control; the streets were properly laid out, there would be a public square, the focus of all Greek cities; a temple for the tutelary deity, a council chamber, sometimes even a theatre; one had a monument to Peritas, a favourite dog he had hand-reared, after whom he had named the town. Most were called Alexandria. The settlers came from the multitude that followed him: veterans who had picked up a woman on the march and bred a family; merchants and craftsmen, attracted by the trade route or the lack of rivals; disabled men ready to settle down with their bounty, their loot and their bit of land rather than face the long drag home; some travel-weary whores to serve the garrison. In later days, if discontent broke out it was in the garrisons; they had no real stake in the place, and a monotonous job while their comrades were with Alexander, getting adventure and wealth.

The campaign against Bessus had been much hampered by the fierce and treacherous Satibarzanes, satrap of Ariana, who, after Gaugamela, had pursued Bessus' and Nabarzanes' original plan of first making peace and then rebelling. In the spring of 329 he was in flight, soon to be killed in hand-to-hand combat by Erigyius, one of the boyhood friends exiled by Philip for their devotion. Alexander, resolved to settle with Bessus for good, and get north into Bactriana before he was expected, early in the year led his army over the still icy heights of the Hindu Kush.

Historians have agreed that as a feat of leadership and endurance it far surpasses Hannibal's crossing of the Alps. Its hardships were to a great extent foreseeable; he must have felt an unshaken confidence in his men's devotion, which events confirmed. He may not have allowed enough for altitude. Provisions ran short; wheeled transport was impossible and the ground grew only alpine herbs; dead mules were eaten raw for lack of cooking fuel; the glare caused snow blindness, and at 11,000-odd feet there must have been some mountain sickness. But Alexander was always to be seen as cold and hungry as anyone, stopping for a joke, or to haul some numbed man out of a drift. Xenophon too had shaken listless soldiers from the drowsy hypothermia that turns to death; one had complained because his hard-tried commander hit him. No one complained of Alexander.

He had by now taken Bessus' measure; he could not have risked struggling down head-on into a fresh and determined enemy. He cast his spell on foes as well as friends. Lean and weary, he was forerun by a name of dread. Irresolutely, Bessus stripped the countryside into which he came; leaner, but resolute, he still came on. Bessus' nerve broke; he fled across the Oxus, burning his boats behind him. Local resistance collapsed; Alexander rested and fed his men. As satrap of Bactria, he appointed the indestructible Artabazus.

It was a breathing spell between a cold hell and a hot one. Alexander detached old veterans and the unfit for discharge home, before marching into the grilling desert round the Oxus. They marched by night, the day being unbearable. The men overspent their water ration in the arid air. The distress of the camp followers must have been extreme. Curtius tells how some of the carriers, who had found a little waterhole and filled a skin for their children, passed Alexander sweltering, and dutifully offered him a cupful. Having asked where they were taking it, he told them to give it to their sons; he would not drink till there was enough for everyone. This recalls a still more famous incident; both are typical, and, human nature being repetitive, no doubt both are true.

At last they reached the river, Alexander standing unrested and unfed, after his last lap, to see everyone safe in camp. The river was wide, the ferry boats had been burned; but Xenophon had taught him on the Danube the lore of the Euphrates, and it served for the Oxus too. The tentmakers set to work stuffing the tent hides into rafts, and the crossing took five days.

Fate treated Bessus just as he had treated Darius. His levies had been melting by desertion. Two of his chiefs decided he was hindering the war. Leaving him in a village fort, held by two servants, they sent Alexander word that he was there for the picking up.

Not to dignify the event by his own presence, Alexander sent Ptolemy, with orders to treat Bessus like a common criminal. The point was to be made that this was not, and never had been, a Persian king. Bessus' fatal mistake was not to have surrendered along with the realistic Nabarzanes, who had secured his amnesty before Oxathres arrived. Now the brother of Darius waited, expectant, for the vengeance that was his price of fealty. Bessus was stripped, a Persian's greatest disgrace, and stood by the road, his hands tied to a wooden yoke. Halting his chariot, Alexander asked why he had betrayed and murdered his benefactor, his kinsman and his king. With less dignity than Darius' when all was lost, he answered that the whole suite had agreed on it, to get safe conduct from Alexander. It was the wrong approach to a man who had pardoned, and taken into his army, a batch of rebels he saw marching to execution with conspicuous courage. He ordered Bessus a flogging, which no doubt Oxathres witnessed, and his custody in chains till a Persian court could try him.

No other pretender appeared. Alexander marched
northeast to the immemorial boundary of the Jaxartes
River, where civilization ended and the steppes began.
Here stood a line of ancient forts, built to keep off the
Scythians, fierce nomads whom even Darius the Great
could not subdue. Alexander was quick to decide that the
frontier had been rightly drawn. He had the rare vision
to perceive that, if prejudice were broken down, two
great civilizations could cross-fertilize; but he knew barbarism when he saw it, and his concern was to keep it
out. It was evident to him that at the first sign of weakness, the Scythians would be across.

Having replaced the horses that heat or cold had killed,
he marched back west towards Samarkand. In a clash
with tribesmen an arrow split his leg bone. Unable to
ride, he saved delay by getting into a litter. First carried
by the infantry, it roused the jealousy of the cavalry, who
demanded to dismount and share the privilege. He let
them take it in turns.

The Jaxartes campaign cannot here be followed in detail. Samarkand, the royal city, was occupied, the river
forts were reduced and manned. The country seemed
quiet, and Alexander summoned the chiefs of Sogdiana
to a council. At once suspecting a treachery which to
them seemed a matter of course, they rose in revolt instead, overran his new towns and laid siege to Samarkand.
His relieving force was cut up, its commanders proving
inadequate, and he had to raise the siege himself. During
these operations, leading from the front as usual, he was
knocked about. His larynx was bruised by a stone—a
dangerous injury—and for a time he lost his voice. A
head blow gave him a spell of clouded vision. From this
may derive a curious quirk of the Alexander legends,
that he had one grey eye and one black. One dilated pupil
is a common feature of concussion; some local report of

him, in a state when most people would have been in bed, may have lodged in folk memory.

On the further shore of the Jaxartes a horde of defiant Scythians appeared. He got a mixed force over, put them to rout, and chased them far across the plains. Like Darius the Great, he found them slip through his fingers. A worse mishap, because more lasting in its results, was that in the heat he drank whatever water he found, and got a crippling bout of enteritis. So no doubt did other soldiers, not without some fatalities, for Alexander was seriously ill. The army soon learned in the thirsty lowlands that the only safe drink was wine.

Oxathres returned to Ecbatana, to preside over Bessus' trial by a court of Persian nobles. His nose and eartips had been cut off, the Persian mark of the criminal. The execution too was traditionally barbaric, by impalement or the cross. Oxathres had the body cut in pieces and strewn for wild beasts to eat. His brother at last avenged, his loyalty rewarded, he certified by his presence the legitimacy of the new Great King, to whose court he then returned.

The mass of administration now surrounding Alexander was as much Persian as Macedonian or Greek. Inevitably, people had to wait for audience; inevitably, Macedonians had to take their turn with Persians. Bagoas, a decorative addition to the royal household, was one not universally approved. Persian officers, satraps and envoys were increasingly in evidence, performing those deep obeisances so offensive to Greek tradition, before a King who did not discourage it.

Alexander had had by now the experienced advice of Artabazus, survivor of four reigns, and of Bagoas, familiar with court procedure from very close to the throne. The deference accorded a foreign king would be measured by his own sense of his dignity; there could be no question of ceasing to exact from Persians so essential a token of respect as the "prostration." But Alexander was thin-skinned; even if no one had told him, he would hardly have missed the fact that the scornful glances of un-bowing Macedonians were not being lost on his newer subjects.

Consulting with Hephaestion—whose unshakeable devotion the advent of Bagoas had not flawed—he considered how the matter could be regularized. It would be difficult, and would have to be done with tact.

Herodotus, writing a century earlier, said of Persian customs:

> When they meet each other in the streets, you may know if the persons meeting are of equal rank by the following sign: if they are, instead of speaking they kiss each other on the lips. Where one is a little the other's inferior, the kiss is given on the cheek; when the difference of rank is great, the inferior prostrates himself on the ground.

All Persians were inferior to the King, most of them greatly inferior; there is an area of debate about the depth of obeisance required of persons about the court. We read of Persians high enough placed to be Alexander's dinner guests making full prostration before him; but he also took over the important institution of the Royal Kindred. The Persian kings had admitted to this privileged caste large numbers of noblemen to whom they were not related, thus making them "a little" his inferiors, with the right to kiss his cheek. Alexander must certainly have conferred this at once upon, for instance, the venerable Artabazus, and royal princes like Oxathres and Bistanes; probably on many more. But he kept it in his gift, not to be taken for granted.

In the time of Darius the Great two Spartan envoys,

men of the highest birth, had risked death sooner than
make *proskynesis* before him (they were magnanimously
spared). If any rite of bending was intermediate between
prostration on the ground and the kinsman's kiss, it was
deep enough to give Macedonians the same sense of
servility. About this Alexander had no illusions, as his
proceedings show.

Persians were willing to bow down before a king,
Macedonians not. Neither race must be humiliated. The
faces of Macedonians could be saved by upgrading the
status of the person to whom they bowed. From a king,
there was only one step up. Let them bow before a son
of Ammon who partook of the god's divinity.

In an issue like this, the complex mind of Alexander,
baffling to men who shared his culture, is inaccessible to
ours. Except in Egypt, where it had millennial sanction,
he had never made use of his divine prerogative. His use of
it now was practical, statesmanlike, and in a sense highly
civilized. On the other hand, it was not a form; he believed
in it. It is worth remembering that millions of men, in
three continents, would agree with him before many years
were out.

Having told his plan to his closest friends, apparently
without opposition, he confided it to leading Persians;
they had put up with enough and were due for some
compensation. A number of them were invited to a
banquet, along with Macedonians of rank. Arrian, who
may here be using either Ptolemy or the chamberlain
Chares, gives the most reasonable account of this event.
The sophist Anaxarchus made a speech in praise of the
King. (He came from the Thracian city of Abdera. The
Athenian tradition called him a flatterer of Alexander.
He ended up being pounded to death with iron clubs by
a Cypriot king about whom he had been rude, a fate he
met with defiant courage. If he did flatter Alexander it

must have been because he liked him, a possibility which can never be excluded.) He listed his unexampled achievements, correctly predicted that he would be offered divine honours as soon as he was dead, and asked why he should not receive them in his lifetime. On cue, the friends jumped up with assenting cries, ready to make their reverence. At the critical moment, Callisthenes intervened.

In a longish speech, he urged the impiety of offering gods' rights to men. Most of the Macedonians had been taken unprepared by the proposal; at this support for their indecisive reluctance, they broke into applause. Alexander, faced with the prospect of an unpleasant scene, sent round word that he would not insist. Everyone sat down. Then the Persian guests, who knew the real intention and were determined to acknowledge it, got up and performed the *proskynesis* of their own accord. As one of them took his turn less gracefully than the rest, a Macedonian guffawed with laughter. It was the last straw for Alexander; he strode down the hall and threw the man off his banquet couch on to the floor—certainly, for the Persians, an innovation in court etiquette.

This volte-face of Callisthenes' may, or may not, have been simply maturing within him. All sources agree on the effusiveness of his official chronicle. But he was a product of the Lyceum, keeping in touch with Aristotle, who must have heard with mounting disgust of honours and offices conferred on Persians, the assumption of "barbarian" royal dress, and the scandalous Bagoas. After the long delays involved in getting private mail from Attica to the Oxus, Callisthenes may have been urged to make a stand.

Alexander remained tenacious of his purpose. His next move cannot be called arrogant; it showed both sensitivity and tact. He arranged a small party, for distinguished Macedonians and Greeks alone. Hephaestion lobbied each beforehand, making sure they knew what to expect and would not object. One was Callisthenes.

A brief ceremony was planned around the loving cup. Each guest would stand and drink, then make the *proskynesis* before Alexander, rise, and come forward to receive a kiss. Thus, in return for a single prostration formally acknowledging his right to it, Alexander would accept them all into the Royal Kin. His return of the kiss —in Persian terms the salutation of equals—was a personal gesture from friend to friends. Offering what was perhaps the most signal proof of his long devotion, Hephaestion bowed down the first of all.

All went smoothly till it came to Callisthenes, when Alexander "happened" to be talking to Hephaestion, and "did not notice" that he came up for the kiss without first making his bow. That the obvious joker in the pack had really been overlooked is of course incredible. A neat little piece of face saving had been arranged, allowing Callisthenes to keep his philosophic pride without official cognizance. Any odium it incurred among the others was his own affair.

Like many intelligent men, Alexander had not left margin enough for others' dullness. As Callisthenes came for his kiss, someone called out that it had not been earned. Diplomacy thus frustrated, the King turned his face away. Callisthenes completed the social disaster by saying rudely, "So I go off short of a kiss." Thus Chares the chamberlain, who must have been an eyewitness.

Hephaestion, who had certainly done his best, had no alternative but to assure the other guests afterwards that Callisthenes had agreed to bow. He may indeed simply have changed his mind, a contingency provided for in vain. There was no further attempt to introduce *proskynesis* among the Macedonians.

Alexander had now not only been twice snubbed pub-

licly by Callisthenes; he had been baulked of an important
political aim. Had he become the Oriental tyrant of
Athenian propaganda, this offensive and obstructive person would speedily have suffered a fatal colic, so easily
passed off as the virulent local dysentery. No clearer
evidence is needed of Alexander's aversion to secret
murder than Callisthenes' continued life. None of his
privileges were withdrawn. He even kept his office of
tutor to the royal squires. Alexander could still be trusting
to the point of naïvety.

He did test the sophist's popularity by asking him one
evening to give in sophistic style first a panegyric exhibi-
tion speech on the Macedonians, then a speech in their
detraction. The second, which the company considered
the more vigorous, was much resented. Alexander, striking while the iron was hot, remarked that it had simply
shown ill will.

The *proskynesis* issue was one handful of fuel on an
already smouldering fire. It had not yet touched the rank
and file, with whom Alexander's stock had never been
higher; but the staff was divided sharply. Young officers,
like the frontier subalterns of Kipling's India, could frat-
ernize when East met West, and enjoy it among the other
adventures with which Alexander had enriched their lives.
Philip's old guard clung bitterly to their victor's status,
and saw it daily eroded.

It is fairer to see Alexander as a great original than to
despise them for reaction. If prejudice is prejudgment,
they could claim to judge by results. They had won against
odds; had fought better, were better led, and thought they
had better traditions. Macedonian restraints on the royal
power, though crude, were valuable. The image of the
Oriental was linked in their minds, not without the truth
evident in Herodotus, to the cruel caprices of despotic
power slavishly endured, of which the prostration was a

symbol. Alexander's friends would have bowed, as they wore his presents of Persian dress, because they knew, loved, and partly understood him. To Philip's men it was all anathema; and their condemnation made the King's party sharply defensive. Though his personality kept it in check, friction bred faction, and still did when he moved his headquarters from the Oxus plains, where he had wintered, to the delightful climate of Samarkand. Ironically, when stress reached breaking point in tragedy, it was not because Alexander had distanced himself from his countrymen with a Great King's hauteur, but precisely because he had not.

Artabazus had lately asked leave to retire from the satrapy of Bactria, which he began to find fatiguing. This exalted and wealthy office had been conferred on Hephaestion's co-commander and Alexander's kinsman, Cleitus.

If it seemed to discharge a debt of honour to him and to his sister, it also removed a vocal and stubborn conservative from the high command. Unlike Parmenion's posting at Ecbatana—a staff job, officially temporary—it had high prestige, but was also permanent. Cleitus had rank already, military and social; he may not have found the golden handshake flattering. However, he accepted it, and would soon have gone his way. The anger of Dionysus determined otherwise.

On the god's Macedonian feast day Alexander gave a banquet, especially to share with his friends a consignment of prime Hyrcanian apples. For reasons unknown, he dedicated the feast to the divine warrior twins, Castor and Pollux. Cleitus, invited, had begun a sacrifice of his own, perhaps to the more orthodox divinity, when he heard the dinner trumpet and put it off. The two sheep he had ready to butcher, sheeplike, came trotting after him. Alexander thought this escort of sacrificial beasts a disturbing omen, and ordered the priests to pray for Cleitus' safety.

Accustomed by now to the axiom that "you can't drink the water," men must already have slaked their thirsts with wine before they arrived; and Macedonian feast days always meant heavy drinking. Someone sang a lampoon on the commanders who had failed to relieve the city; a tasteless black joke, seeing they had been killed, but countenanced by Alexander who had succeeded where they had failed. Feelings built up; his friends began to exalt his exploits over those of Castor and Pollux, perhaps with the *proskynesis* still in mind. With everyone drunk, the debate grew quarrelsome and aggressive; the friends, abandoning the Twins, turned to the still more explosive theme of how Alexander had surpassed his father.

Cleitus noisily disagreed. Having lived close to the royal family through Alexander's lifetime, he must have been dense not to know, even when in liquor, that he was playing with fire. He would have been safe with Alexander the King of Persia, whom he so resented. Fatally, he had aroused instead the furious youth who had hurled a goblet at his father's wedding.

Alexander's response was wholly Macedonian. When Cleitus shouted and argued, he argued and shouted back. Cleitus mocked his Persian dress and his cult of Ammon; complained that "barbarians" must be petitioned for leave to see him; taunted him with having saved his life at the Granicus. Alexander shied an apple at his head, then, the insults continuing, looked about for a weapon. His friends, like true Macedonians, held him back by force while he cursed and struggled; resourceful Ptolemy eased the protesting drunk outside. This common bar-room brawl ended as so many have done among lesser men. Cleitus came bursting in again with a new insult he had

just thought of; Alexander, blind with rage, snatched a
spear from the nearest guard and ran him through the
heart. At the sound of his death cry, the noise in the hall
was succeeded by a deep silence.

Such was the act of homicide invariably called by
historians "the murder of Cleitus." Today, with equivalent
evidence of drink and provocation, it would receive a
sentence of two or three years, with remission for good
conduct.

No judgment on it has been harsher than Alexander's
own. He had killed Parmenion as a king, responsibly.
This time he had killed as a man, who could not hold his
drink or keep his temper. As a king, he had illegally
killed a Macedonian asserting his right of free speech.
As a Greek, he had killed a benefactor and a guest; aspects
whose enormity we can scarcely now assess. His shame
was proportioned to his pride; for a time he found himself intolerable. Plutarch may be right in saying that
in the first shock he had to be restrained from running
himself on the spear he had pulled out of Cleitus. For
three days he would not eat or drink, till there were fears
for his life, perhaps also for his sanity. People came to
his room without his leave, as if he were helpless with
some dangerous illness. The philosophers offered rational
or soothing words. The Macedonian soldiers, alarmed by
his desperation over what must have seemed to them a
very common mishap, called an Assembly of their own
accord, condemned Cleitus for treason, and sent to let
Alexander know that his act had now been legalized.
Consoling as their forgiveness must have been, he did not
yet forgive himself, and met comfort with cries of self-
reproach.

More effective first aid was brought by the priest of
Dionysus. Each of the Olympians had his own weapon of
retribution: Zeus wielded thunderbolts, Poseidon waves

and earthquakes, Aphrodite disastrous passions. Dionysus' weapon was madness. Neglected on his feast day in favour of other deities, he had come like some uninvited fairy in those folk tales which are the detritus of old religions, and cast his malign enchantment. Alexander had done the deed when, literally, he was not himself.

From this he took some salve to his self-respect, and gradually came back to life again. The theory had something in it, even though the spell had been cast on the god's behalf by his votary Olympias, twenty-odd years before.

Any fairly short account of Alexander's crowded life must often seem to leap from drama to drama. Yet these events were brief in time; long weeks and months were spent in varied action, much of it now lost to us; in campaigning over wild and difficult country where, once off the caravan trails, men of his race had never stepped before. After operations of the most physically exacting kind, while his men were resting, he merely changed his tasks; seeing the usual envoys and petitioners and couriers, administering not only the old army but its constant inflow of foreign auxiliaries about whose methods and capacities he had to know; seeing that their native officers got along with his own commanders. He had to see surveyors' reports, and those of the scouts on whose intelligence he would advance into uncharted lands. Everything of importance fell on him. He could not delegate to an establishment he was in process of constructing as he went.

He was founding more cities, deeply concerned with them both as viable communities, and as his own memorials. Kandahar still echoes his name. On choice of site hung the settlers' welfare, even their lives. That Hephaestion was often given a free hand to establish towns when Alexander was busy is striking evidence of his real abilities.

Alexander had plenty to do. The character and terrain of these wars can best be reconstructed from the memoirs of nineteenth-century soldiers who found men and mores largely unchanged, and, coming from a society more sensitive to shock, took less for granted. We learn in passing that Alexander put down a local custom of leaving out the sick and senile for the hyenas. He could not wait to see whether survival offered them a better fate.

His legend was already forming in his tracks. Two thousand years later, Afghan chiefs would be claiming descent from him, and even that of their horses from Bucephalas, rather elderly now to be at stud. Forces which had held out against his officers would melt into the hills at the mere rumour that he himself was on the march towards them. Spitamenes, one of Bessus' betrayers, a tough and resourceful guerrilla leader, died of such news. His officers heard that Alexander was coming, and in panic sent him their chieftain's head. Curtius says that his wife removed it while he slept; adding that she was also his mother.

The country was full of precipitous cliffs and summits, fortified from remote antiquity in the perennial cycles of blood feud and tribal war. From time to time some especially sensational and ingenious siege gets detailed description. It was impossible for Alexander to hear that a strongpoint was impregnable without regarding it as a personal challenge. This showed a perceptive grasp of war psychology in Sogdiana, where courage, strength and success were essentials of status and of survival.

The most notorious of such pinnacles was the Sogdian Rock; high, sheer, and riddled at the top with caves well stocked with food and water. Its chieftain, Oxyartes, was away raising the countryside, leaving his family and gar-

rison in the charge of his son. The single path to the top
was entirely commanded from above. The area was under
snow.

Alexander offered a parley. Two envoys climbed down,
laughed in his face, and told him not to waste his time
unless his men had wings. That settled the matter. He
called for volunteers who were expert climbers, and got
300. At night, helped by the snow which would have
etched out all the ledges, they were to ascend the steepest,
unguarded face, a "very severe." The first man up would
get 12 talents, a sum on which to be comfortable for life;
the next 11; and so through the first twelve. Iron tent
pegs for pitons, mallets, and ropes got them up, in spite
of snow-numbed fingers, with a loss of one in ten. In
Sogdiana, to have conceded failure might have cost lives
by the thousand.

Stunned at dawn by the sight of an unknown force
above him, the chief's son surrendered, and everyone was
spared. A feast was offered, at which the ladies of the
family performed a dance for the conqueror. Among them
was the chief's daughter, Roxane. Alexander fell in love
with her at first sight. Quixotically renouncing the right
of capture which neither friend nor foe would have questioned, he asked for her hand in marriage.

Political expediency has been suggested, but does no
convince. No doubt had she been disastrously unsuitabl.
—married for instance—he would have mastered his feel
ings; but everything points to an authentic *coup de foudre*.
The obvious state marriage would have been with Darius'
daughter, as he knew, for he later made it. Any daughter
of Artabazus would have been more eligible than this
chieftain's child. It would seem that falling in love with a
woman was a new and exhilarating experience, and, ever
the explorer, he was eager to pursue it without delay.

It is unlikely she had any female predecessor. Recent

archaeology has revealed the proud, aristocratic refine-
ment of the ideal type admired by the Persian rulers of
these regions; and she was an acknowledged beauty. Perhaps she reminded him of his mother, with whom she had
traits in common, whether or not he had time to find it
out. After such a childhood, it is a wonder his heterosexual
instincts were not destroyed instead of merely retarded.
The epicene graces of Bagoas may have been tilting, im-
perceptibly, his sexual bias.

Roxane's father was summoned, made alliance and gave
consent. The Macedonians, after the initial shock, would
have remembered Philip's succession of campaign wives,
and presumed that his son would choose in due course a
proper consort. The Persians, their royal house passed by,
must have raised their eyebrows. (The highborn family
of Artabazus remained tranquil, suggesting that the seduc-
tion and humiliation of his daughter Barsine was still
unborn in the mind of its propagandist author; in real life
they could not have swallowed the insult.) The Sogdians
were delighted. At the marriage feast the young girl was
handed her ritual piece of the bridal loaf by the strange
fair-haired chieftain who had sliced it with his sword—
ancient and still-surviving symbol of his power to protect
and maintain her. Tasting the bread, she pledged herself
to a man with five years to live, during most of which
he would be on campaign in conditions where only his
fighting force could follow him. Her married life must
have been measured in months.

Within weeks, he was off to another siege of sensational
difficulty. His new father-in-law having mediated a peace
treaty, he returned to his bride. The story of the marriage
is much neglected by the sources, in itself significant. Only
an accident of history has disclosed that in a month or
two he was already sleeping alone.

That it took him four years to give her a child admits

of various explanations. She is said to have had a still-birth in India, begotten therefore early in their marriage; we hear of no others. He may have been attentive, but infertile; her attraction may have been fitful; or it may have long ceased, and only some premonition of his early death made him bestir himself to beget an heir. The certainty is that he never became uxorious. With Hephaestion he remained in love, at a depth where the physical relationship becomes almost irrelevant; and years later Bagoas was still his recognized *eromenos*. He had been disinhibited, not reversed, and had now achieved the normal Greek bisexuality.

Among those most scandalized by the match must have been Callisthenes. Like his teacher Aristotle, he saw Alexander's mission as that of Hellenic war leader, and thought he had long since betrayed it; Macedonian tolerance of royal polygamy was not shared by southern Greeks, and the thought of Greek lands being some day ruled by a scion of barbarian stock must have been monstrous. Callisthenes adopted an ostentatious austerity of life; a protest admired by the disaffected. Alexander himself paid it little heed. With the spring he had moved from Sogdiana south into Bactria to consolidate his conquests, India in the forefront of his mind. Between this and his new wife, he had enough to think of without the tedious scholar, who was left undisturbed to his instruction of the squires.

His most receptive student, a youth called Hermolaus, was one day attending Alexander at a boar hunt, when for reasons never made clear he speared a boar which the King had marked as his own quarry. For this he got an exemplary sentence: a beating before his fellows, and forfeiture of his right to ride. Since officers who over-punish in fits of petulance are not regarded by their men as Alexander was, it would seem obvious that Hermolaus had been accumulating a bad record. Not enough is known of the royal hunting etiquette to show whether Alexander was now being hard on him for something which might otherwise have been overlooked, or if his offence was flagrant. He was bitterly resentful, and, according to the depositions later, complained to Callisthenes, who spoke in praise of tyrannicides. At all events, Hermolaus formed a plot with five other squires, one of whom was his lover, to kill Alexander as he slept. Six squires made up a night watch; they had therefore to get themselves into the same watch, unobtrusively, one by one.

The ease with which they did so would have staggered any one of the Greek tyrants, of whose precautions such fascinating accounts exist. The squires' arrangements took them about a month. Night duty was only served for one night at a time, which meant that they must act on their night assigned, or wait the best part of a fortnight for their next turn. Yet their plans took no account whatever of Roxane or her anteroom attendants. She had been consigned to the harem, where the assassins had no apparent fears of her husband sleeping.

The lack of evidence about their relations leaves an important gap in our knowledge of Alexander. It is clear, however, that close and affectionate communication had been integral to his other loves. To Hephaestion he confided everything; Bagoas had been encouraged to reminisce about his former life. Roxane cannot have had a word of Greek; the sources are silent about Alexander's Persian. Beyond a few endearments picked up from Bagoas, it was probably elementary. Beauty, however dazzling its first impact, may have turned out to be not enough.

On the night arranged for his murder, Alexander was at a party. The squires awaited him, hoping he would be drunk. Fairly late he got up to leave, but was waylaid going to bed by a slightly crazy Syrian woman, a clairvoyant he had taken up because she had given him some true predictions. He let her hang about his quarters, the third of his mother-figures. Ptolemy, much inclined to ignore Alexander's more disreputable connections, does not admit, as does Aristobulus, that she told him it would be bad luck to turn in before the morning. A born night bird in any case, he got the party going again, and came to bed at dawn. The relief guard arrived, but the anguished conspirators on some pretext still stood by, hoping against hope for their chance. He was sober enough to thank them charmingly for their courtesy in waiting up for him, and give each a tip, before he fell into bed. Hermolaus was ready to wait till their turn came round again; but one of the others now felt unhappy enough to confide in a lover of his, from whom he had kept the secret. The youth was at once sent off to make a clean breast of everything; which he did, in great distress, to Ptolemy whom he found in the royal tent. Alexander, when with some difficulty he had been shaken awake, pardoned the youth, and ordered all the others arrested. Curtius includes Callisthenes; in Arrian, he is only accused after the interrogation of the squires, and Ptolemy does not hesitate here to speak of torture.

They, as Macedonians, were tried before the Assembly. Hermolaus' defence is said to have been a denunciation of Alexander; just possible in a fanatic with nothing left to lose and no concern for his fellows. They were all condemned by general assent to stoning, which the Assembly carried out. Callisthenes, a non-Macedonian, had no title to a trial and got none. According to Ptolemy he was first tortured—probably to learn if the plot had its roots in Athens—and then hanged. Whether or not he had helped to plan the murder, he had created its moral climate. Alexander's logic made no distinction between the theorist killer and the man with the knife.

If he had spent longer in Athens, he might have known what this act would cost him, and thought twice. He had embittered the most influential body of opinion formers in his world. Anti-Macedonian and anti-monarchist already, the men of the Academy and the Lyceum now sank their rivalries to execrate in concert the martyrdom of free-minded philosophy. His barbarian marriage was derided; wild rumours of sexual debauch were swallowed whole; military operations were converted to atrocities. Blatantly forged letters of his abounded. One of them purported to say that the squires had not implicated Callisthenes; even the absurdity of his exonerating a man he had just condemned was not questioned by the logicians, it would have been ideological heresy. The Athenian Alexander, passed on to Rome, has bedevilled history ever since.

His death had been devised with treachery and cowardice, things he abhorred and could not understand. But killing Callisthenes was the one great strategic blunder of his career. He did not live to know the worst of it.

INDIA

In 327 Alexander mobilized his largest army, augmented with troops from all his new dominions, perhaps as many as 120,000 men, for his march on India.

It had every lure to which his nature responded. Darius the Great had failed to hold on to his Punjab satrapies, and now could be surpassed. Heracles, one of Alexander's great examplars, had been there; so had Dionysus, that god of half-human birth, wandering in his divine madness. (Alexander's instinctive genius preserved him from ever trying to suppress the Dionysiac in his nature—that way real madness would have lain.) India called also to the explorer in him. Not only were its marvels legendary; its further shore was, in all Greek belief, the end of the earth.

By now he must have crossed caravan routes that led to China. He may have seen and fingered its silk. But trade goods changed hands along the way, often with the simplest barter signs; the Persians did not know much more than he. His geographers noted all information within their reach; none of it had shaken his belief that the endless Stream of Ocean, the world's girdle, lay a few months' march away. He had no notion of the southward depth of the Indian subcontinent, and supposed that from its eastern shore it would be no great voyage to the Euphrates. Having learned that the Indus harboured crocodiles, he believed for some time that it flowed into the Nile.

In Sogdiana he had had his first contact with the fabled land, a state visit from the King of Taxila in the Punjab; a former satrapy, which its present ruler did not want to lose. He bore splendidly exotic gifts, "such as the Indians most prize," which no doubt included pearls and rubies. His train of twenty-five painted and bedizened elephants made a great impression; astutely, as a last prodigal gesture he sent them back over the passes on his return home. This foretaste sharpened Alexander's appetite for discovery, and his men's for loot.

The quality of Hephaestion's military record now appears. Under him and Perdiccas, Alexander put more than half the army; including apparently most of the new levies, a touchy job. In his charge were the noncombatants, among whom must have been Roxane; Alexander could not have taken her where he was going, which was to control the flanks of the immemorial gateway by which all the rest would enter.

Sir Robert Warburton, who had a similar task in the 1880s, wrote in his memoirs: "To those who are not acquainted with this highway, I must explain that formerly the Khyber Pass, thanks to the quarrels and exactions of the Afridis, was always closed to caravans, trade and travellers, except when some strong man forced them to keep it open for the time being; and when he passed away, or the whim left him, the pass was closed again." This one, when he passed away, was remembered for two millennia.

The campaign began in autumn. Sir Robert, describing operations in winter, says, "So cold was it that the rushing water froze on my pony's feet and flanks wherever it touched the animal." Alexander had much fierce fighting among the hill forts, where the tribesmen shut themselves up at his approach, ready to emerge behind him. Demands for their surrender were taken in bad part; but they were unused to sophisticated siege techniques and most of the assaults were brief. He got two arrow wounds, in the shoulder and ankle; neither of them severe, but his men reacted savagely, as they did to anything that endangered him. He had one narrow escape when an assault bridge, thrown across to the walls of Massaga, collapsed under the weight of men pressing up to fight beside him; luckily the drop was not too deep. On the death of the tribal chief the rest surrendered; including a force of about 7,000 mercenaries from another region. Alexander granted a truce, and negotiated with these men to join his army, which they agreed to do. In the night, however, they started to make off. Alexander decided he could not expose his men to the risk of treachery; he surrounded the Indians and cut them down. It must have been a grim enough business; but not deserving of the propagandist version given by Diodorus, which, disregarding Ptolemy's first-hand witness, makes it an act of calculated revenge.

The brave and attractive Sir Robert, seeking to defend the tribesmen of his manor from the charge of irremediable savagery, writes,

The Afridi lad from his earliest childhood is taught by the circumstances of his existence and life to distrust all mankind; and very often his near relations, heirs to his small plot of land by right of inheritance, are his deadliest enemies. Distrust of all mankind, and readiness to strike the first blow for the safety of his own life, have therefore become the maxims of the Afridi. . . . It took me years to get through this thick crust of mistrust. . . .

All frontier campaigners agree that the fate of their prisoners was appalling.

> When you're wounded an' left on Afghanistan's plains,
> An' the women come out to cut up what remains,
> Jest roll to your rifle an' blow out your brains . . .

This last resort of Kipling's soldier was not available to Alexander's. Though—as Ptolemy admits—the mercenaries may have meant only to get away home, it is understandable that he would not take a chance on it.

Alexander's famous exploit of this campaign was the assault upon Aornus, the "Birdless Rock," a 7,000-foot massif in a curve of the Indus, its precipices carved by primeval floods. The feat astonished Sir Aurel Stein, who rediscovered it. It was unbesiegeable, having natural springs and space for farmland. It could not be bypassed, being full of warriors from miles around who would have threatened his communications. It could only be stormed. Guided by natives hostile to the defenders, Ptolemy seized an outer spur. Alexander brought up his forces, but a wide ravine still barred the way. He got his men to fell the neighbouring pinewoods, and heap up loads of timber with earth thrown on; from this mound his catapults could reach the walls while he filled in the gorge. When missiles started reaching them, the defenders began slipping away at night; he let them go, glad to make the assault less costly to his men, and was the first in the steep climb to the top. Many of the enemy were overtaken. There was an Indian legend that "Heracles" (probably the mighty bowman Rama, with his monkey bridge builders) had attempted the Rock in vain.

Effort and triumph must have left their traces. The ruler of Nysa and his nobles, anxiously seeking peace, came to his tent and found him still in his armour, dusty from the ride and spear in hand. "They were wonder-struck at the sight of him, and fell to the ground, and were a long time silent." He raised them up and reassured them. Prompted no doubt by some astute Greek trader or settler—many such had preceded the Macedonians—they begged him to spare their city because Dionysus had founded it; hence their abundant ivy, unique in those parts. Their goodwill was their soundest recommendation; but Alexander and the Companions had a delightful ramble in the sacred park of the local Indian god, hailing Dionysus in ivy crowns.

Meantime, the experienced Hephaestion had run a pontoon bridge across the Indus; no mean achievement, for it would bear an army across a wide and powerful stream. Alexander, reunited with his lover and (though not for long) with his bride, was received by King Omphis of Taxila with such a huge parade, complete with war elephants, cavalry, drums and gongs, that it looked like an advancing army, and a dreadful misunderstanding was averted just in time by Omphis' riding out in front unarmed. Alexander reciprocated; friendly signs sufficed till the arrival of the interpreters.

Nearchus, Alexander's admiral and one of his exiled boyhood friends, wrote a monograph on India, from which it seems that the Macedonians made contact chiefly, perhaps only, with the Aryan conquerors from the north, who still preserved traditions of their ancient nomadic life. The Nyseans were so fair they were not known to be Indians; the men of the Punjab are described as very tall. Community of race, however, had not kept the Punjab kingdoms, any more than the Greek states, from chronic war; a fact Alexander already knew and had exploited. Alliance with Omphis meant the enmity of his powerful neighbour Porus, whose land lay east of the next river arm, the Hydaspes. Alexander, after putting on an impressive parade, began to prepare for battle.

He made a point, however, of visiting the local ascetics, or naked philosophers as his men called them. Buddhism was now two centuries old, and though its sphere was further east, its influence may have inclined these Hindus towards the "middle way"; they did not practise crippling mortifications, but lived without possessions, fed by the community, in detachment from worldly desires. Arrian (who generally uses Nearchus for descriptive passages on India, Ptolemy for war) says that in rebuke of Alexander's ambition they struck their feet upon the ground, meaning that only the earth under his soles could be his for all his restlessness. He admired their independence, and persuaded one of them to join his court, despite the others' reproofs. Known to the Macedonians as Calanus, he was in his sixties; Strabo says that he had taken in his twenties a forty-year vow which had now expired, and was free to do as he chose. It is a great pity we have no record of what he and Alexander discussed together. The strange friendship lasted, as its dramatic end was to prove.

A formal request for Porus' allegiance produced the expected defiance. Alexander mobilized with Omphis; paying little heed to the entrance on the scene of a more insidious foe, the monsoon rains.

He was realistic about human enemies; unlike Demosthenes he never underrated them. This good judgment failed him more than once in respect of weather. His rigorous training by Leonidas in childhood may have conditioned him to think of it in terms of hardship to be put up with, rather than real strategic threat. Someone must have told him how long and heavy the rains would be; he would have replied that soldiers must expect to get wet sometimes, and they all knew he would get wet with them. They had had rest time after their hard fights in the hills (Hephaestion's army had had some too, passed over almost in silence by Ptolemy, who gave his own exploits generous coverage). Any further delay would look like weakness. Through a growing downpour, Alexander led his men to the Hydaspes. It was beginning to rise. Hephaestion had had his pontoons carted from the Indus; but it was already too late to use them except as rafts. Opposite, at the easiest crossing point, King Porus and his army waited, with two hundred war elephants.

For months Alexander had been fighting on foot; but for a pitched battle he must use cavalry, and horses were terrified of elephants. In the field they could be dealt with; the point of crucial danger was the moment of landing. If they were on the bank, the horses would plunge off the rafts in panic, and be swept away.

No operation of Alexander's better displays his many-sided military genius than the battle of the Hydaspes: war psychology, cool nerve, swift reaction in emergency, resource, organization, and the leadership by which total trust is inspired. Day after day, in pouring rain and thunderstorms, with the river steadily rising, he played an elaborate game of bluff. He made large troop movements to likely crossing points, launching boats and rafts in suggestive ways. He built up ostentatious stores, making it known that he thought of sitting out the floods till their winter fall. He kept Porus guessing not only at his plans, but at his quality. He showed every sign of irresolution. He marched his army by night along the bank, to blow trumpets and yell war cries till Porus and all the elephants had marched to meet him; then he retired, leaving the enemy to wait in the wet till morning. He did it night after night. Porus, a warrior of towering stature, began thoroughly to despise him, and stopped moving elephants each time he made a noise. Alexander was now ready.

He chose an upstream bend, where a headland and wooded island would screen him. The rafts were brought

by stealthy land portage. Craterus was left in camp with
a strong contingent, to cross when the elephants were
engaged elsewhere. Under cover of a violent thunder-
storm, Alexander reached his crossing point. Among his
officers, besides Hephaestion and Perdiccas, were Ptolemy,
Lysimachus and Seleucus, three future kings. With the
rafted horses they stole ashore. There was a bad moment
when they found the bank had been cut off by a flood
channel, but they just managed to ford it. A fascinating
detail here reveals the average height of the Greek war
horse: the men were chest deep in water, and the horses
could just keep their heads above. No elephants appeared.

Too late, Porus' scouts alerted him. He sent one of his
sons with a flying column of chariots and horsemen. They
were cut to pieces, a loss he could ill spare; his infantry
superiority was enormous, about 30,000 to Alexander's
6,000; in cavalry he was weak; he had now lost half
(his son, who was killed, as well) and was left with 2,000
to the Macedonian 5,000 or so. He disposed his huge
force on the most solid ground he could find, the cavalry
on the wings, the infantry in the centre, and in front the
wall of elephants, 100 feet apart.

Alexander was never a general to fight his last war
over again. He did not attempt the tactics of Gaugamela.
His usual right-wing station happened to suit his plan;
but when his weary infantry came struggling up through
the mud, he rested them till it was time for the decisive
thrust. Viewing the portentous line of elephants with their
weapon-bristling howdahs, he planned how to make them
fight for him.

At first he let them alone. He set his horse archers
(mostly Thracian) to harass and confuse the left-wing
cavalry, which he then charged with his own cavalry wing.
The Indian right-wing cavalry galloped round to meet
the threat. They were attacked from the rear by Coenus,

a reliable commander of whom more will be heard. Alexander pressed his assault. The cavalry retreated among the infantry, behind the elephants. Now the horse archers shot down their mahouts, and turned their arrows on the bewildered beasts; as they started milling, the phalanx, its moment come, fell on them with javelins and sarissas. (The sufferings of this intelligent and loyal creature in the service of man's aggression is one of history's shameful tragedies.) In pain and panic, bereft of their guides and friends, they flailed and trampled the troops around them, as the Macedonians cordoned the confused and desperate mob in ever-narrowing ground. The Indians had just forced a gap and started to pour out of it, when Craterus, who had meantime crossed the undefended river, arrived with his fresh troops and cut them off. The scene stuns imagination: the great horde of men and beasts, the drumming rainstorms, the neighing, trumpeting and yells, the war horns and gongs counterpointed with thunder; the deepening bog stinking of blood and elephant spoor and river slime; dark faces and fair alike inhuman with mud and rain. Allowing for the chroniclers' usual licence, the Indian casualties were terrible, the Macedonians' light. It was Alexander's last pitched battle; and, as he would have wished, it was his masterpiece.

King Porus was no Darius. On his brave elephant he fought when others fled, till, wounded in the underarm gap of his mail, he turned slowly to join the rearguard in retreat. Alexander had marked him down with admiration, and at the end sent him a royal ambassador; indiscreetly choosing the hated Omphis, whom he at once prepared to kill. Alexander found someone else, and he surrendered. The regal giant gazed down at the victorious enemy who measured beside him like a half-grown boy. How did he want to be treated, asked the muddy lad's interpreter. "Like a king," he answered. "I would do that for my own sake," said Alexander; "ask something for yours." Porus, having measured the inward as well as the outward stature, replied that all had been said which needed saying. His kingdom was restored as soon as he had given allegiance, and later added to. His loyalty was lifelong. It would seem that Alexander, honouring the brave, did not even forget his elephant. Philostratus preserves a story that in a "temple of the sun" at Taxila there was a very old elephant, formerly belonging to King Porus, dedicated there by Alexander, who gave him the Homeric name of Ajax; the people used to anoint this pensioned hero with myrrh, and decorate him with ribbons.

At Taxila, Alexander performed the funeral rites of another veteran, nearer to his heart.

> In the plains where the battle was fought, and which he set out from to cross the Hydaspes, Alexander founded cities. The first he called Nicaea, from his victory over the Indians; the other Bucephala, in memory of his horse Bucephalas who died there, not wounded at all but from exhaustion and old age. For he was about thirty years old and fell victim to fatigue; but till then had shared with Alexander many labours and dangers, never mounted except by him, since Bucephalas would bear no other rider. He was tall in stature, and valiant of heart.

The Romancers, feeling what was due to him, gave him a heroic death in battle; but both humanity and self-preservation would have kept Alexander from going into such an action on a thirty-year-old horse; and Ptolemy, his lifelong associate, must be Arrian's source here. Bucephalas had come a long way from the horse pastures of Thessaly. By the shifting channel of the Jhelum archaeologists still seek traces of his tomb.

Porus' wound did not lay him up. He was induced to

make peace with Omphis, and was soon on campaign with his new King. Alexander was ready to move east, to the sacred Ganges and its mouth in the ultimate ocean; his zest whetted by the real and the rumoured Indian marvels; the banyans which made a wood of a single tree, the sagacious elephants, the tiger skins and pearls and sapphires and rubies, the brilliant dyes of clothes, moustaches, beards and monkeys' behinds; the fishponds and the shrines.

Not all the marvels were pleasing to his soldiers. Greeks might believe that woman was an imperfect form of man, but it seemed excessive to burn her alive on his pyre. Pythons flushed from their holes by the floods were huge, but unappealing. Worse were the poison snakes also enlivened, of all sizes down to the tiny and deadly krait which can lurk in a shoe or round a door handle. Alexander collected the best Indian snake charmers and used their remedies, but many men died painfully. And always, daily, there was the rain.

He was not going to let it waste his time. He marched north against an old enemy of Porus who, hearing of the rajah's reinstatement, had declared war on both of them. His territory was reduced and handed as a gift to Porus; later in the campaign he was released to take it over. With him was sent Hephaestion, to help consolidate the conquest, found new towns and get them garrisoned. No mission could better attest the ability he had shown in diplomacy and organization; he had to set up the administration of a newly subdued province, in conference with a powerful ex-enemy, carrying also the vital responsibility for Alexander's communications. Had he been simply the beloved confidant, he would have been taken along to see the Ocean. Indeed, in view of the outcome he must have been sadly missed.

Alexander marched on towards the foothills of Kashmir,

unaware of its beauties, concerned only to clear his passage eastward. He had been told (correctly) that the king whose lands bordered the Ganges was a low-caste usurper, despised by his divided people. His lands were rich and populous, his elephants particularly large. Alexander was eager to get on. He pressed swiftly across two more rivers, one of them in spate; made a sensational assault on the city of Sangala (unusually defended with a wagon wall), routed hostile tribesmen and arranged the affairs of others who had acknowledged him. He was too busy to notice that, under a well-disciplined outer surface, his men's morale had sunk to zero.

By this time they had probably decided that it rained in India for nine or ten months a year. The miseries of constant soakings were made worse by inadequate clothes. They could well afford the good strong wool or linen they were used to; but when it wore out, they could get only wretched flimsy cotton, with no wear in it nor protection from the armour's chafing, tearing on every thorn; they referred to the stuff as "Indian rags." They were sick of trudging in pulp-wet boots through deep mud churned up by the column; of lame horses with thrushy frogs and worn hooves; of heaving at the wheels of bogged-down ox carts; of mouldy food, mildewed leather, and daily scourings of all their metal for rust. They felt no exhilaration at the thought of larger elephants, or new tribes of warriors, or the half-month march through desert which they heard would lie between. There was one more Punjab river left to cross, the Beas. Camping on its banks, they put their heads together; in significant numbers, they decided not to cross it.

Once aware of their disaffection, Alexander took it seriously. He knew their discomforts and sympathized; but he had dealt with it all before, he had never failed to pick up their spirits and carry them along with him, and had no fear of failing now. He called the regimental officers together; his address in Arrian shows that he knew they were dejected too. He recalled past exploits and victories and their rich rewards; he reminded them that he had always shared the hardships and let them share the spoils. It is a lovely thing, he said, to live with courage, and die leaving an everlasting fame. When they had reached the Endless Ocean, all could go home who wished; it would be easy then; for, he assured them with passionate conviction, it was well known that Ocean flowed into the Caspian Sea. He recalled to them that Heracles by labours became divine.

It was probably one of his best speeches. This time it failed. The cast-iron-reliable Coenus broke the unresponsive silence. With meticulous respect and courtesy, he said the officers had no complaints; Alexander's generosity had left them none; they were already overpaid even for future hardships. But he would presume to speak for the men. Arrian, himself a soldier, gives him a moving directness and simplicity. He spoke of their weariness (it was eight years since he had set out with Alexander); of their homesickness for wives and children left behind; of their many dead. "Most have died of sickness." In an age without antibiotics, bad water and tropical diseases had killed more than the enemies on whom they had never turned their backs. Old enough, probably, to be Alexander's father, he urged him to let his mother have a sight of him. Let him lead his veterans home, with the loot which would set them up as gentlemen in the homeland, and bring out the young men who would follow him to further conquests. When Coenus ended, the rest did not cheer; they wept.

Alexander had no illusions; he had met rock at last. Still undespairing, he dismissed them brusquely, hoping they would think again. Nothing happened. He called them back, told them they could go as soon as they liked and leave him to advance with the auxiliaries; then flung back into his tent, and shut out everyone. Intellectually he may have seen it as Achilles' angry withdrawal; emotionally, in view of their extraordinary bond, it had something feminine, an appeal to their concern over his wounds and illnesses; even over his grief, real as it had been, for Cleitus' death. This time it did not move them. He kept it up for two days; they answered sulk with sulk. On the third, he ordered the sacrificial omens to be taken for crossing the river. Whether by Ammon's guidance or his son's, all the omens were adverse. He gave it out that he would turn back.

Their anger vanished. They were all his again. They shouted and cried with joy. Many came to his tent invoking blessings on him, saying that this, his sole defeat, was the victory of his kindness. Though the word defeat must have stung, he kept, as he would to the end, his sense of style. He made an occasion of it, holding games and horse races, dedicating the army to the twelve Olympian gods, to each of whom he raised a tower-tall altar (they have defied discovery; perhaps all he had was mud brick), marking the limit of his enterprise. Then he returned to Hephaestion's new cities, where he could unburden himself to the one man who would understand.

The bitterness he felt was probably lifelong. It is not unlikely he could have reached the Bay of Bengal; his intelligence about the route was sound. There is no telling, however, what further knowledge the journey might have brought him of the vast Far Eastern land masses forever beyond his reach, or with what sense of diminishment it might have shaken his soul. The gods may have been kinder than he knew.

THE MARCH TO BABYLON

If the Macedonians expected an easy march through the Khyber and peaceful Sogdiana, they had reckoned without Alexander, who told them acidly that they must at least allow him to leave India, not bolt from it. He had just had reliable information that the Indus did not flow into the Nile, but into the Endless Ocean. Baulked of reaching it eastward, he would not be stopped from getting to it in the west. There was more to this than the thirst of the explorer; like most of his "longings," it had a practical side. From the Indus mouth he had been told of a seaway direct to Persia. It was said in his day that "the sea unites, the land divides"; it was quicker by water wherever water was, and frequently less dangerous. There was promise of a splendid trade route, cutting out the long, hard caravan trail beset with bandits; the coast road was said to be difficult; the obvious answer was the sea. Some states in the western Punjab had not paid allegiance yet; he would therefore voyage down the river till he met resistance, deal with it, reach the Ocean, and send the fleet to Persia while he marched beside it to keep it supplied from land, noting future sites for harbourage. His friend Nearchus, from the seafaring island of Crete, was given the post of admiral.

For the intermediate Indus voyage, Hephaestion would march along the left bank, in command of most of the army, the elephants, and the huge train of noncombatants; including, presumably, Roxane after another brief re-union. Her husband can hardly have taken her to the Beas through swollen torrents and drenching rain; nor would he be taking her now in a war galley on a crocodile-infested river known to have dangerous rapids. For some-thing like a year, she must have spent more time in Hephaestion's custody than in his. On the right bank, Craterus would lead a rather smaller force. Hephaestion was now his equal in rank; rivalry had been felt, and there had been some kind of friction, which Alexander had smoothed over with mingled firmness and tact. This sep-aration gave them time to cool off, and no more is heard of it.

While the fleet was preparing, one more name was added to the long roster of the dead from sickness, of whom Coenus had spoken: Coenus himself. Cholera was no doubt endemic in India then as now. He had voiced the men's discontent, not incited it; and Alexander gave him a state funeral.

The embarkation was a spectacle on which Nearchus' memoir lingered. They were seen off in state by Porus; on whom Alexander had bestowed no mere satrapy, but a tributary kingship over all the conquests between Taxila and the Beas. There were 80 warships, but the whole fleet reached a miscellaneous 2,000. The horses were on rafts, probably Hephaestion's pontoons again, decked over; a marvel to the Indians, who had never seen a horse afloat. Nearchus gives the names of the trierarchs, honorary com-manders of the processional ships (the working captains were the pilots) and privileged to decorate them: mostly high-ranking Macedonians, including Hephaestion, who must have joined his contingent later, and Ptolemy. Be-sides some Greeks, there was, perhaps significantly, one Bagoas "son of Pharnuces" (so spelled by Nearchus); not the young favourite, but a Persian prince. Pharnaces, brother of Darius' wife and half-sister Stateira, had fallen at the Granicus. This compliment to the cousin of Alexander's future bride—the only Persian so honoured —may show his dynastic plans already forming.

At the dawn embarkation, Alexander poured libations to the river spirits, to Heracles, and the gods he usually honoured. In the first light the trumpets sounded, the chantymen timed the rowers; the high river banks gave back the sound; the Indians on shore, entranced by the show, followed it singing for miles.

Alexander stopped along the way to receive homage from various towns which had already promised it. Then they came to the dreaded confluence of the Hydaspes and Akesines, where the gorge was deep and narrow. "Even from far off one can hear the tumult of the waves." The scared rowers paused; the pilots shouted to them to pull as never before, to avoid being slewed abeam into the rapids. Somehow they shot them (the horses must have been disembarked) at the cost of some broken oars and one collision, from which part of the crews were saved. Alexander made camp, sent on the ships, and assembled his troops from both sides of the river. Ahead were the lands of the recalcitrant Mallians who had defied his envoys. In no mood for delay, he did not offer a second parley. Leaving Craterus in charge of his base and the noncombatants beside the river, he advanced with a pincer movement, sending Hephaestion five day's march ahead and telling Ptolemy to keep three days behind. Alexander and his men, avoiding the beaten road, made a short gruelling dash through desert, the quarter whence he would be least expected. His cavalry surprised the men of the first Mallian city still in the fields, and mowed them down as they were. He was as impatient, now, as his men to be done with India.

If he had hoped that one harsh example would end resistance, he was wrong. He had only hardened it. This was Brahmin country, and religion increased hostility.

A savage new campaign was more than his men had bargained for. Retreat would have been suicidal now; but as they stormed walled town after walled town, he found a loss of élan. For him there was only one answer to this —example. When they hung back from a breach, he leaped into it alone, and held it till they were shamed into pressing round him. The breach was forced, and many Indians burned themselves in their houses. Those who fled far were mopped up by Ptolemy and Hephaestion; but many took refuge in their chief city, on the site of modern Multan.

Leading ahead with his cavalry, Alexander managed to contain a greatly superior force which intercepted him, till the phalanx arrived to complete the rout. He then invested the city. It was the last focus of resistance, so Ptolemy and Hephaestion were sent back to the base. Alexander's second-in-command was Perdiccas, with whom he now divided his forces so as to assault the city from two sides. (Ptolemy, though absent, does not fail to point out that his hated rival was late for his assignment.) When Alexander forced a gate in the outer wall, the Mallians all fled to the inner citadel. He chased them through the streets to its walls, and ordered an immediate escalade.

Scaling ladders were brought, but, he thought, were being set up half-heartedly. He snatched one himself, planted it against the wall, and ran straight up it, holding his shield over his head, without a look to see if anyone followed. Reaching the battlements he used the shield to shove off the men above him, clawed his way on to the wall, and cleared a space with his sword. Now three of his officers scrambled up to his help: Peucestas, Leonnatus, and Abreas, a tried hero whose exploits had been recognized with double pay. The men below, seeing them stand on the wall a mark for every missile, began crowding up the ladder. Alexander had worked his spell again, but all too potently; the overburdened ladder broke, before any could reach the top. The four remained stranded; Alexander already recognized by the enemy, "not only by the splendour of his arms but by his superhuman courage." Their section of wall was in missile range from adjacent towers; also from below, there being a mound on the inner side. On to this mound, into the thick of the enemy, he jumped down alone.

Arrian gives his reasons, so typical that he may have told them himself to Ptolemy or Nearchus. "He felt that by staying where he was, he would be at great risk without achieving anything fameworthy; but if he leaped down inside the wall, that in itself might scare the Indians; and if he had to be in danger he might then sell his life dearly, after doing great deeds fit to be heard of by men to come." He did indeed scare the Indians to a distance, after killing some hand to hand; but from there they pelted him with weapons, while he had only stones to throw back. Meantime his brave companions jumped down beside him. Peucestas carried the Homeric shield from Troy, apparently his usual office though this is the first we hear of it. By the time he lifted it over Alexander, it sheltered a man at the point of death. The Mallians were big men, using powerful longbows; a three-foot arrow had gone through his corselet into his lung.

Even then he had fought on, dragging himself erect by clutching at a tree he had been using to guard his back. The movement caused a massive haemorrhage, with pneumothorax, a collapse of the punctured lung; on which he fell senseless. "Air along with blood blew out of the wound," says Arrian, a very good observation of the

bloody bubbles seen in this injury, often fatal even without subsequent exertion. The gallant Abreas died from
another "clothyard shaft" which pierced his skull.

All this time the Macedonians were frantically clamber-
ing up on each other's shoulders or anything they could
find. From the top, they stared at the inert body with
cries and wails, which changed to frenzied battle yells.
Transported with fury, grief and shame, they went through
the citadel like some scourge of the Apocalypse, killing
everyone they found, even the children.

Alexander, the arrow still in his lung fixed by its barb,
was carried out of the battle. The cultured Curtius gives
him a polished little speech, encouraging his friends to
operate. Their hesitation, at least, must have been real,
since the wound must be cut open to release the barb,
whose withdrawal was likely to kill him on the spot. He
was still pinned to his corselet. Feebly drawing his dagger,
he signed with it to saw through the shaft, since the flights
would not pass the hole in the cuirass. They managed this;
Perdiccas later claimed that it was he who, at Alexander's
special request, opened up his side. Someone else (possibly Ptolemy!) said a doctor did it; the likeliest hero is
Peucestas on the spot. The barb was tugged out; the
inevitable fresh haemorrhage followed; blood loss, agony
and shock induced nature's anesthetic, and he lost con-
sciousness again.

When the soldiers, returning from their massacre,
learned he was still alive, they stood about his tent all day
and through the night, till told that he was sleeping. His
amazing constitution had won, for now; but like Achilles
he had paid for glory with length of days. He had almost
certainly a splintered rib; certainly a torn lung, its pleura
perforated through both walls; and lacerated intercostal
muscles. In healing, all these damaged layers, normally
mobile, would knit together with adhesions of tight, ragged

scar tissue. Arrian, the only reliable source here, does not say which side it was; but with every arm movement and any hard breathing he must henceforth have felt the wound; and in three years it would kill him.

Meantime, as in his own camp hope revived, the army at the base had had word that he was dead. A reassurance was sent, but disbelieved; the men took for granted that news so appalling would be concealed by the high command. They expected not only a general Indian rising, but, being Macedonians, an immediate internecine struggle for power. We hear nothing, however, of any rivalry being renewed between Craterus and Hephaestion; he must have been too grief-stricken to care. All this could not long be kept from Alexander; who at once decided that if nothing but his physical presence would convince the army, the army would have to see him. With a week-old unhealed wound into his lung, he had himself carried to the river, about ten miles, to make the journey by water. Going upstream, the heave of the oars must have jarred him; but in a few days he was there. Nearchus described the scene.

> As soon as the ship bearing the King began to near the camp, he ordered the awning to be furled from the stern, so that all could see him. Even then the men doubted, thinking Alexander's corpse was being brought there; till at last, when the ship had moored [his sense of theatre had not deserted him] he raised his hand to the crowd; and they cried aloud, some holding up their hands to heaven, some towards Alexander; and uncontrollable tears were shed in their astonished joy. Some of the bodyguard brought him a litter as he was being carried off the ship; but he ordered a horse to be fetched him. And when he mounted it, and everyone saw him, the whole army clapped their hands repeatedly, and the banks and river-glades threw back the sound. Then when

Alexander was near his tent he got off his horse, so that
the army could see him walking. They all ran to him
from every side, some touching his hands, some his
knees, some his clothing; others just looked from near
by and blessed him as he went; some threw garlands on
him, of whatever Indian flowers were then in bloom.

Physically it must have half-killed him; emotionally it
must have been meat and drink. However, he had given
them the fright of their lives; and, not unreasonably, the
officers reproached him. His part was taken by a rustic
Boeotian subaltern, who said in the broad speech of his
people that deeds are the measure of a man. Alexander
expressed his gratitude; but a more solid comfort was the
unconditional surrender of all the Mallians, whether from
awe of his valour or terror of his men. Their powerful
neighbours, the Oxydracae, against whom he had not
struck a blow, surrendered also. No doubt he gave impressive audiences, seated, to envoys unaware that he
was as weak as a child and coughing blood at every effort.
The relative cool of winter helped his long convalescence.
He never relaxed control of the campaign. As soon as
he could be moved, he continued his progress down river,
along the way receiving embassies from his new lands,
with princely gifts of every kind from pearls to hand-
reared tame tigers.

He had also a visit from his father-in-law, Oxyartes.
Some homesick troops of the Bactrian Alexandrias had
tried to desert on the rumour of the King's death; but
probably the real motive was to learn if his daughter was
pregnant yet. Since leaving Taxila, with one brief interval
Alexander had been at war in conditions which could
not have admitted of taking her along; and since his
wound he would scarcely yet be ready for an active sex
life. He extended Oxyartes' satrapy to the edge of the

Hindu Kush, with nominal rule over the still unsubdued lands down river. His garrisons would of course be Macedonian commanded. He could hardly have been installed much further away from court. Alexander may already have had thoughts of a second, more royal marriage.

While convalescing at a camp somewhere below the Indus-Chenab confluence, he redisposed his forces. Despite his wound, despite—no doubt because of—warnings about a dangerous route, he was still resolved on leading the coastal march in support of Nearchus' fleet. It offered an irresistible mix of usefulness, challenge and romance. Cyrus the Great, and Semiramis the warrior Queen of Assyria, were both said to have come to grief there, barely getting through alive. His own plans elaborately laid, he looked forward to the triumph of bringing *his* expedition through safe and sound. It must, however, be light and mobile; it was to be provisioned by supply columns sent after it from the base.

There could be no question of bringing the main army with its elephants, masses of heavy transport, time-expired veterans, walking wounded, and noncombatants of every kind. Apart from the gruelling conditions, it could not be fed. It was now entrusted to Craterus, to be returned to Persia with the minimum of hardship. Once more Roxane was someone else's charge; only the much-enduring women of the common soldiers would follow their men along the coast.

Arrian says the whole force was rafted over to the left bank of the river—an operation which must have taken weeks—because the going that side was easier and the tribes more peaceful. This clearly points to a riverside march into Taxila, where the needed stores coud be picked up before tackling the Khyber, the main road Alexander had been at such pains to make secure. Yet it has been supposed that he launched this huge, slow-moving and highly vulnerable force directly northward (away from the river) into country never traversed by his troops, uncharted, mountainous and partly desert: the trail over the Mulla and Bolan passes to Kandahar, on which, as recently as the eighteenth century, a Persian army was in desperate straits. The "land of the Arachotians," which Arrian says Craterus traversed, is very vaguely defined and probably reached the Indus. He and his force reached their Persian rendezvous late, but in excellent fettle, testifying to a roundabout and less inhospitable route. After their departure along the river, Hephaestion remained as Alexander's undisputed second-in-command; a rank he would hold for what was left of his life.

The last obstacle between Alexander and the sea was the land of the lower Indus and its ancient, now shifted delta. One of the rajahs there, Musicanus, had withheld submission, but gave it when Alexander came; the next made but brief resistance; the third, Sambus of Sind, had sent homage beforehand, hoping for the destruction of Musicanus, his hated enemy. Angry and alarmed to find him spared, and incited by the local Brahmins, Sambus revolted, then took fright and fled. His family surrendered, blaming the Brahmins, whom Alexander hanged. During these operations Musicanus, breaking his treaty, rose in arms; probably his own Brahmins had proclaimed a holy war. As always after breach of faith, Alexander attacked à l'outrance; the towns were stormed, the men killed, the women enslaved. The Indians' use of poisoned weapons embittered the war. These lands were vital to his communications for the coastal march, and he was determined to secure them. (In this he was unsuccessful.) No personal exploit of his is here recorded, though he took the field. For the first time he must have felt the loss of that inexhaustible energy he had taken for granted all his life. He was to need all that remained, in the months ahead. Of the disabled men shepherded home by Craterus, not a few must have been fitter than the King.

The country once subdued, Hephaestion took charge of turning the chief city of Pattala into a fortified port; but no doubt he joined Alexander for his long-awaited visit to the Ocean. So, probably, did the young Bagoas, whom Alexander had not dispatched with Craterus' convoy. A dancer who kept up his practice, he had a resilience which would stand him in good stead.

The royal flotilla sailed down the north arm of the delta; but the monsoon had come round again, and it was met by a storm of wind. The ships were driven aground, and several wrecked; the natives had fled, and no local guides could at first be found. While they waited, a more dreadful portent than the storm occurred: the water sank away. Acquainted till then only with the landlocked seas, they were unaware that for the first time in their lives they were seeing the ebb tide. Greece being the seismic area that it is, some must have heard about the sinister withdrawal which precedes the *tsunami*. But after some anxious hours, the waters returned, and stayed at their former bounds. The gods had been kind, but no one had known enough to secure the stranded ships, which were badly knocked about. At length, pilots found and repairs done, Alexander put out to an offshore island, where he sacrificed to the gods whom, he said, Ammon had instructed him to honour. Then at last he emerged into open sea. Here two bulls were slaughtered and thrown in for Poseidon; and along with his libations Alexander offered the golden bowls he poured them from.

But it was only half the event he had hoped to celebrate. This should have been the eastern ocean, and its shore the end of the world; better recompense for short breath and a chronic catch in his side. It was about the time of his birthday; he was thirty-one.

Since it was for the sake of the seaway that Alexander had planned his march, the interests of the fleet were paramount. Greek ships avoided moving at night, even in known waters; in these, where the very stars were strange, it was unthinkable. Their inability to carry more than a few days' stores has already been noted; hence the necessity of victualling them from land, and protecting them when they had to beach. Thus the march had to follow the coast, not seek the easiest route inland. As long as the monsoon blew, the wind would be adverse for the ships; the march must therefore start in early autumn. Though Alexander had been warned about desert conditions, his Indian experience probably caused him to expect much more relief from autumn than he would get: cooler weather, and water from mountain snow torrents, such as were still swelling the Punjab streams. He filled in the end of summer with operations against the tribes to the north of the ancient Indus mouth and on the site of its present one, in order to secure his new harbours. Over these people, the Oreitians, he left a Macedonian satrap, who had charge of a supply train for the expedition. After it had set out, there was a revolt and this man was killed. The supplies were no doubt looted; none reached Alexander, nor, till afterwards, did the explanation.

The men of the fleet, setting out into unknown waters, were heartened to know that Nearchus, one of the King's best friends, was being hazarded in command of them— at his own eager insistence, as he himself recorded. In the event, the fleet had by far the best of it. Their hardships were dreadful, their perils great; they got from Alexander neither the provisions he had meant to leave for them, nor the wells he had meant to dig; to survive they turned pirate, raiding the sparse hovels of palaeolithic aborigines for their wretched food; they ended the voyage sun-blackened, gaunt, salt-crusted, unrecognizable ragamuffins; but almost all survived. Nearchus had twelve healthy years ahead of him.

Arrian writes that of all his sources, only Nearchus said that the full difficulties of the route were not known to Alexander. But Nearchus would have known best: Alexander's co-leader, with whom he had plotted the expedition, the arrangements for food depots, watering stations, seamarks and rendezvous. And Nearchus must be right; for had Alexander foreseen the horrors awaiting him, he would not have let camp followers join the march, still less the women and families of the soldiers. Nearer and further Asia must have been scattered already with the unmarked graves of these poor victims, not all of whom had even chosen their lot; many women had been carried off from fallen towns by men of alien races without a word of their native speech, whose children they had borne behind the nearest bush, dying or trudging on. But neither Bactrian frosts nor Indian fevers had taken the toll of them which was now to come.

The army set out with a flourish. Phoenician merchants followed it, having heard rumours of spices, one of their most precious trade goods. They were rewarded at first by a wilderness of myrrh and spikenard, whose bruising by the soldiers' feet scented the air. But it was already inhospitable land, whose thorn bushes were so savage they could drag a man from his horse. Soon it was true desert, and no food convoys had come. Alexander as arranged sent troops to look for harbours, water and forage. What they found would have helped only the still unborn science of anthropology; the coast dwellers, as Nearchus later agreed, were "more like beasts than men"; covered with hair on body as well as head, using no tools but stones, living on raw fish, drinking from brack pools dug out with their clawlike nails; quite possibly an isolated pocket of Neanderthals. When a few victuals were found inland, Alexander kept faith with the fleet, and sent down a load to the shore to be left with a seamark; but on the way, the half-starved troops of the convoy broke the seals and ate it all. Their officers reported their need; Alexander accepted it and gave no punishments. It was growing clear already that the ships must shift for themselves; he would have enough to do with those in his own charge. They had sixty days of it; the most dreadful in most of their lives.

They came into a waste of soft, wind-piled sandhills, "letting them sink as if into wet mud or untrodden snow." Horses and mules sank deeper than the men, and were more distressed, labouring over the ridges under burning sun. Autumn had brought no coolness. At long intervals there was water; the scouts would announce the length of the next march; though they moved by night, the sun was often up before they got there, and they had to press on or die. Mules and horses, foundering from exhaustion, were at once devoured, and soon their death was being expedited. Alexander was told, but turned a blind eye. His self-reproach is evident only from his conduct. He could not allow himself, as after Cleitus' killing, the luxury of seclusion.

The loss of the baggage animals and their useless carts had a grim consequence: there was no transport for the sick, or those who collapsed from sunstroke. They could not be carried by men who could barely walk. Once fallen out, they simply waited for death; "most of them sank into the sand like men lost at sea." Many died too from immoderate drinking when they came to water; they would wallow in it, fouling it for the rest. Later Alexander camped some distance from it; though not till after the march's worst disaster. They had found a wide stream bed with a summer trickle, and made camp on the scoured sands. Rain falling in distant hills caused a sudden flash flood. Instead of the hoped-for relief it was lethal. He had ordered a night of rest; the surviving women and children had dossed down close to the stream; without warning, the wall of water carried more than half away. Next day was spent in the gruelling heat searching for the dead, to give them some minimal rite of passage. Had Alexander not been up in spite of his own fatigue, he too might have been drowned; his tent was swept off, and he lost all he had in it, depending on his friends for a change of clothes. He must have needed the small comforts that were gone; the ordeal would long since have begun to tell on him. Though at least he could be sure of a decent horse, he cannot have been fit for an all-night ride under such conditions; and all responsibilities fell on him. He was lucky to have brought Hephaestion; if only *he* had lived to write his memoirs! The value of his support, never put on record by his rivals, is shown by Alexander's marks of honour later.

The column dragged on, the dying fell out, crying their names in case some friend might hear before the vultures settled. Despair was killing like a disease. Till now Alexander had ridden, and must have found that more than enough. Now he did what his nature compelled him to: dismounted, and began to lead the march on foot.

He did it, Arrian says, "with great difficulty, and as best he could." This fixes the incident to its proper place in his story, for at no earlier time is such an observation likely to have been made. Arrian adds that he did it so that the troops should bear their toil more easily from seeing it shared by *all;* in other words, he had dismounted all the officers and would not make an exception of himself. On one of the long marches which went on into the heat of the day, he was seen to be "much distressed with thirst," as well he might be; a man gasping for breath cannot shut his mouth against dust. He must have been much distressed with pain too, which he did not mention. His plight was evident; for when some of the skirmishers found a tiny puddle in a stony spruit, they hurried to him at once with the contents scooped in a helmet. It was an act of self-sacrifice to which he responded in kind; he thanked them, and poured away the water. It was as good as a share, Arrian says, to every man who saw it.

The account is detailed and factual; both Ptolemy and Aristobulus were on the expedition, and Nearchus got his information just after it. Yet there has been an odd tendency among biographers to suppose that because a slightly similar incident happened at the Oxus crossing, the story must have been transferred. It could rather be claimed that the first supports the second. The Oxus incident was largely his common form. It has been well said that when he had outdistanced other rivals he would still be the rival of himself; and in the Makran desert he was under special pressure to be so. At the Oxus the whole situation is less extreme, the hardship temporary; he does not pour away the water, for there will soon be enough for everyone, but just sends it on to the children it had been meant for; a fit young man, acting like a good officer. In Makran, he is half-dead on his feet, every breath an agony; he cannot conceal it from the onlookers. But men are dying like cattle, arguably through his misjudgment; he will not be seen taking privileges which might have saved their lives; and, even if it kills him, he will not fall below his legend. Nothing could be more typical. If one thing is certain about Alexander, it is that he valued his pride above his life.

As well as his pride he had kept his head. Dismounting the officers, which made him feel forced to walk, was

much more than a gesture. Led, not ridden, a few horses
were kept fit enough for work in an emergency. To this
piece of foresight, what was left of the expedition was to
owe survival. The crowning misery of a violent dust storm
changed the contours of the area, and wiped out all the
landmarks known to the guides. They had no knowledge
of steering by the stars, and owned that they were lost.
Alexander saw, in this despairing moment, that if they
wandered about they were doomed. The sea was on their
left and they could steer to it by the sun. With the last
usable horses, he led the scouting party himself. Man after
man fell behind as in the noon heat the horses failed; with
the last five he reached the sea. There was greenery near
the shore; they dug and found fresh water. The news was
brought to the army, and its ordeal was over. The guides
now knew the way, and they were soon in inhabited land.

Alexander had bettered the disastrous records of Cyrus
and Semiramis, whom, Nearchus' memoirs said, it had
been his ambition to outdo; but not by much. He had
brought more survivors through; but it had still been a
débâcle. Two factors had gone to it: the inadequate intelligence about the route which Nearchus speaks of, and
the failure of supplies. The Macedonian satrap responsible
for the stores was dead, as Alexander learned when he
sent to have him arrested. For the rest of the disaster he
sought no scapegoat; during the march and after, he took
the whole burden on himself. He did not even blame the
gods for it.

At last, however, abundant supplies were coming in
from the regions round; and in Carmania he saw to it that
his men were feasted, rested and amused. All the sources
speak of a Dionysiac progress towards the capital, with
free drinks at every halt; also of Alexander travelling
with friends on a purple-winged dais lashed to two chariots. Arrian adds that Ptolemy and Aristobulus omit this

last; yet it would be very like Alexander thus to disguise the fact that he had barely the strength to sit a horse. If the Mallian arrow had left him with any hope of making old bones, he had poured it away, like the water, on the Makran sands.

Any rest he got now was purely physical; he began at once to learn that while some loyal or prudent satraps had been collecting horses, camels and stores for him, others had written off his return and freely abused their powers. He heard evidence and prepared to do justice; but he kept the festival going, and found time to join in. To this we owe a remarkable testimony to the popularity which his conduct in the desert had won him, despite all that his men had suffered. Plutarch (supported by the anecdotist Athenaeus) says he watched a dancing contest in which Bagoas—who must quickly have got into shape again—carried off the prize. Still in his costume he crossed the theatre to Alexander, who kept him to sit beside him. "At which the Macedonians clapped and shouted out telling him to kiss him, till finally he took him in his arms and kissed him warmly." This story says a good deal for Bagoas, who must have refrained from everything which gets royal favourites hated; but even more for the deep affection felt for Alexander himself, extending its indulgence to whatever he set store by, even his "barbarian" eunuch.

At about this time, Craterus arrived with his multi-racial army, the elephants, Roxane, and several rebellious or oppressive satraps arrested on the way. Alexander put to death, for gross injustice to their subjects, one Persian and one Macedonian; his equal esteem passed the acid test of an equal standard. Arrian says that the chief reason for his rule being accepted by the diverse peoples he had conquered was that "he would not let them be wronged by those set over them."

But such cares were trivial compared with his anxiety for the still missing fleet. He had marched to provision and protect it, and had done neither; the thought of all these lives, among them an old and close friend's, being added to the toll, was preying on him. At last a local governor dashed in with the news that the fleet was beached; but in his eagerness to get in first for the reward, he had sent them no help or transport, so nobody arrived. Alexander, furious for his false hopes, had the man kept under arrest. At last Nearchus and a few friends, getting along as best they could, were passed by some of the scouts sent out to look for them, who had taken them for ragged vagrants. They made themselves known and were conveyed to Alexander, who embraced Nearchus and burst into tears, supposing them the sole survivors. When he heard the whole fleet was safe he wept still more with relief, saying that since its loss would have cancelled all his previous good fortune, this news was worth more to him than the conquest of all Asia. Few Greeks, and certainly not Alexander, cultivated a Roman *gravitas;* but this scene suggests the nerve storm of a debilitated system after almost unbearable strain.

There was a thanksgiving festival with a great procession, Nearchus, kempt and garlanded, riding in front with the King. Among the prizes and promotions, Peucestas, who had held the Trojan shield over Alexander at Multan, was appointed to the small top-ranking Royal Bodyguard till he could be given his real reward—the satrapy of Persia, held by a usurper with whom Alexander had yet to deal. Hephaestion was now sent off with most of the army by the pleasant coast road to Susa, to give the men from the desert a further rest. Alexander's rest, such as it was, was over. He rode up country to the royal heartland of Persia, Cyrus the Great's Pasargadae, Darius the Great's Persepolis. On whether he took Roxane, the sources are silent. He did take Bagoas, and Calanus the Indian philosopher; each in his own way must have proved himself in the fiery test of the desert. At Pasargadae, the satrap of Media brought him one Baraxis, perhaps a relative of the royal house, who had proclaimed himself king in Alexander's absence. He hanged him, and executed several governors who had outraged their vassals. His severity did him no harm in folk tradition; one of his epithets in the Persian romance is "redressor of wrongs." But it was exploited by the Athenian propagandists; and here the credulous Curtius, checked against first-hand evidence, shows how far they were prepared to go.

Aristobulus the architect described in his memoirs how eager Alexander had been to visit Cyrus' tomb as soon as he had conquered Asia. Presumably he did, while near by at Persepolis, for Aristobulus was then commissioned to inventory its contents: a typical Achaemenean royal burial, with a gold sarcophagus on a dais, surrounded with rich grave goods, jewels, weapons, and sumptuous clothes. Alexander had continued the traditional sacrifice to the hero's spirit of a horse a month. Most of the mausoleum still stands, and testifies to Aristobulus' accurate description. Its builders, as a precaution against grave robbers, had narrowed the entrance after the sarcophagus was inside. But Alexander on his return found it broken into and plundered; chunks even hacked off the coffin to get it through the door, and Cyrus' bones scattered about. Alexander would have honoured him even as an enemy (he would probably have preferred him to Darius); the callous insult to his (and Xenophon's) ideal hero enraged him. The shrine's guardian magi claimed total ignorance, and torture got nothing out of them. (Some time later the crime was traced to a Macedonian.) Aristobulus describes in detail how he was instructed to make all good exactly as he had first noted it, even to the ribbons spread upon the dais, and then to wall up the doorway. A later generation of robbers had to burrow under its threshold.

Alexander proceeded to Persepolis, where the usurping satrap Orxines was brought before him. He had appointed himself on the lawful satrap's death, and his subjects now accused him to Alexander of "killing many Persians without cause," and of plundering temples and royal tombs, presumably the rock-cut tombs of Persepolis. He was convicted, hanged, and succeeded by Peucestas, who was already thoroughly Persianized, spoke fluent Persian, and became highly esteemed.

Curtius' version was clearly concocted a very long way from Persia. But calumny often exploits a scrap of truth, and it may be a fact that Bagoas took some part in Orxines' trial; he had known, and could identify, Darius III's palace treasures, some of which may have been among the looted grave goods. The Curtius story is as follows. Orxines, a noble and virtuous satrap, public-spiritedly takes charge of Persia during Alexander's absence; and, on his return, arrives to do homage with a train of splendid gifts for him and all his retinue—except Bagoas, to whom he sends a special message that he does not honour catamites. After this typically Oriental approach to a royal favourite, the naïve and trusting Orxines awaits the reward of probity. Soon after, the tomb of Cyrus is opened (for the first time, it is here assumed); and the dead monarch, in the best traditions of Sparta or republican Rome, is found interred with only his old scimitar, bow and arrows. Alexander, utterly besotted with Bagoas, believes his lying story that Darius had told him the tomb was full of gold; this must be the source of Orxines' wealth. On this evidence he is condemned; Bagoas approaches him as he is led away, at which he exclaims scornfully that it is a new thing in Persia for a eunuch to rule. This at a court where, not two decades back, a eunuch Grand Vizier had been supreme, and had killed two kings! It is seldom that the process of blackwashing Alexander can be traced in such close detail.

At Persepolis, viewing the fire-blackened palace ruins, he expressed regrets. It would no longer have seemed to him the ideal climax for even the most successful party. But, as he made his way down to Susa, another burning lay before him. Calanus, who had never been ill in India, had some grave internal malady, perhaps cancer. Impatient of a long-drawn end disturbing to tranquillity, he asked of Alexander his own chosen death. Alexander pleaded with him in vain; then, knowing he would contrive it if it was refused, resolved it should be worthily done. At Susa, he commissioned Ptolemy to erect a splendid pyre. The cavalry and the royal elephants paraded. Calanus, too weak to mount the horse provided for him, was carried on a litter, singing hymns to his gods. Alexander had supplied rich funeral offerings to be burned with him, but he gave them away to friends and disciples, having no more need of possessions in death than in life. Telling them to rejoice, not mourn for him, he lay down on the pyre. When it was kindled, Alexander ordered the trumpets to sound, and the elephants to blare their royal salute; but there were no cries to drown, Calanus burned unflinching. Arrian says that Alexander was distressed because of his friendship; the rest "felt nothing but astonishment." However, the drinking bout for the wake suggests a fairly violent reaction. Alexander as usual got himself up to bed (the most hostile sources have no instance of his ever being carried there); but thirty-odd men died "of the chill"; probably from finishing under the tables on a winter night.

Arrian and Plutarch both refer to a story that Calanus' friends came up to take leave of him as he approached the pyre; but he would bid no farewell to Alexander, saying that they would meet again in Babylon.

A happier feast was the reunion with Nearchus and his fleet, which had arrived by river; the men of this much-enduring Odyssey got another festival. Awards for valour in India were given; and Hephaestion was now raised over even the highly valued Craterus to be chief Chiliarch; in Persian terms, Grand Vizier. Till now, no office had carried absolute precedence next after Alexander; he had smoothed the earlier rivalry by saying that Craterus was the King's friend, Hephaestion was Alexander's. But a shared ordeal leaves its mark on any human relationship; and this tribute must have expressed Alexander's feelings after the desert march. That Craterus accepted it without pique is evident from the perfect trust in him which Alexander showed to the end.

In Susa a few more untrustworthy satraps were deposed or, when too criminal and dangerous, killed. The replacements were, overall, more often Macedonian than Persian; men proved in command under his eye. These choices turned out well; but any Greek hopes that he would now discard "barbarian ways" soon faded. Hurried along, like so many short-lived men of genius, by a kind of creative urgency, he was planning for a new generation in which such distinctions should disappear.

Before marching east he had left in the Susa palace the Queen Mother, Sisygambis, and her grandchildren. The boy, who would now be about fourteen, does not reappear in history; he must simply have been merged in the Iranian nobility during the succession wars. Both his sisters were of marriageable age. Alexander now married the elder one, at a ceremony of such importance that she could only henceforth be regarded as his chief wife. For this was much more than a wedding; unlike the burning of Persepolis, it was a genuine manifesto. Eighty other

couples shared it; chief officers and friends to whom he
gave, with large dowries, girls from the highest families in
Persia.

Roxane must have been in the city. What she said is unknown; what she thought, she wrote in blood after his
death. She bided her time. None of the chosen bridegrooms, nor the kin of the chosen brides, demurred;
Alexander's will sufficed. His own bride was called either
Stateira (her mother's name) or Barsine; the sources dif-
fer. Her sister, Drypetis, was given to Hephaestion; Alexander wanted them to be linked in kinship through their
children. Craterus got a niece of Darius; Ptolemy a
daughter of Artabazus; Nearchus a grandchild of his by
the Greek general Memnon and the other Barsine, alleged
(though improbably in her lifetime) to be the mother of
the dubious pretender. The list reveals that all this time
the children of the dead guerrilla chief, Spitamenes, had
lived under Alexander's protection; his daughter was
given to Seleucus, who, unlike most of the others, did not
desert her when Alexander was dead, or set her aside for a
more politic marriage; she became a queen and the
mother of a dynasty.

The court chamberlain, Chares, wrote a book of anecdotes called *Stories of Alexander;* among its surviving
fragments is an account of the wedding feast. On the wide
platform before the palace was erected a pavilion 800
yards in circumference. Its columns were 20 cubits high
(the cubit varied; they would have stood about 30 feet)
jewelled and gilded. Gilded curtain rods supported side
curtains woven in patterns. There were a hundred couches
with silvered legs for the chief guests; the carpets were of
purple, scarlet and gold. Arrian says the weddings were
solemnized in the Persian manner; chairs were placed for
the bridegrooms in order of rank; after the healths had
been drunk, the brides entered and sat down each by her

groom, who took her by the hand and kissed her, Alexander doing so first. The army and the lesser guests were entertained in the court outside. Even the bridal chambers were provided by Alexander, including bedsteads plated with silver (the royal one had gold). The feast lasted five days, said Chares; the most famous exponents of every art performed. Once more Alexander honoured the actor Thettalus, who had taken such risks for him in Caria long ago. The subject-allies sent gold crowns to the huge value of 15,000 talents; these masterpieces were probably melted down to meet the still huger expenses.

Aristobulus averred that Alexander also linked himself with the older royal line of Ochus, by marrying his daughter Parysatis. If he did, it is unlikely to have been on this occasion, unless on a later day of the feast. He was sensitive to ridicule, and the only precedent for simultaneous royal bigamy had been set by the wildly unpopular and much-satirized Syracusan tyrant, Dionysius I. There is no word from Ptolemy, one of the bridal party, about this marriage. Yet it is hard to see why Aristobulus should have invented it.

The manifesto of the weddings was on the grandest scale. Alexander regularized, and dowered, the marriages of all his common soldiers who had taken Persian concubines, some 10,000. Not a few had wives in Macedon; but it legitimized the children, whom he looked upon as his wards.

Even less is known of his relationship with Barsine-Stateira than with Roxane. The one established fact is that in the following year, when Alexander died in Babylon, Roxane was there, but Stateira was at Susa. Remembering his lack of height, it is worth noting that Darius, a very tall man, had married his half-sister; so this family trait is likely to have been passed on. Roxane's name means "Little Star."

Among Alexander's boyhood friends, honoured with the noblest brides, one face was missing. Harpalus had fled. In Alexander's absence he had moved to Babylon with its enormous treasure hoard, and had had charge of the mint. Already an aesthete, he had discovered in himself a love of profusion equal to Alexander's own; and the difference of his now owning the money must have seemed trivial when there was so much. He had annoyed, rather than oppressed, the people, who resented being asked to pay semi-divine honours to two Athenian courtesans whom he had successively set up like royalty. It is uncertain whether he had counted on Alexander's death, or just on his indulgence. They had been very close; Harpalus had stuck to him through his disgrace and exile, a thing he never forgot. In spite of colossal peculations, confession and charm would probably have got the sinner off lightly, if he had kept his head. He lost it when he heard about the purge of disloyal satraps, and bolted to Greece with 6,000 talents of specie, 30 ships, presumably bought in Asia Minor, and about 6,000 Greek mercenaries of similar provenance. He had earlier shipped grain to Athens to relieve a famine, and counting on goodwill there, had formed the harebrained plan of financing a revolt. More than 300 talents went in bribes to politicians (Demosthenes got the most, to his later downfall). After complex intrigues, they decided against it but kept the money. Olympias, a more terrifying enemy than Alexander, had ordered Harpalus' arrest, and he fled by sea with his men, one of whom eventually murdered him in Crete, no doubt for his gold. If Alexander had made any real effort he could have had him seized, and his trial would have been a mere formality; even after disillusion, something of old gratitude must have remained. But the offering by a court dramatist of *Agen*—a satire-farce on Harpalus and his goddess queens, with a passing swipe at the Athenians, and Alexander as *deus ex machina*—was not unwelcome, for fragments still survive.

After the dowry payments, Susa overflowed with money; and the traders who lived off the soldiers thought it opportune to foreclose on their ruinous debts. They had lived with the riches and recklessness of buccaneers. They were now in trouble; and Alexander with one of his huge gestures announced he would settle up for them all. But they took it with a new suspicion. At Susa he had acquired not only a Persian bride but, automatically, a Persian court; over and above which, he had introduced Persian soldiers into the most exclusive regiments. The Macedonians began to feel slighted. He was, and ought to remain, their Alexander, not the barbarians' Great King. Word went round that his offer had been made in order to find out, for disciplinary reasons, which of them were overspending their pay. Names were slow to come in. When he learned why, it hurt both his feelings and his pride. He said with dignity that the King must never lie, nor should his subjects ever suppose it. The sentiment was so Persian that it might have come from Cyrus; but he backed it up with proof. Writing things were removed from the money tables; any man who produced a debtor's bond was paid, in the certainty that no record had been made of it. It cost him 10,000 talents, some of it in false pretences; and for the time it won them over. But their amour-propre was soon to be shocked again.

Five years before, while still in Bactria, he had laid down a project which now matured: 30,000 Persian boys had been enrolled in their several provinces, trained in the use of Macedonian weapons (which had seemingly included teaching them Greek) and put into Macedonian dress. This seedling army was now ripe, and had been brought to Susa for his approval. Now about eighteen, they had been hand-picked for grace and physique. When

in their handsome panoplies they manœuvred before
Alexander, he was so pleased with their dash and skill
that in an unguarded moment he called them his Successors.

How many of these boys, half a century on, must have
told their grandsons that once in their youth, in distant
Susa, with their own eyes they had beheld Sikandar! Thus
are legends born. But the veterans of India, weatherworn,
gnarled and scarred, looked sourly at the polished parade.
There were already far too many Persians in the army. A
campaign wife had been all very well in Bactria; a Persian
royal wedding was another thing. They hated seeing a
good Macedonian soldier like Peucestas cheerfully setting
up a satrap's court with the King's approval, talking Persian like a native, going about disgustingly in trousers.
They had been furious when a mixed regiment with Macedonians in it had been put under Persian officers. Now
came a whole corps of Hellenized Persians, presuming to
wear *their* clothes and show off with their weapons. It
was not Alexander's successors they saw here, but their
own; he was "devising every means of doing without
Macedonians"; he was "getting entirely barbarized." Old
grouses and new were angrily milled over, but discipline
still held.

Alexander, as it happened, was occupied just then as
a Greek with Greeks. He had sent to the cities of the
League of Corinth—the states which had originally appointed him as war leader—requiring them to give him
divine honours.

There are rooted misinterpretations of history with
which the truth seems never to catch up. There will always be people who believe that Canute was serious when
he ordered the tide to turn, though all his own contemporaries knew it was a moral object lesson; and people
who will go on supposing that this request of Alexander's

marked the onset of megalomania. Not only had such honours voluntarily been offered him years before by several liberated cities of Asian Greece; they had often been conferred on men with poorer claims. The oligarchs of Samos, less than a century earlier, had granted them to the brutal Spartan general, Lysander, for maintaining their tyranny. In a moment of sentiment, Harpalus had even set up a posthumous cult of his first hetaira as Aphrodite; he had been laughed at, not stoned for blasphemy. Divine honours, however solemnly awarded, carried no specific rights or immunities. To the rationalist intellectuals of the day, they were an important distinction, like a Nobel Prize; to the many for whom religion still had meaning, they implied that the recipient had risen above the normal limitations of humanity, to a point where the gods must have had a hand in it. The birth legends which so swiftly adhered to Alexander after his death were not propaganda, but hagiography.

He himself, as so often, was thinking on two planes at once. Within, he felt in himself the divine spark hailed by Ammon. Objectively, he needed for purely political reasons the status its recognition would give. He did not ask it in Persia or Macedon, in neither of which, for different reasons, it would have been understood; in Egypt, he already had it; he wanted it in Greece where it could be used. And he got it without trouble, not because he had inspired any reverence there, but because Greek politicians were profoundly cynical. What they did respect was power. Even Demosthenes shrugged it off with "Let Alexander be the son of Zeus. And Poseidon's too if he likes." Ritual religious embassies, with the ritual tributes, were planned to set out next spring. Without awaiting them, Alexander moved at once to the real object of the exercise. Unconstitutionally, but imperiously, he ordered the cities to receive back their exiles.

No other man could have done it. Exiles were products of the blood feud. Party strife in the Greek city-states went back to before the time of the sixth-century tyrants, whom it had put in power. After every fifth-century coup, leaders of the ousted party were expelled, lest they get even with their enemies. So, often, were too-powerful rivals; some had retaliated by getting even with their country, like that baleful meteor Alcibiades. Others had welcomed foreign invaders in return for support. In the fourth century it had continued; Greek Asia was full of exiles. Darius' 50,000 mercenaries had been partly made up of them; lest Alexander should have let the problem slip his mind, he had lately learned that Harpalus had been able to raise no less than 6,000 of such desperate men for his wildcat gamble. And there were still some 20,000 of them adrift, ready tools for any adventurer who could feed them. Alexander's demand for their recall meant, of course, recall with immunity; common murderers and temple robbers were barred. When the herald gave out the news at the next Olympic Games, there was a furor of cheering.

Overall it worked, averting much misery. But in the cities there was some perturbation. In that individualistic society, it meant getting back one's personal enemy, knowing just who had worked his downfall; biding his time, and his sons along with him. Sometimes it meant the unwelcome restitution of his land. Last, and most seriously, it undermined the policies of Antipater in the southern states. He had ensured their subservience to Macedon by supporting many harsh oligarch governments, and large numbers of the exiles had been expelled by them. Alexander was getting into touch with the West after a long and busy absence; firmly, though civilly, he was letting it be known that he did not approve of everything that had been done in his name.

In the spring of 324, after several months crowded

with these activities, he made his way towards the beautiful hill palace of Ecbatana, the Persian kings' summer resort. Probably he felt the need of rest. At all events, he had one of his longings, to explore the Tigris; it would take him the first stage by boat, while the army marched under Hephaestion's command. Before making for the hills, they were to rendezvous at Opis. This river town lay on the Royal Road to the Mediterranean; and it was here that Alexander planned to discharge his oldest veterans, with substantial long-service bonuses. It took him a good deal out of his way; but it was unthinkable to him that anyone else should see them off.

After a couple of weeks of almost unprecedented leisure, doing nothing more active than seeing waterways cleared, he got to Opis and ordered the parade. But in his short absence, the Macedonians on the march had had time to work up their grievances. Once freed from the disagreeable prospect of the Ganges campaign, and fresh after the easy return west with the inland contingent, tough old sweats in their seventh decade had no wish whatever to be discharged; they took it as an insult, prompted by his barbarian leanings, and they had enlisted their comrades' sympathy. Unsuspecting, Alexander mounted the dais on the parade ground, and thanked them for their faithful service. He had just promised them bonuses which would make them the envy of their neighbours at home, when the storm broke about his head. His voice was drowned by furious shouts from the serving troops of "You can discharge the lot of us!" and "Go marching with your Father!"

This was the kind of situation in which Roman emperors were to die like butchered boars; or, if strong enough, restore control with a bloodbath of decimations, beheadings, floggings to death. What Alexander did was to leap straight down off his dais at the yelling crowd.

His generals jumped down after him. (Hephaestion, standing next him, would have been the first.) If he had been mobbed, there would have been nothing they could do but die with him. Nobody touched him. Striding here and there he pointed out the ringleaders (so Arrian says, and Ptolemy must have been down there) and ordered their arrest. They were led away, no one obstructing. He then went back on the dais and made a speech. The army listened. Whether, in the short remainder of his life, he looked back on this as more remarkable than the storming of the Birdless Rock, there is no knowing. Perhaps he simply took it for granted.

It would be strange if his speech had not stuck in Ptolemy's memory till old age. It is magnificent, with a natural momentum far different from the frigid, baroque flourishes of Curtius' compositions; it should be read in full in Arrian. They could discharge themselves one and all, he told them; but let them first remember how Philip and Alexander had raised them from the poverty of mountain shepherds harassed by neighbour enemies ("of whom you were scared to death") to be masters of the world. It was a resounding roll of victories. He challenged them to name any wealth he had not shared with them, or hardships either. ("See here—let anyone who has wounds strip and show them, and I'll show you mine. I've no part of my body without them—at least, in front.") He reminded them that not a man had been killed in flight as long as he had led them. After a ringing peroration, he bade them go back and boast in Macedon of having abandoned him among the races they had conquered. "You will be famous among men and a pleasure to the gods when you tell the story. Go!" He flung off the platform, rode back to the royal lodging, and slammed his door.

He had made his impact. The Macedonians hung

about in camp, not knowing what to do with themselves next. Nobody left. For two days he did not appear. Then Persians were seen going in. Rumour came out. He had taken the troops at their words; he was replacing them. Alongside the great traditional Macedonian regiments, the Foot Companions, the Silver Shields, the Companion Cavalry, there would be Persian corps bearing their names. Only those who were now his kindred (the Royal Kin of the Persians, and his fellow bridegrooms) were entitled to give him the greeting kiss. The Macedonian rank and file, many of whom had joined the shouting in a mere gust of crowd excitement, now pictured young Successors marching under their old standards before they had reached the sea.

Then came the climax of this extraordinary episode. The Macedonians ran in a body to the royal terrace. They flung down their weapons and their shields, the sign of surrender in the field. As unarmed suppliants, they stood before the doors, crying to be let in. They promised to condemn the men who had incited them. They vowed to remain there day and night, till Alexander pitied them. After a while he came out. By then they were weeping, and he could not hold back his tears. He stepped forward, struggling for words. A cavalry officer called Callines spoke first. What had hurt them, he said, was his having made Persians his kin with leave to kiss him, a privilege no Macedonian had enjoyed.

> Alexander answered, "But I make you all my kinsmen, I call you that from now on." When he had said this, Callines came up and kissed him, and anyone kissed him who wished. Then they took up their arms again, and went back cheering and singing paeans to the camp.

The instigators of the mutiny were condemned to death as agreed. Arrian comments on Alexander's having ordered their arrest, "For his temper had worsened at this time"; a startling light upon his earlier tolerance, but probably true; increased fatigue and recurrent pain do make for irritability. T. E. Lawrence says in *The Mint,* "After that Handley crash in Rome the X-ray showed one rib furred like the bristles of a toothbrush against the wall of my chest, and much lung-pumping thrusts its thin dagger-pain into my heart." The wall of Alexander's chest had been perforated; his rib is more likely to have had spikes than bristles; and his X-ray would probably have shocked a thoracic surgeon. But whatever his recent anger, its sequel had deeply touched the romantic in him. He had made it up like a lovers' quarrel; but it needed a bigger gesture. With his usual mixture of drama and practicality, he offered public thanksgiving at which both Greek seers and Persian magi officiated, followed by an enormous open-air feast of reconciliation. All the Macedonians (Arrian must mean all the officers) sat round him; next came the Persians; the foreign auxiliaries took precedence by their military records. He and his comrades drank from the same loving cup. "And he prayed for all kinds of blessings, and for harmony; above all between Greeks and Persians in their common land. It is said that nine thousand shared the feast."

After this, 10,000 elderly mercenaries were affectionately seen off without trouble; paid for their travel time, with a bounty of a talent each. Alexander took into his care the children of their campaign wives; he knew what their lives would be as foreign bastards in Macedon, and promised to have the boys brought up as Macedonians and good soldiers. He would present them to their fathers when they were men. Why not? He was only thirty-two.

Contained in the veterans' departure was an act of great political significance. They went under the command of Craterus, allegedly in need of sick leave (perhaps really

so; he was given a deputy in case of his incapacitation);
but appointed, when he reached Macedon, to assume
the Regency.

Antipater had held this office ever since Alexander's
boyhood in every absence of two successive kings, except when it was held by Alexander. For ten years he had
been the virtual master of Greece. He was now ordered
to come out with the draft of fresh troops from Macedon.
What plans Alexander had for him is uncertain, since he
never came. Alexander may have merely wished to separate him from Olympias as he had once temporarily
separated Craterus and Hephaestion. The constant friction
between Queen and Regent was an old story; but new
factors had accumulated. There was the restoration of
the exiles thrown out by Antipater's puppet regimes;
there was his continued close friendship with Aristotle,
from whom since the squires' conspiracy Alexander had
been estranged. Olympias, though mischievous, was not
a fool, and may have sent information which her son took
seriously. Arrian says that he never at any time expressed
the least ill will to Antipater; who, however, was extremely
perturbed when the royal courier reached him. While
Craterus was crossing Asia at the easy pace his health
and his veterans' needed, the Regent sent off his son Cassander to plead his cause. The two men must have met
somewhere along the road; and the encounter can hardly
have been amicable.

Meantime, Alexander was traveling on from Opis to
Ecbatana; and here Arrian, nearly all of whose text has
survived, has a frustrating gap in an important human
story. The text reads, after the tear in it, ". . . Hephaestion. It is said that yielding to these words, Hephaestion
was reconciled with Eumenes; unwillingly, Eumenes being willing." It may be inferred that these words were
Alexander's. Plutarch, an inveterate muddler whose

chronology hardly exists, says that during the Indian campaign Hephaestion and Craterus drew their swords upon each other and a faction fight was about to start, when Alexander rode up and stopped it, rebuking Hephaestion publicly and Craterus in private. The course of subsequent events makes it seem much more likely that this incident belongs to Hephaestion's quarrel with Eumenes.

Eumenes was a distinguished Greek, one of the Susa bridegrooms. He had been private secretary in turn to Philip and Alexander, and under the latter had held command in the field as well. He was a shrewd and capable man, active later in the succession wars. He had had a little brush with Alexander which has had serious consequences for history. After the desert march, Alexander's immediate supply of money had run out, and he asked his friends for a whip-round loan. Eumenes' contribution was very mean; and since Alexander was known to return such favours with interest, he was annoyed. With simple, not to say crude, Macedonian humour, he arranged for Eumenes' tent to catch fire, in order to observe the salvage. It amounted to 1,000 talents in specie, an enormous fortune; but the royal archives and correspondence had gone up in smoke, a loss scholars are still lamenting. If Eumenes already disliked Hephaestion he may have blamed him for the idea. Later, when Susa was crowded out for the festival, Hephaestion, then high in power, had billeted a visiting musician in the house reserved by Eumenes; and there had been a row, in which blame cannot be apportioned since no more details survive. This feud must have smouldered on the march to Opis; and seemingly in the incident missing from Arrian it broke out in flame. Alexander may have lost his temper—especially if he thought that faction among the troops had contributed to the mutiny—or he may have acted in cool-headed judgment to prevent a dangerous brawl. Arrian's account of his words would be worth much more than Plutarch's, who says, in his Craterus version of the story, that Alexander reminded Hephaestion to whom he owed his position, and threatened death to whichever of the men opened the feud again. Whatever really happened would be of deep interest, especially in view of its sequel.

Alexander with his court, including Roxane but not Barsine-Stateira (she must have remained with her grandmother in the Susa harem), rode up towards Ecbatana, viewing on the way the royal horse herds, and a parade of "Amazons" laid on by a local satrap, of whom he had once inquired about this fabled race; perhaps the idea of them appealed to his ambisexual nature. They now appeared, classically correct down to the bared right breast, and armed with the traditional small axe. Though they manœuvred dashingly, Alexander did not think their unaccustomed weapons would avail them much against sex-starved soldiers, and had them escorted protectively out of camp.

Ecbatana, the beautiful city romantically described by much-travelled Herodotus, must have been a cold lodging for poor Darius' last winter; it was in summer perfection now. Alexander, though busy with future plans (he wanted the Caspian explored in the hope of a northeast passage to India), relaxed at last in this Persian paradise—the word itself is Persian, and means a beautiful park. Ever averse to doing nothing, he invited along the usual crowd of distinguished artists, and held competitions, banquets and games. No doubt drink flowed freely, though not more than often before. It is important to remember that the behaviour pattern of heavy drinkers, after the point of disinhibition has been reached, is always essentially repetitive. Had Alexander become increasingly addicted, we should certainly hear of outbreaks of violence, similar to the one which caused Cleitus' death. It may be inferred that his penitence was more than temporary; it taught him a dreadful lesson.

During these festivities, Hephaestion went down with a fever, but after a week was mending. Alexander left the palace to preside over an athletic contest for boys. A message reached him that Hephaestion was suddenly worse. "They say the stadium was full of people"; leaving them to stare at his abrupt departure, he hurried to the sickbed, but was still too late.

Against danger, wounds, extremes of weather, hardship, fatigue, sickness, the pressure of responsibility, the fear of his own death, he had willed himself into invulnerable fortitude. This blow struck him where he was without defence, and his reason barely withstood it. For a day and a night he lay upon the body, till his friends dragged him off by force; for three days he could only lie weeping or mute, fasting and unapproachable. The tragedy he had enacted to impress the soldiers at Opis was changed to bitter reality. When he roused himself it was to a wild extravagance of mourning. He sheared all his hair like Achilles for Patroclus (the usual tribute was a single lock, tied into a grave wreath). He had the manes and tails of all the horses clipped as well, and the ornaments removed from the city walls.

The sources give no reason to suppose that the lovers had been still estranged when Hephaestion died. But the self-reproaches of bereavement are pitilessly retrospective; everything is remembered. Not long since, Alexander had put kingship before friendship, perhaps with good cause; but such things are re-lived with agony. Certainly for a time he was barely rational. It is, however, by no means certain that he was irrational to hang Hephaestion's doctor.

Plutarch says that while this doctor (a Greek called Glaucias; the trusted Philip must have been dead) was at the theatre, the patient broke his diet (unspecified) and had for breakfast a chicken and a bottle of wine. (The Greeks normally took wine at breakfast.) Arrian mentions wine alone. Whatever he had, he died very soon after, since Alexander lay on the body "the greater part of the day." Arrian, who uses a number of sources for this event which unluckily he does not name, quotes one as saying that Alexander put the doctor to death for giving a noxious drug. Not only was this a reasonable suspicion then; it still is today.

This sudden crisis in a young, convalescent man is very hard to account for. Peritonitis from burst appendix is not an instant killer. Typhoid suggests itself; it causes hunger pains, solid food will perforate the ulcerated intestine and the patient can die of bleeding; but this process would be considered rapid if it took as little as six hours; and Alexander must have galloped back from the stadium in something more like minutes. Such a swift collapse *could* be produced by an atypical, massive haemorrhage; but it is far more consistent with poisoning, and would certainly seem so to Alexander with the medical knowledge of his day. The doctor's position was invidious. He could have given the wrong medicine while everyone was at the festival; told the patient (afterwards denying it) that he might take a meal, which could then be blamed for the death; and then gone off where he could not be found—this was anyway reprehensible—leaving the drug to work. It was no doubt the vain search for him which caused the fatal delay in sending for Alexander. Like all powerful men Hephaestion had enemies, and this Alexander knew. Patroclus must be avenged, and Achilles was in no state to split hairs about it. But after his first frenzy he would know that Glaucias, if guilty, could only have been an agent; and with him had died the knowledge of his principal.

Theoretically, Craterus could have planned it from a distance; but towards him Alexander never showed the least impairment of trust, which shows that any conflict between him and Hephaestion must long since have blown over. It was Eumenes who lived in terror from day to day. *His* feud had been recent, long and hot. Plutarch, who wrote a separate Life of him, says Alexander had quickly regretted having supported him against Hephaestion. Regret had now turned to wormwood. He was harsh to anyone who had been at odds with the dead man, but most to Eumenes, whom he suspected of rejoicing. Considering his state of mind, Eumenes must have wondered how soon he would wake up one morning convinced that he knew the murderer. The secretary, a prudent man of affairs, protected himself by instituting elaborate and costly memorial dedications. Alexander, who had known him all his life, must, as he came to himself, have abandoned his suspicions; for he relented at these tributes, and devoted himself to his own offerings. To a man of his time they were a form of communication with the departed, the only one now left him; and, in spite of Calanus' teachings, action was the only release he knew.

He forbade all music in court and camp; he ordered mourning in every city of the empire; he dedicated to Hephaestion his late regiment, to bear his name in perpetuity and carry his image as its standard. Architects and sculptors were set designing memorial shrines and statues for the larger cities. Alexandria's were to be outstanding; and here the extravagant Pseudo-Callisthenes is for once of value; he can at least be listened to when describing his native town. Arrian quotes, and rightly

deplores, a letter purporting to be from Alexander to
Cleomenes, satrap of Egypt, the man later turned out
by Ptolemy. It says that in return for the proper care of
Hephaestion's shrines, Cleomenes will be granted immunity for all offences, past *or future*. The document is of
some importance, since if Alexander wrote it he must
have been temporarily insane; but in the form here given
it is certainly spurious (there is a reference to the Pharos,
built eighty years later); and the nature of the immunity
really granted can be guessed from Pseudo-Callisthenes.
Describing Ptolemy's foundation of a state cult temple
to Sarapis and Apis, he defines the status of its High
Priest, his regalia, and his stipend. "And he would be
inviolate and free from every obligation." Alexander
knew as much as Ptolemy about Egyptian religious procedure; his real instruction must have been to set up such
an inviolate priesthood for the cult of Hephaestion.

Saddest and most desperate was an embassy to
Ammon's oracle at Siwah, asking for Hephaestion to
be granted divine honours. (Hence of course the priesthood.) It was more than an aggrandizement of the dead.
How else could the deified son of Ammon be reunited,
in the world to come, with the mortal son of Amyntor of
Pella?

Concerned with all this he forgot his distraught suspicions. Among those on whom they fell, there is no
word of the one with the strongest motive of all; who,
comforting him in his loss, must have most rejoiced at it.
He was not to know that she had resolution and ruth-
lessness enough to have brought it about. That was not
revealed till after he was dead. Then it was clear that no
one can have hated Hephaestion as bitterly as did
Roxane, who murdered his young widow the moment her
hands were free.

Before leaving Ecbatana, the crowd of artists gathered

for the festival was summoned from its mourning silence
to compete in funeral games. The funeral itself was to be
in Babylon, by Homeric fire. The embalmed body was
entrusted to the convoy of Perdiccas, the new Chiliarch,
a connection of the Macedonian royal house and bearing
one of its traditional names. Alexander himself, restless
to be gone and dull his grief with action, led an expedition
against a brigand tribe, the Cossaeans, who had long
plagued the road between Babylon and Susa. The Persian
kings had never succeeded in subduing them, finding it
cheaper to buy them off. He went after them in their
winter forts—in summer they lived as nomads—and
forced them to surrender. (With his usual respect for
the brave, he recruited a corps of them later.) Ptolemy,
his co-commander, reported it a tough mountain campaign, in which Alexander was active. His chest wound
must have been relieved by the months of physical rest.
Yet this war may have been his death warrant. It kept
him in the hills for two months at the time when Persian
kings had held court in Babylon for its mild winter season.
He reached it in spring, and stayed on into its hot, un-
healthy summer.

"We defy augury," says Hamlet just before his death;
recalling Alexander, whose noble dust he mused upon
in the graveyard. Alexander had had his first augury
already. A certain Apollodorus, who had a bad con-
science about some peccadillo of his committed in
Babylon while Alexander was in India, asked his brother
Peithagoras, a haruspex diviner, to read his future in
the sacrificial entrails, explaining that he stood most in
fear of Hephaestion and the King. The seer wrote to
his brother, by then in Ecbatana (there had perhaps been
a wait for an auspicious day), saying he need not fear
Hephaestion; the lobeless liver of the victim foretold his
death. He died the day after Apollodorus got the letter;

which so impressed him that he wrote back to Babylon, asking what the omens might be for Alexander. In due course the same reply came back. Evidently in the meantime Apollodorus had got over whatever fear of the King had troubled him; he went to him in sincere concern, and begged him to beware of dangers, though without disclosing the full story of the omen, or its gravity. Alexander thanked him kindly, and rode off, taking no notice, to the Cossaean war. More auguries now awaited him.

The first were fortunate. Coming down into the Euphrates plains, he was met by envoys from peoples beyond the frontiers of his empire: Carthaginians, Libyans and Ethiopians; Scythians, Celts, and the semi-barbarous Italian Tyrrhenians, Bruttians and Lucanians. They not only asked for treaties of friendship with him; they brought him their disputes to settle, as if he were an oracle above contention. Later, Arrian says, it was much disputed whether Rome had sent an embassy; he himself thought not. But Alexander certainly knew something of the Romans; his brother-in-law and uncle, Alexandros of Epirus, had fought for two years in Italy on the side of the Tarentine Greeks against the Bruttian and Lucanian incursions, till killed by treachery. He had been in alliance with Rome, and his dispatches must have reached both his sister Olympias and Alexander himself, who, whether the Romans sent him envoys or not, must already have had his eye on them—especially if not. Here history's greatest If briefly appears, and vanishes.

Men from these faraway places had never been seen by him or his people before. With new vistas, new prospects opened. But his next message from fate was personal. Nearchus, who had preceded him to Babylon, came anxiously to meet him. (Nearchus' memoirs are a deplorable loss to history. Their surviving fragments show a vivid style, a talent for description, and a deep, perceptive affection for Alexander.) He brought a message from the priests of Bel, the great god of Assyrian Babylonia, who divided sky from earth and set the courses of the stars. His priests were astrologers; and they had descried a most adverse aspect of the heavens for the King's entry into Babylon. They begged him to pass it by.

At the Tigris crossing they met him themselves, and, says Arrian, drew him apart from his companions. Presumably through an interpreter, they warned him not to continue his westward march, but to turn east. At that time of year this would have been the normal progress of a Persian king going to Susa. This one, however, had plans which could only be carried out in Babylon. He replied with a line of Euripides which said (whatever the interpreter made of it) that the best prophecies are those that come true. A sceptic he had never been; but he liked his own way, and had survived bad omens before. He had had one at Gaza, and had not bled quite to death; he had had one at the Oxus, and recovered from his cholera or whatever he had got. Yet at Multan, where he had been a hair's breadth from death, he had had no warning at all. And he had a present suspicion of ulterior motives. His vast gift to the temple restoration fund at his earlier visit had produced, he heard, no temple. Bel's tithes had been coming in ever since Xerxes' demolition; when the new structure rose, they would have to go to its upkeep instead of to the priests. After Harpalus' defalcations, he must have wondered about the building fund itself. Babylon had no reputation for austerity.

But even a suspect god should be given some benefit of doubt; so he decided to enter the city, at least, from the eastern side. He led his men round, but found the way barred by swamps. Floundering about in Euphrates mud, in deference to a mercenary ruse, would have been humiliating; it made up his divided mind. Arrian, perhaps here echoing Nearchus, says, "So partly from choice, and partly not, he disobeyed the god." Not long after his entry into the city, he sent for Apollodorus' brother, the seer Peithagoras, and asked what sign had made him send his warning. Evidently Apollodorus had been afraid to say; but one man of integrity perceived another. The omen was described; Alexander asked its real meaning, and was told, "Something very grave." His only outward response was to express respect for the seer's honesty. Aristobulus said in his memoirs that Peithagoras himself had told him this.

Ever since Hephaestion died and he hanged the doctor, it cannot have been far from Alexander's mind that Achilles had not long outlived Patroclus. Immortal Thetis, reading the fate of her mortal son, had warned him that if he avenged his friend his own death came next; he had paid the blood debt, and its price. But only a part of Alexander's mind lived with Homeric parallels. Swift-footed Achilles, a poet's great creation, had not himself ever created anything. He had not been a king, an explorer, a builder of cities or of peoples. Alexander looked westward, and planned for his next few years.

Roxane had come to Babylon, obviously by the easy Royal Road from Ecbatana, for she cannot have gone roughing it in the winter war. She was pregnant. Odd, and perhaps very significant, is the absence of any comment from Alexander, any known word about his plans if the child were male. And here a look at the map suggests an important possibility. He had "rested his men" after the campaign; and the easy route back to Babylon would be by way of Susa. Here were installed Barsine-Stateira, the young Drypetis (perhaps only since Hephaestion's death), and Sisygambis, whose influence had always been so great. If he passed through, he must have visited them; and he may then have decided that his heir should be of royal Persian blood. It is possible that at the time of his death, Darius' daughter was some months pregnant. This would make Roxane's motive for her murder much more pressing than mere revenge.

Babylon was geographically central to Alexander's empire; he intended it for the capital. Soon after he was gone it would sink into provinciality; by the first century it was in ruins. He had created in Alexandria the true centre of the Hellenistic world. But the Babylon of his day retained the traditions of royal pomp which Persia had inherited from Assyria. He half-Hellenized and enhanced it. His state pavilion was set up in the "paradise"; around him on couches with silver feet (probably the ones from the Susa wedding) sat his chief officers and friends. Near his throne stood the perfumed incense burners, ancient protection of Persian kings from the almost universal human stink (the courtier addressing Darius the Great on the Persepolis relief is holding up his hand to ward off his breath from the royal face). The beloved Bagoas now took his doubtless exalted place in a whole hierarchy of palace eunuchs, many of whom must have held office since Ochus' reign. Here was the royal harem, which they had probably taken upon themselves to replenish with youthful beauty of either or neither sex.

To the state pavilion came the sacred embassies from Greece, to acknowledge the son of Ammon. Their tributes were mainly the exquisite golden crowns of which a few lesser examples have ·survived to hint at the best; wreaths of wheat or barley ears, berried olive sprays, flowers, wrought with the delicacy of nature. Here too, at a time not exactly known, came Antipater's son Cassander as his father's envoy.

He was a man in his prime, very able, and with no aversion to war; yet Alexander when setting out for Asia had left behind his Regent's eldest son. Since Antipater was no invalid needing support, a long-standing antipathy seems the only explanation. Indeed, the unsuitability of Cassander for his mission made his father's motive in sending him dubious to the ancient world, which suspected his real task of having been more sinister. But Antipater had no one else to send, his two other sons being already with Alexander; one, Iollas, serving as his cupbearer. Ten years had passed and boyhood quarrels might have been forgotten.

Ten years had passed, for Cassander, in Macedon; excluded from the great adventure with its resplendent prizes; fighting the Spartans in a war which comparison had made to seem provincial; watching Olympias' constant intrigues against his father, whose policies had just been undermined by the Exiles' Decree. Then had come the shattering blow of his replacement and summons to court; to men already resentful and uneasy, a move of implicit threat. Neither father nor son had seen Alexander in a decade; both had contacts with the Lyceum to which the dead Callisthenes had belonged. Now, in the exotic magnificence of Babylon, Cassander saw the men who had been boys when he was a boy seated in state among the incense burners as generals and satraps; and enthroned in gold the precocious lad he had hated and envied in old days at Pella, a world ruler, a god.

Alexander for his part found Cassander no more attractive than before. Their exchanges became hostile almost at once. That Cassander jeered at a Persian doing the *proskynesis,* and that Alexander banged his head against the wall, is probably a transferred anecdote, but scarcely looks far-fetched. Long after Alexander's death, says Plutarch, the sudden sight of his statue at Delphi threw Cassander into a cold sweat. Later he killed Olym-

pias, Roxane and her son; that he would have liked to kill
Alexander is beyond question; naturally enough he is Plutarch's favourite suspect. Even now, in the teeth of the
medical evidence, he cannot be acquitted without reluctance.

With no intention of removing the trusty Craterus from
his new appointment, Alexander had small time for Cassander anyway; his own concerns were too large. His
westward movement was about to start. Its first phase
would be a coastwise exploration of the unknown Arabian
Peninsula, in search of a navigable route to Egypt. The
Egyptian end of the Red Sea he knew about already; also
about Darius the Great's canal from near Suez into the
Nile, which only needed clearing to let a navy through.
Among the papers said to have been found after his death
was a plan for the exploration of the North African coast
and construction of a road as far as the Strait of Gibraltar.
His next objective would probably have been Sicily, a
land then in vulnerable fission; its history had been
among the books sent him by Harpalus; it would have
made a good springboard for Italy. As the embassies had
shown, his reputation had already half-won his future
campaigns. The Carthaginians and the Romans would
have given him hard work; if he lived through that, there
was nothing much to stop him from getting to Britain.

The harbour of Babylon was being enlarged, and a new
fleet built there; the indomitable Nearchus was ready to
command it; Peucestas was training a loyal and disciplined Persian army; an army of young Macedonians was
due to come out with Antipater. The adventure would
start with a march of about three hundred miles from
Babylon to the mouth of the Euphrates. Here they would
rendezvous with the fleet, and turn southward, Alexander
making the supporting march by land. The narrowness of
the Gulf was already known; this time, if the coast should

turn out desert, supplies could reach them by sea. The formidable southern and Red Sea coasts were *terra incognita;* far further from help than Makran, they might have involved him in appalling disasters, though he had probably learned by now when to turn back.

Arrian comments that he was insatiable of conquest. True as this is, his whole career shows that for him power was not an end but a tool. He longed to discover, and what he found to shape creatively. The romantic love of personal heroism, which shortened his life, was also the spell which caused his men to follow him, and is inseparable from his destiny.

But all these great plans fell into the background when Deinocrates, the artist commissioned to design Hephaestion's pyre, dismissed his swarming workmen and announced that it stood complete. All was ready for what still remains the most spectacular funeral known to history. Alexander's own is no exception; his body was too sacred a relic, too great a political status symbol, to be destroyed. Patroclus was to go in the archaic way of heroes; but accompanied by a holocaust of Babylonian riches and Hellenistic art.

That so grandiose a construction was designed for burning, and built in the available time, has attracted doubt only in our century which has seen the death of handcraft. It could have been achieved, if not with ease, certainly with success, at all those courts of sixteenth-century Europe whose huge triumphal spectacles—contests in royal splendour—can still be studied in their architects' detailed drawings. All were created for occasions as ephemeral as this one. Alexander could call upon infinitely greater resources.

The form was Babylonian, a stepped pyramid or ziggurat; the art was Greek. It stood some two hundred feet high, upon a platform a furlong square, set into the vast

Babylonian outer wall. The lowest tier was of combustible palmwood columns, left open for fuel and updraught. Then the carvings began in ascending, narrowing tiers; ship prows bearing armed figures, with red felt banners hanging between to be lifted by the rising heat; then twenty-foot wreathed torches supporting eagles; then a hunting scene; then a battle of centaurs; then alternating bulls and lions; then trophies of arms; at the top, the woman-headed birds the Greeks called sirens, hollowed behind so that, before the burning, hidden singers could give them voices to praise the dead. No apex is described; this must have been the body on its bier. The use of quick-burning soft-wood would much hasten the task of the hundreds of craftsmen and their army of assistant slaves. Parts were gilded; the rest would have been painted, mainly in crimson and blue. For weeks, as the tiers rose, it must have drawn swarms of sightseers; one of whom, like a modern tourist taking snapshots, must have sketched or written the detailed description used by Diodorus. Alexander's plans purposed a permanent memorial, perhaps on the same site; whatever its form, the work not of weeks but years.

This, it might seem, was the one occasion on which he used his almost limitless power in the cause of pure self-indulgence. But for the modern sceptic one factor has disappeared: the continued presence of Hephaestion himself, wandering as Patroclus did while he awaited the fire's release; knowing of the plea for his divinity which would rescue him from some separating, inferior station in the land of the dead; understanding—had he not always understood?—the tokens of devotion and offerings of remorse.

The site of the pyre had been covered with baked tiles, to preserve the ancient Babylonian brickwork, mortared with bitumen, from the fierce heat. For the men from the west, the stupendous spectacle of the blaze must have been the memory of a lifetime; and Alexander's other tribute, a quiet and solemn little ceremony, would largely have passed them by. But for the Babylonians, it may have been more startling than the other. He ordered that during the day of the funeral the sacred fires in the temples should be extinguished. It was the logical expression of what he had said to Sisygambis years before: "He too is Alexander." Custom reserved this rite for the death of the Great King.

Alexander plunged back immediately into action. He looked forward, indeed, for as long as he had breath to tell his mind. Even the intention of the funeral had been concerned with Hephaestion's present and future fame on earth, and his enduring life in Elysium.

All this time, the new fleet had been training on the Euphrates. Himself intensely competitive, Alexander seems to have been adept in stimulating among his men keen rivalry without ill feeling; the contests with which he now enlivened the work, turning exercises into races with trophies to be won, were very popular. He was busy too with the reorganization of the army. His racial fusions were starting to work more smoothly. Peucestas had arrived with his high-grade Persian troops; promptly, and it seems with no opposition, Alexander began assigning them to units under a mixed officer corps of Persians and Macedonians. Troops from the satrapies of Asia Minor were pouring in.

The Persian Gulf expedition was almost ready to start. Today it can be safely assumed that uninhabited land is uninhabitable; there was then plenty of spare room, and on his coastal march he planned to make harbours and found colonies. His North African scheme did not, of course, depend on an Arabian sea route; if this search had to be abandoned, he could simply have started his march from Egypt. Once more exploration and pioneering were paramount in his mind.

Nothing is so wise after the event as legend. But it seems that several, at least, of Alexander's death omens were recognized as sinister at the time. It has been noted that Aristobulus had the testimony of the diviner at first hand. Another portent was the occupation of the throne, during the King's brief absence, by some man of obscure condition who seems to have been deranged; he had been under arrest for some unknown offence, but had got away and wandered into the throne room, while everyone's attention was relaxed, Alexander and his officers having taken a refreshment break elsewhere. His first warning of the event was the distraught wailing of the court eunuchs —Bagoas no doubt among them—who had seen the dreadful augury but "because of some Persian custom" could not remove the man; perhaps their incomplete manhood would have made the omen worse. Long before he conquered Persia, Alexander had known that to sit on the Great King's throne was a capital offence; he had said so in joke to the frost-numbed soldier he had been warming in his chair. Now the seers told him it was something worse than disrespect, a symbol of disaster. The man was tortured, to learn if he was the instrument of a plot; the poor wretch could only say that he had felt like sitting there, he knew not why. This made the bad luck more threatening, and to avert it he was killed; probably a kinder fate than the lot of a madman in those days.

It has been suggested that, because of previous bad omens, some Persian well-wishers had sent the man, an expendable criminal, to act as a royal scapegoat (as the disingenuous Bessus had proposed to stand in for Darius); and that Alexander had him killed in error, instead of letting him carry the bad luck away. But there seems no reason why this prophylactic measure on his behalf should not have been discussed with Alexander beforehand and the right procedure explained. It would appear that the incident was one of those portents, the product of genuine chance, which in the ancient world carried the greatest weight.

Nearer to the mark, in a realistic sense, was a sign less forcible to those who saw it; for us it has the force of being connected with the likeliest actual cause of Alexander's death.

Among the countless activities which make it incredible he could have found time for the dissipations alleged in Athens, he was concerned for the farmers on the land downstream from Babylon. They got poor irrigation, because the Euphrates was inclined to drain uselessly away from them into bogs and lakes. He took a flotilla and sailed down that way with his engineers to see what could be done. A practical system, which could be adjusted to the flow, was worked out; while he was about it he saw a good site for a town, and arranged to found one. Then he sailed back towards Babylon by way of the floodlands. Their channels were winding and complex; some of the ships were temporarily lost in them; over the years they had invaded the ancient burial grounds of the Assyrian kings, who had ruled there before the conquests of Cyrus the Great.

Alexander, who seems always to have enjoyed messing about in boats, had taken the tiller of his own ship, then under sail in a bit of wind. He was wearing the *petasos*, or Greek sun hat, with a hatband in the royal colours, purple and white. The wind caught the hat, whirled the band off, and tangled it into a clump of rushes beside a tomb. Hindsight remembered the tomb as ominous; the chief concern at the time was the loss of the royal diadem, the symbolic *mitra*. A ready seaman swam over and retrieved it; then, to keep it dry going back, tied it unthinkingly around his head. This was agreed by the seers to be not only a shocking solecism but a dire omen. He was beaten for it; but Alexander, typically thinking that his initiative should be recognized as well as his fault, gave him a talent of silver. (Some unnamed sources had him beheaded; but Aristobulus the engineer, who must have been on the expedition, is here to be believed.) None of the ancient writers recognized, even by hindsight, the more significant fact that into these swamps and channels must have drained the entire sewage effluent of densely populated Babylon.

The authenticity of the Royal Journal, which gives the daily course of Alexander's last illness, has been much debated. Some scholars point out that it is improbably frank for a court document; others suggest that it was expanded later, to refute the rumours that he had died by poison. So indeed it does; and it is hard to believe the whole account is not genuine, seeing that the case history it describes is so straightforward as to be almost classic, with a consistency far beyond the medical knowledge of the time to invent.

Whether it would have made any difference if he had taken care of himself at the outset is anybody's guess; as are the reasons why he did not. Certainly his conscious mind was not seeking death. He had conceived enough new plans to have filled a normal life span. We are here on psychosomatic ground where we know, essentially, no more than did Pythagoras, if as much. Alexander's whole life story shows that his sense of his own being was often mysterious even to himself. But it had a power he felt like a force of nature. Something more basic than vanity, something of which vanity was no more than a side effect, had brought Ammon's oracle home to him with recognition. He had grown beyond, but never out of, Homer;

and a central part of him had been Achilles ever since he had sat on old Lysimachus' knee. Patroclus had died; as far as vengeance could reach, he had been avenged; the terms of Achilles' death fate had been fulfilled. While still a boy, Alexander must have known by heart the words of the ghost returning as a dream:

> And I call upon you in sorrow, give me your hand; no longer
> shall I come back from death, once you give me my rite of burning.
> No longer shall you and I, alive, sit apart from our other
> beloved companions and make our plans, since the bitter destiny
> that was given me when I was born has opened its jaws to take me.
> And you, Achilleus, like the gods, have your own destiny . . .

The rite of burning was over. From such a furnace no pinch of mortal dust can have been recovered; much is said of Hephaestion's monuments, nothing of his tomb. Now Alexander was in a state of constant movement; by day organizing a fleet and an army, giving ceremonious audiences in the pavilion of the silver couches; at night, plunging into the distractions of the symposium or the banquet, the only way of unwinding his tensions he had ever known. If he was ready to die, his intellect had not acknowledged it. But his instincts were always powerful, often strikingly perceptive. For a decade and more his body had been cruelly overloaded; his mind for much longer, probably most of his life. While his mind pondered the omens of a throne or a purple ribbon, his instincts may have been wiser; a message may have reached them that it was his mind which could wear out first.

What he is likely to have said to himself, as he dressed for dinner and felt the first shivers of fever, is simply that

it was nothing much; like something he had picked up in
Bactria and thrown off in a couple of days; nothing to
make a fuss about. But it is perhaps significant that the
last event of his life which Arrian records before its onset
is the return of the envoys from Siwah, bringing Ammon's
oracle about Hephaestion. He did not quite qualify for a
god; but he could be worshipped as a divine hero. His
cult was authorized; his shade had the entry to the Elysian
Fields; and the difference of rank had never mattered
much. This may have been the occasion of the letter to
Cleomenes in Alexandria. It was decreed also by Alexander that all business contracts, whose form invoked gods
to witness them as God is invoked on the witness stand
today, should be inscribed "In Hephaestion's name."

Plutarch and Arrian, between them, tell the rest of the
story. Plutarch says that Alexander gave a splendid enter-
tainment in honour of Nearchus. Arrian says he had held
ceremonies that day, on his soothsayers' advice, to ward
off the evil omens. Both agree that when bedtime came,
Medius of Larissa invited him to a late-night party, promising it would be a good one.

This is the first we hear in the sources of Medius, except for the fact, recorded by Nearchus, that he had enjoyed the privilege of commanding a trireme on the Indus
cruise, indicating, since he held no high command, that he
must have been one of Alexander's friends. He was accused by ancient writers of flattery, perhaps in a book he
wrote which has disappeared, or perhaps merely because
he had won Alexander's favour. To have become a valued
companion since his bereavement must surely have needed
more than flattery; some imagination and tact; even the
most hostile sources make no sexual suggestions. Unlike
Cassander, Medius had no known motive whatever for
wishing Alexander dead, and every reason for wanting
him alive; he was a generous friend. In Cassander's rec-

ord, one murder more or less can be only a matter of detail; but Medius, whether or not an admirable man, is almost certainly a gravely slandered one.

As Alexander's host two evenings running, he had opportunity. That he was the lover of Iollas, Alexander's cupbearer, is most likely a canard meant to furnish him with a motive; Iollas, even if guilty, could have acted on his own at any time, nor could a festive occasion have freed him from responsibility. Both Arrian and Plutarch dismiss as absurd the tale that Alexander was poisoned at Medius' party; as, on the medical evidence, well they may. Both therefore mention only to reject it a story that on draining a "cup of Heracles" Alexander gave a sharp cry of pain, and had to leave the feast. It may indeed be just a propaganda story concocted during the succession wars to smear Medius or Perdiccas; but it is interesting that, if true, it would fit the clinical picture very well. It goes without saying that any poison which could produce such an effect as soon as it was swallowed would have its victim dead in convulsions well within the hour. But a "cup of Heracles" was a very large beaker, drained without heeltaps. In a Babylonian summer the wine was probably well chilled from a snow pit. A draught like this, flung down on a hot night by a man with a rising temperature, could easily cause an instant, violent stomach cramp. On no other occasion is Alexander ever said to have cried out with pain; anything so uncharacteristic has a certain persuasiveness, for in such a spasm it could have been involuntary.

If it happened, nothing much need have been thought of it at the time. Later, it would have raised dreadful doubts in the minds of Medius and his guests; mutual suspicions; personal fears. Small wonder if the incident was hushed up, and the hushing up bred sinister rumour.

Enwrapped in much mumbo-jumbo, Plutarch has prob-

ably preserved an essential truth: "the poison was water."
Most likely it was only the water of downstream Euphrates, laden with the untreated excreta of a dozen diseases.
But this, of course, is not what Plutarch meant; and
Iollas, Cassander's brother, the royal cupbearer, remains
a dubious figure still. Man did not wait for Pasteur to
learn that water could be lethal; he could connect cause
and effect. Florence Nightingale, who to the end of a long
life refused to believe in germs, was well aware that certain pumps and wells in London were dangerous. Em-
piric knowledge like this must go back to the dawn of
civilization; it was common currency in classical times. It
is an extraordinary fact that not only did the kings of
Persia have their drinking water drawn from a special
spring; they had it boiled. No one knows why, or whether
the lost science of some earlier age had been preserved as
ritual. Nor is it known whether Alexander kept it up at his
Persian court; very likely it was just continued as routine.
But, unless turbid, all water looks much alike. It may
have been the instrument of many undiscovered murders
which have passed for—as in a sense they were—natural
deaths. Its disadvantage was that it was not infallible; the
infection might not take, or the victim might recover. Its
advantage was the enormous one of being undetectable—
unless someone talked; and, according to Plutarch, someone did. That the poison was water was, he said, confided
by Antigonus One-Eye to a certain Hagnothemis, of
whom, unfortunately, nothing else is known.

He claimed that the water was sent by Antipater on
Aristotle's advice, and carried by Cassander. It was alleged to have been drawn from an outlet of the Styx at
Nonacris, its lethal power residing in its intense cold,
which would eat through anything except an ass's hoof,
in which it was conveyed.

Antigonus is little heard of while one of Alexander's officers; he became a king in nearer Asia. He bears a good character, but had later contacts with Antipater and could have heard something then. The Styx is innocuous; the obscure Hagnothemis may have been a compulsive liar; but Pseudo-Callisthenes, in a fanciful account of the murder, puts in the remarkable detail that the ass-hoof container had been *boiled*. Just as country wise women were using substances containing penicillin long before its principles were known to science, so malevolent empiricists may have found that a boiled container would preserve a microbiotic strain from destructive contact with other organisms; while the jelly formed in the hoof would make a perfect culture. Tainted water could surely have been found within a few miles of Babylon. Many such infections produce no dystentery, only fever and increasing weakness, just as the Journal describes; without a timely antibiotic, they can still end fatally.

After the party, Alexander slept most of the day. This statement has made the Journal suspect to some historians, who take it simply as the description of an all-day hangover. But extreme fatigue is typical at the onset of severe infections, often the first thing complained of. Feeling tired and off-colour, he spent the day in bed to be rested for the evening. Medius had asked him to dinner, and he went.

It is this second party which brings in question his psychological state. Here is a man with a religious respect for omens. He has had several bad ones, warning him of the gravest danger. He has spent part of the previous day in solemn ceremonies to avert it. He is planning to start on a major expedition within two weeks. He has had as good a grounding in medical science as any layman of his time. He knows he is starting to run up a fever. Yet he gets up, goes off to an informal dinner party of no ceremonial importance, and sits up half the night over the wine. All in all, it seems very odd behaviour.

Though he left late, he left before the end. Late as it was he had a bath, and for the first time felt really ill; he had a bed made up for him in the bath house by the pool, and spent the rest of the night there. In the morning he had to be carried by litter to perform the daily offering at the household altar; but he proceeded as if he had a trifling indisposition which need not impede his plans. The march was still scheduled to start in three days and the fleet to sail in four. In the sweltering heat he took another bath, after which he felt much worse; it probably brought on a rigor. He was now in high fever, but continued to organize the expedition, only postponing its departure by a few days. He began to seek in the grilling river plain the cool and shade he had known in boyhood, having himself ferried across the Euphrates to the "paradise" with its trees, and sleeping at night beside the palace bathing pool. By the ninth day he could scarcely make the offering when he had been carried to the shrine, but was still briefing his officers. Nothing is said of any doctor attending him; he may have lost faith in them since Hephaestion's death. Had he had one, the man, however blameless, would surely have been named in legend as a party to his murder. The whole account presents an extraordinary picture: stubborn mistreatment of an illness he should by now have known was dangerous; and stubborn refusal to admit the danger into his conscious thought.

Plutarch has a detail here which again casts a shadow on Iollas: "Aristobulus says that when he was light-headed with fever, he drank wine and thereon grew violently delirious." This certainly suggests that he had not been regularly drinking it; people with fever usually lose

all craving for alcohol and reject it in favour of something more refreshing; a wise provision of nature. If it was
offered him when his mind was wandering, no matter by
whom, there is a strong suspicion of malice. For a man in
his condition it was little short of poison, and may have
had a critical effect.

His delirium cannot have lasted long; but his sickness
was advancing, and on the tenth day he could deceive
himself no longer. He ordered all his chief officers to be
summoned before him, and the junior ones to assemble
outside the doors; and had himself carried back from the
garden to address them. But before he got there, the fatal
complication, whose approach he must have felt when he
gave the order, had taken hold. He could not make himself heard.

A man with lower powers of resistance would have de-
veloped pneumonia much sooner. Now it would have
spread from his damaged lung into the scar tissue of his
chest wound, and invaded the lung lining as pleurisy. He
was probably in great pain. It is evident that though his
mind was clear at the end, from this time on he could only
manage a whispered word or two.

He was now too ill to be moved from the royal bed-
chamber. All this time, the soldiers who had seen him
carried about had been fairly optimistic; most of them
must have had a bout of fever somewhere in Asia. But
what the officers had seen could not be kept secret. When
on the second day he did not appear, the men began to
say, as they had said three years before upon the Indus,
that his death was being concealed from them. They
mobbed the palace gates and demanded to see him for
themselves. They were just in time.

It can only have been on his orders that they were let
inside. A door was opened at the far end of the room, so
that they could pass through in single file; and thus Alex-

ander held his last parade. As the first man entered, he turned himself towards them, and held himself there till the last man had gone by. Not one of them went without acknowledgment; "he greeted them all, lifting his head though with difficulty, and signing to them with his eyes."

Ever ready to die in war, he must long have been prepared to die in pain, and resolved it should not diminish him. The exhaustion must have shortened his last hours, but it is unlikely that at this stage he could have recovered. The necessary suffering he accepted in return for what had been essential to him all his life: to be equal to his legend; to be beloved; and to requite it extravagantly, regardless of expense. Whether sustained by pride, by philosophy, by belief in the immortality of his fame or of his soul, he met his end with no less dignity, fortitude and consideration for others than Socrates himself. And he, till he drank the quick painless hemlock, was a healthy man with a long, fulfilled life behind him; Alexander carried it through with a great design in ruins, and in the distress of a mortal sickness.

No pretence was now maintained that he was not near death. Peucestas and six other friends spent the night in prayer for him at the temple of Sarapis, a much-metamorphosed Egyptian Asclepius whose cult Alexander seems to have brought to Babylon, where it was merged in that of some local god. Asclepius' patients slept in his sanctuary to have healing dreams; Sarapis was consulted by vigil, giving his oracular verdict at dawn. In unselfish concern for the friend whose life he had saved in India, Peucestas was absent from the death chamber, and from the shadowy power struggle already forming.

Alexander is credited with remarking ironically that he foresaw a great contest at his funeral games, but it falls a little too pat; he had never been a wit and had now no breath to spare for it. He took off his royal ring and handed it to Perdiccas, which in itself did no more than appoint a temporary deputy—he did not give up easily—though it was accepted as the appointment of a Regent. But the time came, as it was bound to come, when his generals asked him, "To whom do you leave your kingdom?"

It has been widely assumed that he was being asked to choose a successor from among his chief officers. But by now, if Barsine-Stateira was pregnant, he may have confided a secret of such dynastic importance to high-ranking friends like Perdiccas and Nearchus. If so, he had two unborn children of unknown sex; and, in case they should both be male, was being confronted by Macedonians with the age-old question of the polygamous Macedonian kings.

Arrian gives his answer: "Hoti to kratisto"—to the strongest; words which acquired the force of prophecy during the succession wars. But it can also mean, "To the best." He was dying; explanations were beyond him; he may have meant that when the children were of age, the Macedonian Assembly should choose between them. Superlative for comparative in colloquial speech was probably used as loosely then as now. That is, if "kratisto" was what he really said.

Normally pronounced, "kratisto" and "Kratero" are not very much alike. But whispered by a man rattling and gasping with pneumonia they could be confused quite easily; especially if it was convenient. Craterus was the man highest in Alexander's trust. He had already been appointed Regent of Macedon. If he was now meant to take over the Regency of the empire, on behalf of the unborn heirs, it would hardly be welcome news to Perdiccas, present holder of the royal ring. Probably Alexander's words were barely audible, except to someone leaning over him. There may have been an expedient mistake.

Early next morning, Peucestas and his friends returned from the healing shrine. They had asked the god whether it would help Alexander if he were carried into the sanctuary; but the oracle had replied that it would be better for him where he was.

No doubt the deity was concerned for his professional reputation; but his advice was sound. It allowed Alexander to produce, for the last time, that basic ingredient of all the multiform legends which his death was in process of bringing to birth—his indestructible sense of style. Curtius, for once renouncing rhetoric, gives his parting words. When Perdiccas asked him at what times he wished to have his divine honours paid him, he answered, "When you are happy."

A dark mist crossed the sky, and a bolt of lightning was seen to fall from heaven into the sea, and with it a great eagle. And the bronze statue of Arimazd in Babylon quivered; and the lightning ascended into heaven, and the eagle went with it, taking with it a radiant star. And when the star disappeared in the sky, Alexander too had shut his eyes.

The legend had begun.

POSTSCRIPT

After much wrangling, intrigue, and intervals of actual fighting, it was agreed among the generals that it was unthinkable the throne should pass to anyone not of Alexander's blood. The feeble-minded Arridaeus was brought out to rule under Perdiccas' regency, pending the birth of Roxane's child.

In Curtius' account, confused references are made in the debate to a child of Barsine. That Darius' daughter is referred to seems probable in Plutarch. The most persuasive evidence for this is the action of Roxane. Unlike Alexander when he lost Hephaestion, she proceeded at once to practical matters. She sent off by fast courier a letter to the Princess, forged in Alexander's name, summoning her immediately to Babylon. It must have been by using the royal post relay, which raced day and night, that the news of the death was outrun. If it met her on the road, she did not turn back, still expecting to be met with honour. She arrived with Drypetis her sister, Hephaestion's widow. Roxane had both of them killed, and their bodies thrown in a well. It was precisely what Olympias would have done in her position; when the two queens met, they must have found much in common.

Plutarch says that Perdiccas was her accomplice in the deed; but this is most unlikely in view of the fact that the sex of her own child was still unknown. Faced, however, with the *fait accompli,* and only a single child of Alexander now in prospect, he most probably helped to cover up for her.

The son, Alexander IV, was thirteen years old when Cassander murdered him together with Roxane. No shred of information about his character or appearance has survived.

Olympias had been lynched four years before. Cassander's soldiers, who had themselves voted for her death, could not bring themselves after all to kill the mother of Alexander. Cassander handed her over to the numerous relatives of those she herself had killed. She met her fate, of which the details are mercifully lacking, with unflinching courage.

She had outlived her son seven years. Sisygambis, the Queen Mother of Persia, survived the news of his death five days. On receiving it she bade her family and friends farewell, turned her face to the wall and died by fasting.

ANCIENT SOURCES

In courtesy to their fellow scholars, classical historians naturally and properly take for granted a previous knowledge of the ancient source material. This book is meant for general readers; and the following list may serve as a guide to those wishing to make their own assessments and explorations. Almost all the works are available in translation; the relative reliability of the more important has been discussed in the text.

Arrian, *History of Alexander*

Quintus Curtius, *History of Alexander*

Plutarch, *Parallel Lives:* Life of Alexander

Diodorus Siculus, *History* (Book XVII for Alexander's reign; but also XVI and XVIII for events preceding and following)

Justin, *Epitome of Trogus*

Additional biographical details or anecdotes

Plutarch, *Lives:* Demosthenes; Eumenes; Phocion

Plutarch, *Moralia:* On the Fortune or Virtue of Alexander; Sayings of Kings and Commanders

Strabo, *Geography* (Book XV for many quotations from Nearchus)

Athenaeus, *The Diepnosophists* (discursive gossip)

L. Pearson, *The Lost Histories of Alexander the Great* (collected fragments, with commentary on the writers). American Philological Association, New York; also printed in Great Britain 1960

Works relevant to Alexander's life and times

Demosthenes, *Orations*

Aeschines, *Orations*

Isocrates, *Epistles and Orations*

Aristotle, especially the *Politics* and *Ethics*

Diogenes Laertius, *Lives of the Philosophers:* Life of Aristotle

Works known to Alexander, which certainly or probably influenced his thought

Homer, *Iliad* R. Lattimore's verse translation, published by University of Chicago Press, Chicago and London 1962, is preferable to E. V. Rieu's prosy one, published by Penguin Books, Harmondsworth 1950)

Xenophon, *Anabasis; Cyropaedia*

Herodotus, *History*

Euripides, Tragedies (especially, perhaps, *The Bacchae*, written and first performed in Macedon)

For the legend

E. A. Wallis Budge, *The Alexander Book in Ethiopia.* Oxford University Press. London 1933

George Cary, *The Mediaeval Alexander*, ed. D. J. A. Ross. Cambridge University Press. London 1956

A. M. Wolohojian (trans.), *The Romance of Alexander the Great by Pseudo-Callisthenes* (a recent translation from a good Armenian version). Columbia University Press. New York and London 1969

H. W. Clarke's quaint literal translation (1880) of the thirteenth-century Persian *Sikandar Nama E Bara* is unfortunately scarce.

INDEX

Abdalonymus, 111
Abreas, 207, 208
Academy (Plato's), 39, 40, 54, 188
Achilles, 6, 22, 24, 28–9, 44, 75, 90, 113, 118, 202, 208, 240, 241, 247, 257
Ada (Queen of Caria), 27, 94–5, 97
Admetus, 115
Aegae, 5, 62, 146
Aelian, 33
Aeschines, 49, 67
Agriani, 77, 80, 102, 136
Alcibiades, 39, 232
Alexander III, the Great: accession, 30, 63, 69; ancestry, 24, 28, 121–2; army, 25, 30, 93, 98, 101–2, 127–8, 141–2, 149, 166–7, 200–12, 233–5, 263–4; in Athens, 54; Athens' submission, 86; attitude towards killing, 65–6, 128, 180–1; at Babylon, 139–41, 248–66; in Bactria, 168–9, 185; and Bagoas (q.v.), 154–5, 161, 185, 186, 220, 222, 223; battle tactics, 78, 101–2, 133, 134; birth, 22; birth legends, 8, 22, 24, 122, 231; books, 28, 71–3, 128, 142; and Bucephalas (q.v.), 33–4, 102, 138, 158, 198; Callisthenes' murder, 187–8; in Caria, 94–7; Cleitus' murder, 180–1; at Chaeronea (q.v.), 51–3; childhood, 23–4, 29, 30; daily routine, 125–9; at Damascus, 109–10; and Darius III (q.v.), 108–9, 132, 149–57; death, 4, 266; Demosthenes' view, 68, 82; divinity, 5, 6, 7, 12, 119, 121–2, 174, 230–1; at Dodona, 57; drinking habits, 128–9, 179–80, 239–40, 262–3; early court duties, 29–30; at Ecbatana, 239–44; education, 26–7, 39–43, 44,

46; in Egypt, 118–23; at Ephesus, 94; Exile's Decree, 231–2, 249; explorative urge, 78, 189, 254; father (Philip II, q.v.), 26, 33, 34, 45–6, 54, 55–6 58–65; first colony, 45; friendships, 26, 44, 48–9, 58, 66, 80, 99, 113–14, 128, 141, 143, 162; funeral cortège, 5–6; at Gaugamela, 34, 132–9; at Gaza, 117; Gordian knot, 98–9; at the Granicus, 90–3; half-brother (see Arridaeus); at Halicarnassus, 96–7; and Hephaestion (q.v.), 43–4, 48, 54, 60, 90, 104, 105, 121, 126, 162, 185, 186, 193, 240–4, 251–3; Hermolaus' plot, 185–7; historians' views, 13–14, 16–18, 30–2; humor, 37; at the Hydaspes, 195–8; identification with Achilles (q.v.), 28–9, 44, 75, 90, 240, 247, 257; illnesses & injuries, 99, 104, 117, 118, 171, 172, 207–9, 256, 257–66; in Illyria, 57–58; Illyrian campaigns, 47–8, 80–1; in India, 188 ff.; inheritance, 89; at the Issus, 99–107; at the Jaxartes, 171–2; legends, 7–16, 72, 182; on the Makran desert, 215–20; at Miletus, 95–6; mother (Olympias, q.v.), 23–4, 32, 48, 55, 56–7, 58, 59, 63, 64, 121, 126, 237; at Multan, 206–10; musical interests, 32–3, 38–9, 70, 90; omens, 89, 95, 96, 117, 119, 144, 202, 245, 246–7, 254–6, 258, 261; at Opis, 233–7; oracles consulted, 57, 120–21, 258; at Persepolis, 145–9, 223–4; Persian King, 172–8, 229–30; Philotas' plot, 162–6; physical appearance & dress, 26, 27, 68–70, 92, 160; and

Ptolemy (*q.v.*), 5–7, 30–2;
purge of rivals, 73–5; quoted,
37, 46, 55–6, 70, 89, 103,
104, 109, 116, 133, 197–8,
234, 235, 253, 266; re-
founding of Stagira, 46; as
regent, 44–5, 46–7, 62;
regents for, 10, 237; river
crossings—Hydaspes, 195–6
—Indus, 193, 211—Ister,
78–80—Oxus, 169–70—
Tigris, 130–1; sacrifices &
offerings, 27–8, 80, 87, 89,
90, 93–4, 112, 119, 122, 123,
125, 131, 134, 144, 202, 205,
213, 222, 262; at Sardis,
93–4; sexual nature, 48, 55,
70, 88, 95, 155, 184–5, 239;
at Sidon, 110–12, 113, 114;
Sikandar myth, 8, 9; sister
(*see* Cleopatra); and Sisygambis (*q.v.*), 104–5, 106,
132, 144; in Sogdiana, 182–5,
190; the Successors, 229–30,
235; at Susa, 142–4, 224–32,
248; at Tarsus, 99;
theatrical interest, 70, 71,
123; Theban campaign,
82–6; in Thessaly, 75; tomb,
6–7; Triballians defeated,
77; at Troy, 89–90; at
Tyre, 112, 114–15, 123;
wealth & financial arrangements, 82, 89, 93, 96, 103,
110, 123–4, 140–1, 142–4,
146, 157, 227, 228, 229,
238; weddings, 183–4, 225–7;
wives—Roxane (*q.v.*), 183–5,
186, 190, 193, 204, 239—
Barsine-Stateira (*q.v.*), 109–
10, 226, 227
Alexander IV, 10, 250, 268
Alexander's Feast (Dryden), 17
Alexandreis, 16
Alexandria, 6, 7, 31, 121, 126,
242, 248, 258
Alexandros (King of Epirus),
39, 57, 61, 245
Alexandros (of Lyncestis), 74,
82, 98, 99, 164
Amazons, 9, 28, 239
Ammon, 5, 8, 119, 120–1, 179,
202, 213, 231, 243, 248, 256,
258
Amphissa, 47, 49, 54
Amyntas, 73
Amyntor, 243
Anaxarchus, 174

Andromache, 22
Antigone, 122
Antigonus One-Eye, 260, 261
Antipater, 10, 45, 47, 83, 86, 88,
112, 126, 159, 232, 237, 248,
249, 250, 260, 261
Aornus, 192
Apelles, 69
Aphrodite, 181, 231
Apis, 119, 243
Apollo, 17, 47, 115
Apollodorus, 244–5, 247
Arbela, 130, 138
Aristander, 117
Aristobulus, 13–14, 128, 129, 187,
218, 219, 222, 227, 247, 254,
256, 262
Aristotle, 10, 11, 39–43, 46, 48,
54, 60, 64, 72, 73, 107, 108,
131, 142, 158, 159, 175, 185,
237, 260
Aristoxenus, 70
Arrian (Flavius Arrianus), 13–14,
16, 30–1, 34, 69, 78, 83–4, 85,
91, 93, 94, 97, 98, 100, 101,
102, 104, 115, 119–20, 121,
134, 144, 147, 148, 155, 164,
166, 174, 187, 194, 198, 201,
207, 209, 211, 212, 215, 217–
18, 219, 220, 224, 226, 234,
235–6, 237, 238, 239, 241,
242–3, 245, 246, 247, 250,
258, 259, 265
Arridaeus, 32, 58–9, 60, 74, 76,
128, 267
Arsames, 93
Arses, 61, 68
Artabazus, 29, 87, 109, 150, 151,
152, 155, 156, 159, 160, 169,
172, 173, 178, 183, 184, 226
Artaxerxes II, 29
Asia, 3, 5, 27, 57, 62, 71, 76,
77, 78, 84, 106, 109, 112, 125,
131, 134, 157, 215, 221, 222,
237, 249, 261, 263
Asia Minor, 35–6, 38, 59, 74, 82,
90, 93, 98, 116, 119, 124,
134, 145, 159, 232, 253
Assyria, 106, 130, 139, 211, 246,
248, 255
Athenaeus, 155, 220
Athene, 67, 90
Athens, Athenians, 10–22, 12, 17,
20, 26, 27, 32, 35, 37–8, 39,
40, 45, 47, 49, 50, 51, 53, 54,
58, 62, 66, 67, 74, 75, 82, 83,
86, 108, 110, 112, 118, 131,

144, 147, 155, 156, 164, 174, 177, 187, 188, 222, 228, 229, 255

Attalus, 35, 55, 56, 61, 64, 66, 74–5, 97, 165

Attica, 50, 53, 76, 83, 86, 175

Augustus, 7, 12

Babylon, 3, 5, 11, 99, 101, 112, 130, 137, 139, 140, 141, 146, 147, 225, 227, 228, 244 ff., 255, 256, 259, 261, 264, 267

Bactria (Bactriana), Bactrians, 129, 135, 150 ff., 160, 167, 168, 169, 178, 185, 210, 215, 229, 230, 258

Bagoas (favourite of Alexander), 151, 153–5, 156, 160 ff., 172, 173, 175, 184 ff., 213, 220, 222, 223, 248, 254

Bagoas (Grand Vizier), 61, 68, 142

Bagoas (prince), 204–5

Baraxis, 222

Barsine, 109–10, 184, 226

Barsine-Stateira (wife), 110, 226, 227, 239, 247, 248, 265, 267

Beas, 200, 204

Bel, 141, 246

Benefactors, 167

Bessus, 129, 135, 150, 151, 152, 153, 154, 156, 157, 161, 167, 168, 169, 170, 172, 182, 254

Bistanes, 150, 164, 173

Boeotia, Boeotians, 50, 51, 82, 210

Britain, 250

Bubaces, 150, 152

Bucephalas, 33, 102, 130, 136, 138, 158, 182, 198

Byzantium, 47, 77, 79

Cadmea, 76, 83

Caesar, Julius, 7, 11, 13, 36, 108, 127

Caesars, 19, 140, 160

Calanus, 194, 222, 224–5, 242

Caligula, 12

Callines, 235

Callisthenes, 10, 14, 158–9, 175, 176, 177, 185, 186, 187–8, 249. See also Pseudo-Callisthenes

Callisthenes (Valerius), 15

Caria, 27, 59, 60, 74, 94, 97, 123, 227

Carthaginians, 115, 245, 250

Caspian Sea, 150, 151, 153, 200, 239

Cassander, 6, 10–11, 16, 18, 22, 237, 248–50, 258–9, 260, 268

Celts, 80, 245

Chaeronea, 51, 75, 77, 82, 83, 85, 86, 89

Chares, 125, 174, 176, 226, 227

China, 9, 167, 189

Cilician Gates, 99

Cleitus (the Black), 92, 167, 178–80, 202, 216, 240

Cleitus (Illyrian), 80–1

Cleomenes, 243, 258

Cleopatra (Queen of Egypt), 7, 99

Cleopatra (sister), 23, 61

Coenus, 196–7, 201, 204

Companion Cavalry, 44, 49, 51, 93, 102, 135, 137, 138, 156–7, 159, 167, 193, 235

Corinth, 54, 58, 60, 76, 81, 92, 230

Cossaeans, 244, 245

Craterus, 31, 91, 122, 196, 197, 204, 205, 209, 211, 212, 213, 220, 225, 226, 236, 237, 238, 239, 242, 250, 265

Crete, 203, 228

Croesus, 93

Crusaders, 15, 97

Curtius, Quintus, 12, 34, 44, 104, 115–16, 117, 132, 139, 145, 146, 147, 150, 151, 153, 154, 155, 162 ff., 169, 182, 187, 208, 222, 223, 234, 266, 267

Cynna, 80

Cyprus, 114, 174

Cyropaedia (Xenophon), 71, 106

Cyrus the Great, 9, 71–3, 92, 93, 106, 107, 127, 139, 146, 167, 211, 219, 221, 222, 223, 255

Damascus, 104, 109, 110, 122

Darius I, the Great, 147, 171, 172, 173, 189, 221, 248, 250

Darius II, 8

Darius III, 9, 16, 17, 29, 37, 68, 74, 81, 82, 87, 90 98, 99–100, 101, 102–4, 107, 108, 109, 110, 116, 117, 120, 124, 129 ff., 142 ff., 146, 148 ff., 159, 161, 170, 183, 197, 205, 222, 223, 226, 227, 232, 239, 254, 267

Deinocrates, 251

Delphi, 47, 49, 51, 249

Demades, 86

Demaratus, 58, 92

Demosthenes, 10, 17, 37–8, 45, 47, 49, 50, 51, 53, 67, 68, 74, 81, 82, 83, 85, 86, 194, 228, 231

Diodorus, 4, 12, 34, 63, 64, 66, 73, 100, 114, 115, 137, 145, 147, 162, 164, 191, 252
Dionysius (god), 23, 53, 64, 147, 178, 180–1, 189, 193, 219
Dionysius I, of Syracuse, 25, 227
Dodona, 56, 57, 120
Drangiana, 162
Dryden, John, 17
Drypetis, 226, 247, 267
Dymnus, 162, 163

Ecbatana, 139, 146, 149, 157, 165, 172, 178, 233, 237, 239–44, 247
Egypt, 5, 6, 7, 8, 9, 31, 94, 112, 116, 118–19, 120, 122, 123, 124, 126, 134, 150, 174, 231, 243, 250, 254, 264
Elatia, 50, 51
Eleusinian Mysteries, 86
Ephesus, 94
Epictetus, 13
Epirus, 21–2, 39, 56, 57, 58, 61, 76, 245
Erigyius, 168
Ethiopians, 11, 245
Eumenes, 237, 238, 242
Euphrates, 5, 79, 107, 112, 116, 130, 135, 170, 189, 245, 246, 250, 253, 255, 260, 262
Euripides, 42, 246
Eurydice, 58, 61, 76
Exile's Decree, 231–2, 249

Fuller, Gen. J. F. C., 91

Gaugamela, 34, 131, 132, 139, 141, 144, 146, 150, 168, 196
Gaza, 117, 246
Glaucias, 241, 242
Gordium, 98
Granicus, 90–3, 100, 101, 167, 179, 205
Grote, George, 17, 32

Hadrian, 13
Hagnothemis, 260, 261
Halicarnassus, 96–7
Hannibal, 168
Harpalus, 123–4, 141, 149, 228, 231, 232, 246, 250
Hecataeus, 74–5
Hector (son of Parmenion), 122
Hellanice, 92
Hellespont, 5, 7, 26, 45, 61, 76, 89
Hephaestion, 31, 43–4, 48, 54, 60, 90, 91, 104, 105, 110–11,

116–17, 118, 121, 126, 137, 161, 162, 167, 173, 175, 176, 178, 181, 185, 186, 190, 193, 194, 195, 196, 199, 203–4, 205, 206, 209, 212, 213, 217, 221, 225, 226, 233, 234, 237, 238, 239, 240–4, 247, 251–3, 257, 258, 262, 267
Heracles, 80, 83, 94, 112, 120, 189, 192, 201, 205, 259
Hermias, 40, 43
Hermolaus, 185–6, 187
Herodotus, 139, 173, 177, 239
Hindu Kush, 168, 211
Homer, 20, 28, 44, 52, 71, 90, 113, 118, 158, 198, 207, 244, 247, 256
Hydaspes, 195, 198, 205
Hyrcania, 153, 157, 158, 178

Iliad, 28, 42, 142, 158
Illyria, Illyrians, 22, 35, 36, 45, 47, 57, 58, 65, 77, 80–1, 84
India, 9, 11, 14, 128, 129, 137, 161, 167, 177, 185, 189 ff., 203 ff., 207, 212, 215, 222, 224, 225, 230, 239, 244, 264
Indus, 189–90, 193, 195, 203, 211, 212, 214, 263
Iollas, 248, 259, 260, 262
Isocrates, 36, 38, 39
Issus, 100, 109, 118, 123, 130, 131, 132, 135, 137, 151
Ister, 77, 78–9, 80, 170
Italy, 16, 245, 250

Jaxartes, 171, 172
Judaea, 6, 11, 107
Justin, 12, 76

Kandahar, 181, 212
Kashmir, 199–200
Khyber, 190, 203, 211
Kipling, Rudyard, 177, 192

Lambarus, 77, 80, 102
Lawrence, T. E., 236
League of Corinth, 230
Leonnatus, 64, 207
Leonidas, 27, 28, 141, 145, 194
Lyceum, 11, 12, 17, 40, 159, 175, 188, 249
Lysander, 231
Lysimachus, 28, 113, 196, 257
Lysippus, 69

Maedi, 45, 77
Makran, 218, 219, 251
Mallians, 205, 206, 207, 210, 220

Marathon, 50, 83
Mardians, 158
Mark Antony, 7, 97, 99
Marsden, E. W., 138–9
Massaga, 191
Mazaces, 118
Mazaeus, 130, 131, 135, 137, 140 f.
Medea (Euripides), 65
Media, Medes, 150, 160, 222
Medius, 258–9, 261
Melkart, 112, 123
Memnon, 87, 88, 90, 93, 97, 100, 109, 150, 226
Memphis, 6, 118 120, 122
Mesopotamia, 108, 129, 142
Midas, 98
Middle Ages, 15, 41, 91
Miletus, 95, 96, 97, 114
Montrose, James Graham, 87
Multan, 206, 221, 246
Musicanus, 212

Nabarzanes, 101 ff., 130, 137, 150 ff., 168, 170
Nearchus, 14, 193, 194, 203, 204, 207, 209–10, 211, 214, 215, 218, 219, 221, 225, 226, 245–6, 247, 250, 258, 265
Nebuchadnezzar, 139
Nectanebo, 7, 8, 122
Neoptolemus, 22
Nichomachus, 40, 162, 163
Nicias, 131
Nile, 118, 119, 190, 203, 250
Nysa, 192, 193

Ochus (Artaxerxes III), 29, 38, 43, 61, 87, 100, 109, 112, 119, 145, 150, 151, 161, 227, 248
Olympias, 7–8, 21, 22, 23–4, 26, 27, 32, 39, 44, 45, 46, 48, 55, 56, 58, 59, 61, 63, 64, 65, 76, 88, 121, 126, 181, 228, 237, 245, 249–50, 267, 268
Olympic Games, 22, 70, 232
Omphis, 190, 193, 194, 197, 199
"On Horsemanship" (Xenophon), 33
Opis, 5, 233, 237, 238, 240
Orxines, 223
Oxathres, 103, 139, 156, 161, 164, 170, 172, 173
Oxus, 169–70, 175, 178, 218, 246
Oxyartes, 182, 210

Parallel Lives (Plutarch), 13
Parmenion, 22, 60, 61, 75, 76, 79,

87, 91, 95, 97, 98, 99, 102, 103, 109, 116, 122, 133 ff., 140, 142, 147, 148, 157, 162, 164 ff., 178, 180
Parysatis, 227
Pasargadae, 146, 221, 222
Patroclus, 44, 240, 241, 247, 251, 252, 257
Patron, 151–2, 156
Pausanias, 34, 35, 55, 62–3, 65, 66, 68, 76
Peithagoras, 244, 247
Pella, 20, 30, 38, 43, 60, 77, 89, 243, 249
Pelopidas, 20
Peloponnesian War, 35, 47, 131
Perdiccas III, 19, 20–1, 73, 75
Perdiccas (general), 6, 64, 84, 89, 91, 190, 196, 206, 208, 244, 259, 265, 266, 267
Pericles, 37, 50, 51
Perinthus, 46, 47
Persepolis, 139, 144 ff., 153, 160, 221 ff., 248
Persian War, 61
Persis, 144
Peucestas, 206, 207, 208, 221, 223, 230, 250, 253, 264, 266
Pharnaces, 204–5
Phidias, 94
Philip II, 8, 10, 17, 19–26, 27, 29, 30, 32 ff., 44 ff., 71, 73 ff., 79, 82, 84 ff., 88–9, 97, 99, 108, 109, 121, 123, 159, 168, 177, 178, 184, 234, 238
Philip (doctor), 99, 241
Philostratus, 198
Philotas, 60, 79, 81, 83, 91, 96, 110, 122–3, 144, 162–4, 165–6
Phocians, 47, 49, 50, 83, 84, 85, 145
Phoenicians, 107, 112, 114, 215
Phoenix, 28, 113
Pindar, 85
Pixodorus, 59, 60, 94–5, 96–7
Plataeans, 50, 83, 84, 85
Plato, 10, 39, 40, 42, 43, 45, 54, 73
Plutarch, 13, 23, 29–30, 34, 41, 44, 45, 59, 60, 63, 65, 69, 73, 76, 85, 90, 98, 104, 105, 109, 113–14, 125, 128, 129, 131, 134, 142, 143, 147, 148, 153, 154, 155, 160, 162, 164, 180, 220, 224, 237, 239, 241, 242, 249, 250, 258, 259–60, 262, 267
Porus, 9, 193, 194, 195, 196, 197–9, 204

Poseidon, 89, 180–1, 213, 231
Pseudo-Callisthenes, 14, 159, 242, 243, 261
Ptolemy I, 5–7, 13, 30–2, 43, 48, 79, 84, 86, 89, 91, 101, 111, 120, 147, 148, 155, 161, 164, 170, 174, 179, 187, 191, 192, 194–5, 196, 198, 204 ff., 218, 219, 224, 226, 227, 234, 243 ff.
Punjab, 189, 190, 193, 200, 203, 214
Pythagoras, 256

Red Sea, 250, 251
Roman d'Alexandre, 16
Rome, Romans, 7, 11–12, 15, 73, 78, 101, 108, 127, 134, 140, 188, 221, 223, 233, 236, 245, 250
Roxane, 3, 16, 17, 110, 183–5, 186, 190, 204, 211, 220, 221, 226, 227, 239, 243, 247, 248, 250, 267–8
Royal Journal, 256, 261
Royal Kindred, 173, 176, 235
Royal Road, 5, 139, 142, 233, 247

Sacred Band, 20, 34, 51, 52, 53, 83, 85
Sacred League, 47, 49, 51, 75
Sambus of Sind, 212
Samarkand, 171, 178
Samos, 231
Samothrace, 19, 21
Sangala, 200
Sarapis, 243, 264
Sardis, 82, 93, 96, 109
Sarpedon, 52
Satibarzanes, 168
Scythians, 47, 171, 172, 245
Seleucus, 196, 226
Semiramis, 211, 219
Shakespeare, William, 71, 97
Sicily, 115, 131, 250
Sidon, 110, 111, 112, 113, 114
Sisygambis, 104, 105, 106, 128, 132, 137, 144, 153, 225, 246, 253, 268
Siwah, 57, 120, 243, 258
Socrates, 36, 37, 39, 41, 71, 73, 108, 264
Sogdiana, 129, 171, 182–3, 184, 185, 190, 203
Sparta, Spartans, 20, 25, 35, 49, 54, 110, 112, 126, 173, 223, 230, 249
Speusippus, 39
Spitamenes, 182, 226

Stagira, 40, 46
Stateira, 104–5, 131–2, 154, 205
Stateira-Barsine. *See* Barsine-Stateira
Stein, Sir Aurel, 192
Stories of Alexander (Chares), 226
Strabo, 194
Successors, 230, 235
Susa, 139, 142, 143, 144, 146, 147, 221, 224, 225, 227, 229, 230, 238, 239, 244, 246, 247, 248
Syria, 5, 6
Syrian seer, 186–7

Tarn, Sir William, 17, 89, 148
Tarsus, 99
Taxila, 190, 193, 198, 204, 210, 211
Thais, 147, 148
Theagenes, 85
Thebes, 19–20, 34, 36, 49, 50, 51, 53, 76, 82–3, 84–5, 86, 89, 110, 120
Theophrastus, 11
Thermopylae, 49, 75, 144
Thessaly, 26, 35, 49, 75, 82, 198
Thettalus, 59, 60–1, 123, 227
Thrace, Thracians, 22, 24, 26, 32, 40, 44, 45, 46, 47, 76, 77, 80, 84, 86, 98, 174, 196
Tigris, 5, 129, 130, 131, 233, 246
Triballians, 47, 76, 78
Troy, Trojans, 22, 24, 44, 52, 68, 89–90, 207, 221
Trojan War, 159
Tyre, Tyrians, 6, 112, 113, 114–15, 123, 140

Uxians, 144

Valerius, Julius, 14–15
Vasco of Lucena, 16

Warburton, Sir Robert, 190, 191
Wilcken, Ulrich, 116, 142
Williams, John, 67

Xenocrates, 54
Xenophon, 33–4, 71–3, 79, 92, 101, 102, 106, 107, 126, 127, 131, 133, 139, 147, 169, 170, 222
Xerxes I, the Great, 49, 108, 116, 140, 144, 146, 147, 246

Zeus, 8, 24, 57, 67, 80, 87, 93–4, 120, 122, 143, 180, 231
Zoroaster, 9, 154